General Editor Alastair Service

THE BUILDINGS OF BRITAIN
REGENCY

David Watkin is a Fellow of Peterhouse, Cambridge and University Lecturer in History of Art. Among his publications are *The Life and Work of C. R. Cockerell, RA* (1974), *Morality and Architecture* (1977), *English Architecture, a Concise History* (1979), and *The Rise of Architectural History* (1980).

The Series Editor, Alastair Service, is the author of *Edwardian Architecture* (1977), *The Architects of London: 1066 to the Present Day* (1979), *A Guide to the Megaliths of Europe* (1979, paperback 1981), and other books. He is a Committee Member of the Victorian Society.

Uniform with this volume in the series *The Buildings of Britain*:

TUDOR AND JACOBEAN
Malcolm Airs

Titles in preparation:
ANGLO-SAXON AND NORMAN
MEDIEVAL AND GOTHIC
STUART AND BAROQUE
GEORGIAN
VICTORIAN
TWENTIETH CENTURY

General Editor Alastair Service

THE BUILDINGS OF BRITAIN
REGENCY
A Guide and Gazetteer
DAVID WATKIN

Barrie & Jenkins

London   Melbourne   Sydney   Auckland   Johannesburg

Barrie & Jenkins Ltd
An imprint of the Hutchinson Publishing Group
17–21 Conway Street, London W1P 6JD

Hutchinson Group (Australia) Pty Ltd
30–32 Cremorne Street, Richmond South, Victoria 3121
PO Box 151, Broadway, New South Wales 2007

Hutchinson Group (NZ) Ltd
32–34 View Road, PO Box 40–086, Glenfield, Auckland 10

Hutchinson Group (SA) (Pty) Ltd
PO Box 337, Bergvlei 2012, South Africa

First published 1982

© David Watkin 1982

Set in 10/12pt Goudy Old Style
by V & M Graphics Ltd, Aylesbury, Bucks
Printed and bound by Fletcher & Son Limited, Norwich.

ISBN 0 09 147990 8 (cased)
       0 09 147991 6 (paper)

CONTENTS

1

INTRODUCTION
PICTURESQUE, GREEK AND GOTHIC

Royal Pavilion,
Brighton,
1815–21; Nash.
The fantastic
roofscape of the
Prince Regent's
neo-Moghul
extravaganza
incorporates a
Classical villa of
the 1780s by H.
Holland

There can be no period in British architecture more worthy of study than that covered in the present book. This is a bold claim, but one which does not imply that the architectural quality of the individual buildings erected in 1790–1840 is necessarily as high as that in earlier periods. Buildings like Ely Cathedral or St Paul's Cathedral combine a largeness of poetic vision with a refinement of detail for which we look in vain in Regency England. The characteristic Regency materials are stucco and cast-iron, moulded, mass-produced, and incapable of providing scope for artists like Grinling Gibbons or the master of the leaves of Southwell. Yet we surely find in Regency architecture a variety and an elegance which no other period can equal. A stuccoed Indian fantasy like John Nash's Brighton Pavilion, and a grim monument to the Greek Revival like Robert Smirke's County Buildings at Perth, though exactly contemporary, can seem the products not merely of different ages but almost of different cultures. The terraces and villas of Regent's Park, of Brighton, Cheltenham, Clifton, Newcastle and Edinburgh; the astringencies of Soane; the idyllic parks of Repton; the cottages ornés with their thatched verandahs, and the proud chill mansions with their Doric porticos; the rambling Gothic country houses, and the geometric Athenian churches; the visionary engineering brilliance of Telford, who tricked out his suspension bridge at Conwy with castellated towers – all these were produced in the reigns of the mad King George III and the spendthrift patron George IV in a country turned upside down by the Industrial Revolution and by the egalitarian doctrines of Tom Payne and Jeremy Bentham, but which was yet dominated by a landed aristocracy richer and more confident than ever before or since.

For nearly half the period covered by this book England was engaged in one of the longest and most challenging wars of her history. It is a commonplace to point out that Jane Austen's novels contain scarcely a reference to the contemporary wars against Revolutionary and Napoleonic France of 1793–1815. The rich literary output of leaders of the Romantic movement, like Scott, Byron, Wordsworth, Coleridge, Shelley and Keats, similarly flourished undiminished by the national crisis. How far was architecture affected by the wars? It is often supposed that they greatly curtailed building production but, with the exception of government commissions, it is difficult to reconcile this view with the expansion of the great London estates during this period, or with the proliferation of country houses and villas by architects such as Nash, James Wyatt and William Atkinson.

Clytha Park, Gwent, c.1830; E. Haycock. The portico is of the Erectheion Ionic order

Moreover, in precisely these years the Industrial Revolution created a mood of commercial confidence and expansion which was accompanied by a great increase in population. From the 1780s the mechanisation of the textile industry, the new technology of coal and iron, and the introduction of steam-power, had created new jobs and new money. This naturally led to an increased architectural output which was not, of course, confined to purely industrial building types but overflowed into the civic and domestic field. Improvements in transport which had begun with the growth of canals from the 1760s reached a climax in this period with the engineering achievements of John Rennie and Thomas Telford. Telford's Scottish roads and bridges enabled tourists to visit a country which was being popularised by the romantic imagination of Sir Walter Scott: here one of the creative paradoxes of the age is epitomised. Indeed, it is the collision of reason and romance, engineering and poetry, Greek and Gothic, iron and stucco, that makes the period 1790–1840 so aesthetically and intellectually arresting. If it is the age of John Nash, the Picturesque poseur, on the one hand, then on the other it is that of the stern Utilitarian Jeremy Bentham. While Bentham was busy questioning all established institutions in works like his *Parliamentary Reform Catechism* (1817), King George IV was celebrating his Coronation in 1821 with a medieval banquet and a Ceremony of the Challenge which was a virtual re-creation of scenes from *Ivanhoe*.

If one were to choose two major buildings as characteristic

Tregothnan, near Truro, Cornwall, 1816–18; Wilkins. An early example of the Picturesque Tudor Revival

examples of the architectural contrasts within the period 1790–1840, one could scarcely do better than point to two projects initiated in the early 1820s: Jeffry Wyatville's remodelling of Windsor Castle with its incomparably romantic skyline, and Robert Smirke's British Museum, the epitome of learned Neo-Classical sobriety. Their significance as building types is obvious, while their respective styles embody assumptions about the history of England and the history of culture. Thus it would have been unthinkable in the 1820s for Windsor Castle to have emerged in Greek Revival dress, or the British Museum in Picturesque Gothic. However, when King Charles II modernised Windsor in the 1660s he had not hesitated to adopt the contemporary baroque style for the principal interiors; on the other hand, by the mid nineteenth century museums were built in the Gothic style. The decision taken in the 1820s to elaborate in the Gothic style the medieval parts of Windsor Castle and to Gothicise the seventeenth-century parts was an affirmation of faith in the historic continuity of English government, monarchy and culture on the part of a generation which was not only flushed with national pride after the victories of Wellington but was also, encouraged by the novels of Sir Walter Scott, engaged in a process of romantic historical contemplation.

The Picturesque movement of the eighteenth century was perhaps the major English contribution to European

Right: Glynllifon Park, Llandwrog, Gwynedd, 1836–40; E. Haycock? Characteristic Regency staircase of the imperial type, i.e. rising in one arm and returning in two

Below right: General view of Glynllifon Park – impressive by its size if nothing else

Below: Stracathro House, Tayside Region, 1828; A. Simpson. A rich Roman Corinthian order set in a building of Greek austerity

aesthetics. It is important for our present purposes as one of the principal determining factors on architecture in the period 1790–1840. Unfortunately, it is notoriously difficult to define the Picturesque concisely. From Vanbrugh onwards, eighteenth-century architects had put a new stress on the primacy of pictorial values. The landscape paintings of Claude and Poussin were seen as models not only for painterly technique but especially for principles of composition in which real or imaginary architectural forms were blended with natural scenery. A new awareness of the sense of place, heightened by the developing art of landscape gardening, was accompanied by an increased sense of time; in other words, of the historical reverberations attaching to particular historical buildings and styles.

Writing in his *Philosophical Enquiry into the Origins of our Ideas of the Sublime and Beautiful* (1757), Edmund Burke claimed that 'no work of art can be great, but as it deceives'. The Picturesque represents the triumph of illusion where the styles of other ages and cultures are tried on like theatrical costumes, and where architecture is designed like scenery, and gardens like paintings. Beginning with his *Observations on the River Wye and several parts of South Wales, etc. relative chiefly to Picturesque Beauty* (1782), the indefatigable tourist William

Lennox Castle, Lennoxtown, Central Region, 1837–41; D. Hamilton. A towering essay in the neo-Norman style

Gilpin published numerous critical analyses of natural scenery as though it were the work of landscape painters. This technique was applied to architecture by Robert Adam in the Preface to *Works in Architecture of Robert and James Adam* (1773). He summed up the Picturesque in the word 'movement':

Movement is meant to express, the rise and fall, the advance and recess, with other diversity of form, in the different parts of a building, so as to add greatly to the picturesque of the composition. For the rising and falling, advancing and receding, with the convexity and concavity, and other forms of the great parts, have the same effect in architecture, that hill and dale, fore-ground and distance, swelling and sinking have in landscape: that is, they serve to produce an agreeable and diversified contour, that groups and contrasts like a picture, and creates a variety of light and shade, which gives great spirit, beauty and effect to the composition.

The theories of the Picturesque which had been gathering force during the eighteenth century were codified for the first, and last, time by Sir Uvedale Price in his *Essay on the Picturesque as Compared with the Sublime and the Beautiful: and on the Use of*

Sandridge Park, Stoke Gabriel, Devon, c.1805; Nash. An Italianate villa inspired by vernacular buildings in the backgrounds of Claude's paintings

Studying Pictures for the Purpose of Improving Real Landscape (1794, enlarged edition 1810). For Price the principal attributes of the Picturesque as opposed to the Beautiful and the Sublime were variety, movement, irregularity, intricacy and roughness. Pursuit of these qualities in architecture, planning and landscape design came to characterise much of the work of men like Nash, James Wyatt, Soane, Repton and Wyatville. Nash was acquainted with Price, for whom he designed a small castellated villa near Aberystwyth Castle in the early 1790s. At this time he must also have met Richard Payne Knight who had designed Downton Castle, Hereford and Worcester, for himself in 1772–8, a pioneering building in a Claudean Picturesque mood which profoundly influenced Nash's subsequent castle-style. This is immediately discernible in Luscombe Castle, Devon, which Nash designed in 1799 in association with the landscape designer Humphry Repton, with whom he had entered into a loose partnership three years before. Nash repeated the Picturesque formula of Luscombe in the design of numerous other castles which, if they were often on a larger scale, were always beautifully related to their landscaped settings.

Repton had devised a cunningly attractive technique for persuading potential patrons to adopt his schemes. The watercolours in what he called his Red Books were provided

Tyringham Hall, Buckinghamshire, 1793–c.1800; Soane. (The dome was added in 1909.) Grecian refinement with Soane's characteristic incised lines and a French colonnaded bow

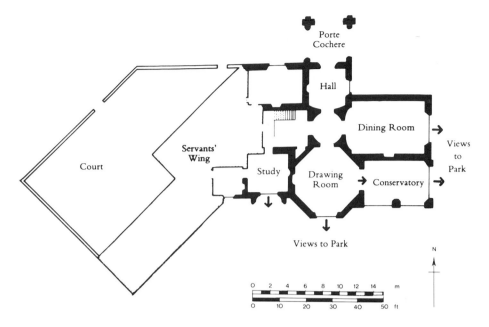

Porte
Cochere

Hall

Dining Room

→ Views
to
Park

Servants'
Wing

Court

Study

Drawing
Room

→ Conservatory

→

Views to Park

N

O 2 4 6 8 10 12 14 m

O   10   20   30   40   50 ft

Luscombe Castle, near Dawlish, Devon, 1799–1804; Nash. One of the earliest of the freely-planned villas which became so popular in the Regency period

with moveable flaps so that the same scene could be shown before and after his proposed improvements. The device was quintessentially Picturesque in its emphasis on pictorial values and in its approach to architecture in terms of landscape painting in watercolour. It was also well suited to Nash's architectural skills, which were akin to those of a rapid scene painter. For example, at the Brighton Pavilion from 1815 he left intact the basic structure of Henry Holland's chaste Neo-Classical villa of the 1780s, but transformed it into an orientalising fantasy which is little more than skin deep. Nash played a different kind of pictorial game at Blaise Hamlet, near Bristol, in 1810–11, where he laid out a set of almshouses not in the familiar institutional row but in the form of cottages grouped round a green as if they comprised a genuine village. Architecture 'as if' is a recurring feature of the Picturesque. Even 'real' architecture was made to seem more genuine by recourse to artificial devices: thus Wyatville was dissatisfied with the inadequately Picturesque skyline of the Norman Round Tower at Windsor Castle and, in the process of remodelling the castle, added a thirty-foot-high false collar on top of the tower. At Virginia Water nearby in 1826–7 he disposed in a wholly fanciful way, so as to form a composed ruin, a quantity of genuine antique columns from the Late Roman city of Lepcis Magna in North Africa.

Nash was unusual in his ability to bring the Picturesque into the heart of a town. His plans of 1811 onwards for Regent's Park and Regent Street fully accorded with Price's principles in their variety, contrast and delicious blending of architecture and scenery, especially in the park with its villas, terraces and two Park Villages, East and West. This rightly represents what many think of as characteristic of Regency architecture at its flashy best. The formula caught on so that towns like Brighton, Hove, Hastings, Plymouth, Bath, Clifton, Tunbridge Wells, Cheltenham and Leamington were developed in the early nineteenth century with delectable combinations of stuccoed terraces, villas, verandahs, conservatories, flowers and trees.

The work of John Soane from the 1790s to the 1820s was a highly idiosyncratic statement of Picturesque ideals. The variety and intricacy of his planning in buildings like the Bank of England, Law Courts, and his own house in Lincoln's Inn Fields, reflect Price's principles, while his obsession with top-lighting produced mysteriously romantic interiors which are quite unlike the work of his contemporaries. They are, perhaps, analogous to the paintings of Turner, who shared Soane's intense preoccupation with light and whose approach to architecture had similarly been profoundly coloured by Piranesi's Picturesque etchings of ancient Rome.

The Picturesque man of taste enjoyed looking at representations of architecture as much as at the architecture itself. Hence the popularity from the 1790s of the coloured aquatint, a process especially associated with the publisher Rudolph Ackermann, who produced the captivating *Microcosm of London* (1808–11) as well as illustrated volumes on Oxford, Cambridge and the public schools. His monthly journal, the *Repository of Arts, Literature and Fashions* (1809–28), is one of the most elegantly characteristic souvenirs of fashionable Regency taste. W. H. Pyne's three-volumed *History of the Royal Residences* (1819) was a pioneer in the representation of interiors and may have encouraged George IV to commission *The Royal Pavilion at Brighton* (1827), a sumptuously illustrated record of the interiors and exteriors of Nash's extravaganza. Illustrated monographs appeared on great country houses such as Eaton Hall, Toddington and Cassiobury, while between 1790 and 1835 over sixty books of designs for cottages, villas and houses of moderate size were published by architects such as Dearn, Elsam, Gandy, Goodwin, Hunt, Laing, Loudon, Lugar, Malton, Papworth, Plaw, Robinson

Right: Daylesford House, Gloucestershire, 1788–93; S. P. Cockerell. French and Indian motifs combine in the west front of a great house built for Warren Hastings

Below right: Chimney-piece, Daylesford House, 1792; T. Banks. A sculptural *tour-de-force* flanked by Indian caryatids

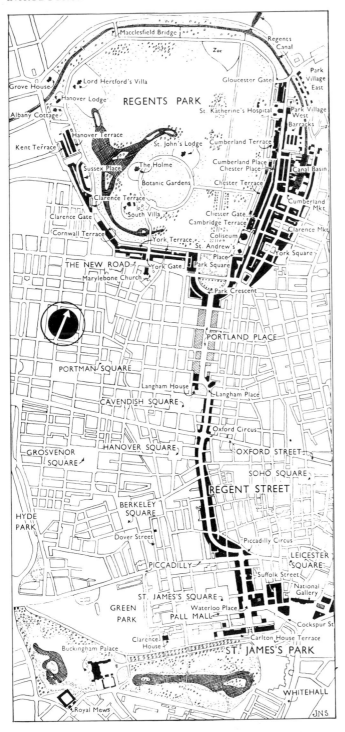

Left: Replanning of central London from Regent's Park to St James's Park, 1811–30; Nash. One of the most comprehensive, elegant and imaginative townplanning schemes carried out anywhere in Europe during these years

Right: Chester Terrace, Regent's Park, London, 1825; Nash. A quiet enclave with its own private road guarded by triumphal arches

and Soane. The establishment of architecture as a profession akin to those of law and medicine came at the end of the Regency period and was accompanied by the founding of journals such as Loudon's *Architectural Magazine* in 1834, the *Transactions of the Institute of British Architects* in 1835, the *Civil Engineer and Architect's Journal* in 1837, and the *Builder* in 1842.

The contrasting interpretations of the Picturesque offered by Nash and Soane are one of the principal architectural highlights of the period 1790–1830. However, this period was also coloured by the Greek Revival. Like the Picturesque, this had its roots in the eighteenth century but only flowered in the early nineteenth century. The first monuments of the Greek Revival were books rather than buildings, in particular the *Antiquities of Athens* (4 vols., 1762, 1789, 1795, 1816) by James Stuart and Nicholas Revett. The impetus to study and measure the long-forgotten remains of Greek architecture had numerous cultural, social and intellectual overtones ranging from the glamour of the Grand Tour and the belief in a Golden

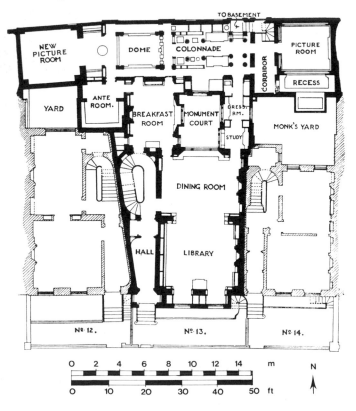

Nos 12–14 Lincoln's Inn Fields, London, 1792–1824; Soane. Perhaps the most complete surviving Regency town house with its complex and uniquely claustrophobic planning

Age, to the development of archaeology as an academic discipline and the hope of reforming the looseness of contemporary architecture by a return to the austere perfections of the 5th century BC. In short, the Greek Revival was as diffuse and, in many ways, as romantically orientated as the Picturesque itself. Thus, following Stuart's return from Athens in 1755 as the leading expert on Greek architecture, the first buildings he was called on to design were garden ornaments and temples in Picturesque landscaped parks at Hagley and Shugborough. So dominant was the Picturesque mode that even the church Stuart designed at Nuneham Courtenay in 1764 was landscaped so as to become a pictorial incident. Horace Walpole wrote in 1782 to William Mason, who was largely responsible for laying out the grounds at Nuneham, 'This place is more Elysian than ever, the river full to the brim, and the church by one touch of Albano's pencil is become a temple, and a principal feature of one of the most beautiful landscapes in the world.'

Before 1800 the Greek Revival was the plaything of a few

Sir John Soane's Museum, Lincoln's Inn Fields. The Breakfast Parlour built in 1812 is the quintessence of Soane's poetic style with its pendant canopy-like vault studded with mirrors

private patrons. Its most striking monument was, perhaps, the church in the park at Packington, West Midlands, designed in 1789 by Joseph Bonomi with the assistance of his patron, the Earl of Aylesford. In the 1790s Latrobe, Soane and James Wyatt all employed the baseless Greek Doric column, but this scarcely prepares us for the full-scale Greek Revival of the early nineteenth century. The change came with Thomas Harrison's Chester Castle, built slowly between 1785 and 1820. It seemed to demonstrate the appropriateness of a massive and sober Greek style for modern public buildings. 1806 was the *annus mirabilis* of the Greek Revival: in that year William Wilkins defeated James Wyatt in the competition for Downing College, Cambridge, and supplanted Henry Holland as architect for the new East India College at Haileybury, while George Dance brought the Greek taste to London with his monumental Ionic portico at the Royal College of Surgeons in Lincoln's Inn Fields. In 1809 Wilkins produced the most templar house in Europe, Grange Park, Hampshire, and in London Robert Smirke built the massively Greek Doric Covent Garden Theatre. From 1810 Greek became the rage so that from one end of the country to the other not only churches and country houses but town halls, law courts, hospitals and museums – the building types which assumed prominence after Waterloo – were designed in a style directly dependent on Smirke and Wilkins. Often they are dull but workmanlike and can thus be seen as a parallel to the official Palladian style of mid eighteenth-century England. An exception was provided in Edinburgh where the dramatic site and the skill of architects like Thomas Hamilton and W. H. Playfair justified its description as 'the Athens of the North'.

Above: Royal High School, Edinburgh, 1825–9; T. Hamilton. Designed and sited with spectacular imagination

Right: Chester Castle, 1788–1822; T. Harrison. Behind this blank unfluted Doric portico lies the elegant semi-circular Shire Hall

Below right: St James, Great Packington, West Midlands, 1789–90; J. Bonomi. Interior. The Earl of Aylesford helped design this early monument of the Greek Revival

The thoroughness with which Edinburgh architects applied Greek forms to a modern city reminds one of the public buildings of Munich by Leo von Klenze (1784–1864) and of his Bavarian followers in Athens. The Greek Revival language adopted by Klenze had been developed in Prussia by the great Karl Friedrich Schinkel (1781–1841) whose influence on British architecture it would be interesting to trace. Schinkel's characteristic trabeated forms can be discerned, for example, in the early works of Charles Barry such as his Royal Institution of Fine Arts, Manchester (1824–35); Buile Hill, near Manchester (1825–7); and shops at 16–17 Pall Mall (1833–4, dem. 1913). Smirke, similarly, has more than a touch of Schinkel, as do later architects such as 'Greek' Thomson of Glasgow and James Hibbert of Preston.

Just as the sharp individuality and exceptional refinement of Soane set him apart from his contemporaries, so C. R. Cockerell, a generation younger, combined scholarship and imagination in a personal style of unique distinction. The surviving oeuvre of Cockerell, like that of Soane, is severely restricted as a result of widespread demolition. Just as Soane's Bank of England and Law Courts are no more, so too we have lost Cockerell's masterpieces of the 1820s and 30s: in London, the Hanover Chapel; Westminster Life and British Fire Office; London and Westminster Bank; and Sun Fire Office; as well as three country houses, Derry Ormond, Lough

Below: St George's Hall, Liverpool; designed 1840–1 by H. L. Elmes and completed with enrichments by C. R. Cockerell, 1856. Principal floor plan. Monumental planning inspired by the Baths of ancient Rome

Right: St George's Hall, Liverpool: interior of the Great Hall with C. R. Cockerell's sumptuous floor of Minton tiles

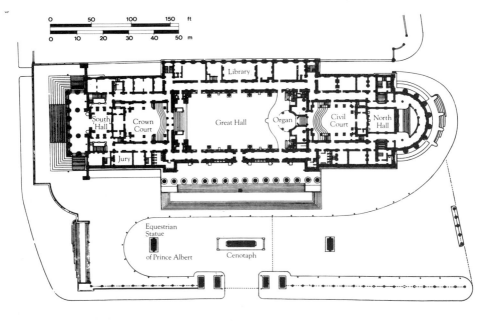

Crew and Langton. Like 'Athenian' Stuart and William Wilkins, Cockerell began as an archaeologist in Greece who, on returning to England, was confronted with the task of applying his knowledge and his ideals to a well-established Classical tradition. Amongst his surviving buildings, the Squire Law Library at Cambridge, the Ashmolean Museum at Oxford, branch Banks of England at Bristol, Manchester and Liverpool, and interiors at St George's Hall, Liverpool, show how successfully he eschewed the arid manner of Smirke in favour of a richer more sculpturally based Classicism which combined the curvaceous line of fifth-century Greece with the surface texture of sixteenth-century Mannerism and the heroic boldness of English baroque as deployed by Wren, Hawksmoor and Vanbrugh.

The desire for greater richness of effect had led Cockerell by the end of his life to a revival of Italian sixteenth- and seventeenth-century forms. The Italianate Revival is especially associated with the name of Charles Barry, who began his career with the Greek and Gothic styles popular in the 1820s: Gothic for Commissioners' churches like St Peter's, Brighton, Greek for the Royal Institution of Fine Arts (now City Art

Below: Reform Club, Pall Mall, London, 1837–41; Barry. With its top-lit colonnaded saloon rising through two storeys, this is architecturally the noblest of London clubs

Right: The two-storeyed central saloon of the Reform Club, looking towards the tunnel-vaulted staircase

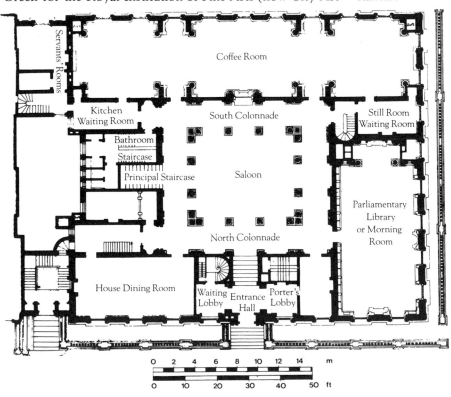

26

Gallery) at Manchester, a masterly synthesis of influences from Smirke and Schinkel. However, with his Travellers' Club in Pall Mall, London, won in a celebrated competition in 1829, and, more particularly, with the Reform Club of 1837 next door, Barry turned to an Italianate Renaissance manner which he further developed at Trentham Hall, Staffordshire (1834-9) and Bridgewater House, London (1846-51). Welcomed as an exuberant and adaptable style, it was widely adopted in the mid nineteenth century for clubs, commercial buildings, country houses and villas.

But Barry is perhaps best known as the architect of the neo-Perpendicular Houses of Parliament. Though not executed until 1840-60, a period outside that covered by the present book, they were designed in 1835-6 and must therefore be accounted for in terms of the Gothic Revival as it had developed by that date. Like the Picturesque and the Greek Revival, the Gothic Revival was a product of the inventive fertility of the eighteenth century. From at least the time of Hawksmoor and Kent in the 1730s a tradition of what might be called 'environmental propriety' had been used to justify the adaptation, extension or remodelling in a supposedly Gothic style of medieval or Tudor buildings. This selection of style on associational grounds is obviously related to ideas which we have seen as characteristic of the Picturesque. However, the belief gradually took root that Gothic architecture, like Classical, had an intrinsic merit. This was given early expression by Horace Walpole when he selected Gothic for Strawberry Hill in 1750 on a site free of medieval associations or structures.

However, the Gothic Revival was slower to develop than the Greek partly because of the absence of the books of engravings of measured details which Classical archaeologists such as Robert Wood, Stuart and Revett had been supplying since the mid eighteenth century. Not until the publication between the 1790s and the 1830s of books on medieval antiquities by John Carter and John Britton was there anything comparable for architects who were prepared to design in Gothic. Equally useful was the handbook published in 1817 by Thomas Rickman under the title *An Attempt to Discriminate the Styles of English Architecture from the Conquest to the Reformation*. Rickman's systematic study in which he established the names by which medieval architecture is still known – 'Norman', 'Early English', 'Decorated' and 'Perpendicular' – helped give the kind of academic respectability to Gothic which the numerous treatises on the orders had long given to Classical architecture. Despite his undoubted knowledge of medieval architecture, Rickman's numerous churches, mainly in Lancashire and Warwickshire, tend to have a brittle Regency feel.

James Wyatt's Fonthill Abbey, Wiltshire, built in 1796–1812 for the colourful recluse William Beckford, was the most spectacular building designed in what one might call 'pre-archaeological' Gothic, that is to say in a fanciful rather than an accurate Gothic. The collapse in 1825 and subsequent demolition of this Sublime extravaganza, with its dramatic cruciform plan and colossal tower, is one of the great losses of English architecture. Far less alluring but even more influential were the papery Gothic country houses of William Atkinson, including Scone Palace, Tayside Region (1803–12), Mulgrave Castle, North Yorkshire (1804–11), Panshanger, Hertford-shire (1807–20, dem. 1953), and Abbotsford, Borders Region (1816–23), a Baronial pile for the high priest of the Romantic movement, Sir Walter Scott. William Wilkins, whom we have already met as an apparently uncompromising Classicist, saw early in his career which way the wind was blowing and switched to Gothic for his new buildings at Trinity, Corpus Christi and King's Colleges, Cambridge. In all

Holy Trinity, Theale, Berkshire. Nave, 1820–2, E. W. Garbett; tower, 1827–8, J. Buckler. The choice of the Early English style was unusual for this date

these colleges Gothic could be justified on the grounds of fitting in with existing medieval buildings, but in 1814–17 Wilkins had already provided a new house at Dalmeny, Lothian Region, on a virgin site in a Tudor Gothic style inspired, somewhat incongruously, by East Barsham Hall in his native Norfolk. The prolific William Burn, a pupil of Smirke, began in the Greek Revival but switched to a succession of Tudor, Jacobethan and Baronial styles for his seemingly endless flow of not specially inspired Scottish country houses. Of greater interest was Anthony Salvin, who had learnt Picturesque principles from his master John Nash and built a number of large neo-Tudor and Jacobean houses, including Mamhead, Devon (1828), Harlaxton, Lincolnshire (1831–53), and Scotney Castle, Kent (1835–43). With its contrived view down a valley to the ruins of the old moated castle, Scotney is one of the high points of Picturesque planning. However, the abruptly asymmetrical façades of the new house give less the impression of Picturesque irregularity than of the kind of 'truthful' functionalism which Pugin was beginning to demand.

Mamhead, Devon, 1828–38; A. Salvin. The Picturesque south front with its neo-Tudor conservatory

Dalmeny House,
Lothian Region,
1814–17;
Wilkins. The first
Scottish example
of Wilkins's
elaborate and
influential neo-
Tudor style

Augustus Welby Northmore Pugin was passionately opposed to the architectural currents represented by the Picturesque and the Greek Revival. He was in love with Gothic and with the Catholic Church and, indeed, could hardly distinguish in his mind between the two. The Greek he condemned as pagan, and the Picturesque as untruthful. Despite his hostility to the architecture of the period 1790–1840 he must be included here because he produced in the 1830s not only his entertainingly polemical book *Contrasts* (1836), but also such richly Gothic buildings as Scarisbrick Hall, Lancashire, St Chad's Cathedral, Birmingham, and St Giles's, Cheadle, Staffordshire. However, the new archaeological seriousness of such buildings as compared to those, say, of Rickman, makes it more appropriate to discuss them in the context of Victorian architecture.

It should also be remembered that the Industrial Revolution was at its height in these years. This not only introduced new building types but meant that some old ones, for example bridge design, now tended to become the preserve of engineers rather than architects. Fortunately there were engineers of genius like Telford, Rennie and Brunel who deployed their functional skills in an architectural language tautened and ennobled by the lessons of the Greek Revival: the suspension bridges at Clifton and the Menai Straits, St Katharine's Dock at London and the Albert Dock at Liverpool are amongst the most masterly achievements of their time in Europe.

The most memorable architectural expressions of the period 1790–1840 lie in four areas: the Picturesque country houses, whether Greek or Gothic; the Classical terraces and crescents of towns like Cheltenham, Brighton, Edinburgh, London and Clifton; the monumental public buildings erected after Waterloo in a solemn Greek Revival style – town halls, court-houses, infirmaries, from Penzance to Aberdeen; and the great bridges of Telford, Rennie and Brunel. The next few chapters will survey the highlights within these categories as well as those of educational, religious and royal building.

Clifton Suspension Bridge, Bristol, 1829–64; Brunel. The original designs envisaged a more richly ornamented structure

2

TOWN PLANNING
AND
TOWN HOUSES

By the end of the eighteenth century the development of the British Empire, marked by Clive's victory at Plassey and Wolfe's at Quebec, had led to a growth in trade which brought new prosperity to the increasing mercantile and productive classes. The Napoleonic Wars encouraged the concentration of commercial activity in London so that the capital rapidly expanded with terraced houses in the centre and elegant villas in the suburbs. What happened in London one day was echoed in the provinces the next. This whole urban expansion in early nineteenth-century England and Scotland stimulated the rise of the building contractor, typified by Thomas Cubitt. The building contractor was distinct both from the old-fashioned builder-architect and from the professional architect who had become established around the mid eighteenth century.

The years 1790–1840 saw the execution of what were perhaps the most handsome town-planning schemes in the history of British architecture. The leading architects were Nash, Decimus Burton and Cubitt in London; Reid, Archibald Elliot and W. H. Playfair in Edinburgh; Grainger and Dobson in Newcastle; Papworth and Jearrad in Cheltenham; and Busby in Brighton and Hove. Contemporaries were conscious of the visual revolution that was being effected in British cities: for example, we can sense the prevailing mood of pride and excitement in two splendidly illustrated publications – James Elmes's *Metropolitan Improvements: or London in the Nineteenth Century* (1827) and John Britton's *Modern Athens! Displayed in a Series of Views: or Edinburgh in the Nineteenth Century* (1831). Though the sparkling terraces, squares and crescents of Regency Britain were second to none in elegance and panache, it could not be claimed that they were possessed of much architectural originality. The modest workman's house in the East End of London or the peer's house in Mayfair followed the same long-established pattern, with a staircase at one side, a front room and a back room on each floor, a small projection at the back containing closets, and generally a basement storey. What was new were the Picturesque experiments of Nash which gave birth to the asymmetrical villa in Tudor or Italianate dress. These, standing in their own grounds, began to line the approaches to major towns from about 1815.

For the origin of Regency town planning we must turn to the informal sequence in Georgian Bath of Queen Square, Gay Street, the Circus and Royal Crescent, laid out by the elder and the younger John Wood between 1729 and 1775. The elder Wood had worked in the 1720s on the design of Cavendish Square in London which, with Edward Shepherd's north side of Grosvenor Square, was the first example of the treatment of

The Paragon, Blackheath, Greenwich, c.1793; M. Searles. One of the most elegant examples of urban design in the Regency period

one whole side of a square as a unified architectural entity, with a central pedimented section like a palace or great public building. The first English example, that is; for J.-H. Mansart had pioneered the idea in the Place Vendôme, Paris, in 1690, and it was taken up by Henry Aldrich in Peckwater Quadrangle at Christ Church, Oxford, in 1707–14.

What was also significant at Bath was the evident pleasure taken in the visual contrast between the successive elements of the scheme, and the way in which the semi-elliptical Royal Crescent, with a plan following the contours of the site, looked straight out on to open fields. These Picturesque considerations were even more in evidence in the breathtaking undulations of Lansdowne Crescent added in 1789–93 by John Palmer.

The kind of comprehensive town planning pioneered at Bath exercised very little influence in the eighteenth century. It was, however, to become a dominant feature of Regency

Carlton House Terrace, The Mall, London, 1827–33; Nash. A colonnade of cast-iron Greek Doric columns supports a palatial row of terraced houses

Norfolk Crescent, Bath, begun early 1790s; probably J. Palmer, with details by J. Pinch. Completed after 1810 by subscription

towns. Themes which had been given their first expression at Bath were carried to London by Nash from 1811 in his plans for Regent's Park and Regent Street. The Bathian experiment of uniting a circus and a crescent in an informal relationship with streets and squares, had been echoed in miniature by George Dance on the Minories Estate near Tower Hill in 1767 and developed by him in 1790 in an unexecuted scheme for the Camden Estate at St Pancras. In 1794 a similar plan was drawn up by an anonymous architect for the Eyres Estate in St John's Wood, immediately adjoining the Marylebone Park on the west. This was engraved and circulated in 1794 and was certainly known to Nash. His comprehensive scheme for the replanning of central London, the most complete in its history, involved not merely the creation of Regent's Park and Regent Street but also the formation of Trafalgar Square and the replanning of St James's Park and the west end of the Strand. It was all prompted by the reversion from the Duke of Portland to the Crown in January 1811 of a lease of 552 acres in Marylebone. Though Nash's first proposals of March 1811 envisaged a rather denser development than that eventually executed, it was regarded as axiomatic from the start that the existing park-like character be retained. Thus Nash's terraced houses round the edge of the park looked across a rural scene which, though containing villas screened by planting, resembled the landscaped park of a gentleman's country seat. Regent Street was similarly planned along Picturesque rather than formal lines with deliberate breaks in the composition and silhouette.

The successive stages in the development of the New Town at Edinburgh represent the most complete surviving example of Late Georgian town planning. Like Nash's London, it had roots in the Woods' work in Bath, though it did not go so far as Nash in the direction of the Picturesque. James Craig's plan for the New Town, adopted in 1767, consisted of two squares, St Andrew's to the east and Charlotte (originally St George's) to the west, linked by George Street; Queen Street ran parallel to the north and Princes Street to the south. The fact that the houses command views south to the Castle and north to the Firth of Forth means that despite its uninteresting layout, the scheme is important for its scenic quality. Charlotte Square was designed by Robert Adam in 1791 as the first instance in Edinburgh of a united architectural treatment for one whole side of a square. This set the pattern for subsequent developments in the city.

North of this area came the Second New Town, with the Royal Circus as its most arresting feature, first planned in 1796 and built from 1802 from designs by Robert Reid and William Sibbald.

To the north and west of Charlotte Square came the spectacular development of the Earl of Moray's Estate in 1822 by James Gillespie Graham. An elongated fan-shaped area on the edge of the ravine above the Water of Leith inspired the unusual shape of Gillespie's three interlocking squares: Randolph Crescent, the oval Ainslie Place and the octagonal Moray Place, an exhilarating concatenation of baroque, Neo-Classical and Picturesque effects. From 1819 came W. H. Playfair's extensive development of the area north of Calton Hill. His Regent Terrace on the slopes of Calton Hill and the broad sweep of Hillside Crescent, both with their insistent lines of Greek Doric columns, bear the unforgettable stamp of northern Classicism.

Much of the authority and dignity of this architecture derive from the fine local stone of which it is constructed. The same is true of the celebrated development of Newcastle from the 1820s by the speculative builder Richard Grainger and a group of architects of whom the most distinguished was John Dobson. In c. 1824 Dobson submitted a plan for developing a

Left: Lancaster House, St James's, London, 1820–38; Sir R. Smirke, B. D. Wyatt and Barry. The staircase is probably the most sumptuous of its date in the country

Below: Charlotte Square, Edinburgh, 1791; Adam. Each side of the square is treated as a unified palatial composition

thirteen-acre site in the centre of Newcastle. Though his scheme was not adopted he built the impressive Eldon Square in 1824–6 with a uniform design for each side. This was followed by the no less extensive Leazes Terrace in 1829, built by Thomas Oliver as part of a large-scale development of terrace houses with smaller houses behind them as at Nash's Regent's Park. Dobson's scheme of 1824 was partially realised in 1834–9 with the development by Grainger of the Triangle, composed of Market Street, Grey Street and Grainger Street facing the Grey Column. With its slow curve on a rising site, Grey Street owes something to the empirical and Picturesque design of Regent Street, though the use of stone and the sparser ornament produce a more sober and monumental effect. Nearby was the Royal Arcade (1831–2, dem. 1963), also attributable to Dobson and Grainger, a nobly sited shopping and office arcade with a glazed domed roof.

Decimus Burton, who had designed a number of the terraces and villas of Regent's Park, carried the urban villa theme to Tunbridge Wells, Kent, where he laid out the attractive Calverley Estate from 1828. His proposed estates at Folkestone and Eastbourne remained unexecuted, though

Below: Moray Place, Edinburgh, c.1822–30; J. G. Graham. An unusually planned square in a style derived from Adam

Right: Grey Street, Newcastle, 1825–40; R. Grainger and J. Dobson. On the left is the portico of the Theatre Royal, 1836–7, by B. Green

Below right: Clifton Vale, Bristol, 1840–3; J. Foster and W. Okely. A late and somewhat mannered example of a Georgian terrace

Left: Pittville
Pump Room,
Cheltenham,
1825–30; J. B.
Forbes. The
quintessence of
Regency panache

Below: St Mary-in-
the-Castle and
Pelham Crescent,
Hastings, 1824–8;
J. Kay. A
memorable
integration of
ecclesiastical and
domestic
architecture

substantial portions of his new town at Fleetwood, Lancashire, were built in 1836–43.

London, Torquay, Plymouth, Devonport, Bristol, Clifton, Brighton, Worthing, Weymouth, Portsmouth and Leamington are all rich in Regency urban developments, but perhaps the most complete surviving example is Cheltenham. Its rapid rise to popularity as a summer spa resort is demonstrated in its increase in population from 3,000 in 1801 to 20,000 in 1826. In c.1824 J. B. Papworth prepared designs for what has been described as 'the first English garden city with houses set among formal avenues and gardens'. Lansdowne Road, Place and Crescent were built on lines largely laid down by Papworth but he was dismissed in 1829–30 and replaced by R. W. Jearrad who practised with his son and brother. Cheltenham is rightly celebrated for its elegant wrought-iron balconies with their filigree anthemion patterns casting delicious shadows on smooth ashlar facing. Papworth's elegant villa-style helped make the semi-detached house socially acceptable, and the Greek, Tudor or Italianate villas of towns such as Bath and Cheltenham are one of the most characteristic contributions of the Regency period. Somewhat heavier than Papworth's style, and so possibly designed by the Jearrads, are Lansdowne Terrace, Cheltenham, with its curious pedimented aedicules on the first floor, and, also of c.1830, Lansdowne Court, a development anticipating the Italianate villas which were to be such a feature of English towns after c.1840.

3

COUNTRY HOUSES

I t is doubtful whether the landed classes have ever enjoyed a period of greater prosperity and security than between 1790 and 1840, despite the Napoleonic Wars and the growing calls for parliamentary reform. The rage for the country house was never greater than in the early nineteenth century. Both money and styles were almost unlimited, so that chaos was only prevented by the fact that architects had had a training in the Classical tradition which generally gave even the most fanciful buildings an underlying balance and refinement. The acquisition of a country estate remained throughout the nineteenth century a way of achieving a stake in the historic continuity of the English scene and thus of becoming part of the governing class. The vitality of this tradition was ensured by the ability of the landed gentry to avoid becoming the kind of isolated caste that they had on the Continent. In other words, there was a flow from landed families into business, and vice versa. This, of course, had been true of English life from the sixteenth century, but it was a process made immeasurably more significant by the growth of commercial and industrial fortunes associated with the Industrial Revolution from the 1780s onwards.

The major country houses were significant as centres of political, social and intellectual life. The country-house party, which was an invention of the middle years of the eighteenth century facilitated by improved transport, assumed increasing significance during the first half of the nineteenth century. The formal disposition on the main floor of state apartments each generally consisting of withdrawing room, bedroom and closet, was replaced from c.1770 by a succession of reception rooms with bedrooms kept to upper floors. The *piano nobile*

Cranbury Park, Hampshire. Tent Room, c.1830; J. B. Papworth. Rare surviving example of a familiar Regency type inspired by the French Empire style

was abolished so that it was possible to walk straight out from the ground-floor living rooms into the garden. An increasingly important part was played in this process by the villa or moderate-sized house often in a suburban situation, a building type which had been developed from the 1750s by Robert Taylor, James Paine and Isaac Ware.

In c.1800–10 John Nash and Humphry Repton led the movement to even greater comfort in the planning and furnishing of interiors. The asymmetrical villa in a Picturesque setting contained furniture scattered asymmetrically through the rooms rather than disposed formally round the edge and brought forward by servants when required. For example, the Grecian couch of the Regency period not only suggests reclining rather than sitting but was also the first kind of sofa not intended to be set with its back against the wall. The comfortable 'lived-in' look established during these years continues to colour people's expectations in the present day of what rooms ought to look like both in grand mansions and in more modest houses. Libraries were now used as sitting rooms, rooms opened into conservatories and verandahs, and there were separate rooms for men, for women, for mixed company, for the family and for their guests.

It was these years, too, that saw the establishment of the

Above: Caerhays Castle, Cornwall, c.1808; Nash. Castellated Gothic pile built for a cousin and acquaintance of Lord Byron

Above right: Clare House, East Malling, Kent, 1793; M. Searles. Villa of surprising animation in both plan and elevation

Right: Bowood House, Wiltshire. The Library was formed in 1821 by C. R. Cockerell in a wing by Adam of the 1760s: a fine example of the characteristic Regency library-cum-drawing room

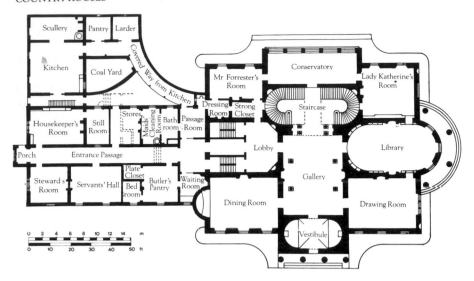

Scullery | Pantry | Larder
Kitchen | Coal Yard
Covered Way from Kitchen
Housekeeper's Room | Still Room | Stores | Maids Cleaning Room | Bath room | Passage Room
Porch | Entrance Passage
Steward's Room | Servants' Hall | Bed room | Plate Closet | Butler's Pantry | Waiting Room
Mr Forrester's Room | Dressing Room | Strong Closet | Conservatory | Lady Katherine's Room
Staircase | Lobby | Gallery | Library | Dining Room | Drawing Room | Vestibule

type of country-house party which survived into the twentieth century. The male guests would shoot or hunt in the morning, sometimes returning to the newly invented institution of luncheon, largely attended by ladies; the climax of the day was dinner, now served in the early evening rather than the late afternoon. Dinner involved the impressive ritual of the procession of family and guests along an architecturally contrived route from the drawing room to the dining room, where numerous footmen and an elaborate display of plate added a touch of feudal splendour. The ladies retired to the

Willey Hall, Salop, 1813–15; L. W. Wyatt. The processional way through the centre of the house is one of the most splendid statements of English Neo-Classicism

Trelissick House, near Truro, Cornwall, 1824; P. F. Robinson. South front. The Greek Revival spread to the extremities of the country

drawing room after dinner where they would be joined at the end of the evening by the men who had been enjoying their wine in the dining room. Even Wyatville's romantic remodelling of Windsor Castle from 1824 was governed internally by the need to provide this kind of comfort and opulent domesticity. As such it was condemned by C. R. Cockerell to whom Wyatville ill-advisedly showed the plans in 1825. Cockerell complained in his diary of 'the usual suite of drawing room, library and dining room ... like an ordinary country gentleman's house enlarged with a bedroom on the same floor and a suite of rooms for his [George IV's] personal friends and family ... but nothing like chambre, anti chambre, waiting chamber, ministers' rooms, salle de Huissiers with all the parade and pomp and circumstance of a court'.

In attempting to pick our way through the confusing avenues of Regency taste as applied to the design of country houses, it may be helpful to begin by recalling the emphasis given in the Introduction to the twin categories of the Greek Revival and the Picturesque. The Greek fashion was especially promoted by Latrobe, Dance, Gandy, Smirke, Wilkins, Cockerell, Dobson and Edward Haycock. Before he left England to transform the architectural scene in North

Longhirst House, near Morpeth, Northumberland, 1824–8; J. Dobson. Chill Classical grandeur in the domed staircase hall

America, Latrobe designed Hammerwood, Sussex (1792), with stocky Ledoux-inspired forms which were echoed by Gandy at Storrs Hall, Cumbria (1808–11). More widely imitated was Dance's rather bald Stratton Park, Hampshire (1803), with its solemn Doric portico. This set the pattern for portico houses such as Wilkins's Osberton, Nottinghamshire (1806) and Grange Park, Hampshire (1809), W. Burn's Camperdown, Dundee (1824), and Haycock's Clytha Park, Gwent (1830) and Millichope Park, Salop (1835–40). The most distinguished of all Greek Revival houses is Belsay, Northumberland (1806–17), designed by its owner Sir Charles Monck. The massive austerity of its exterior is offset by the two-storeyed columnar peristyle which is the convincingly neo-antique climax of the interior.

Robert Smirke pioneered a daunting Greek manner of his own for houses like Kinmount, Dumfries and Galloway Region (1812), and Normanby, Humberside (1825–30), which rely for their effect not on porticos but on the carefully built-up interplay of large cubic masses. In a class of its own is Ickworth, Suffolk. Enlivened externally with friezes based on Flaxman's illustrations to Homer, this vast rotunda was designed by Francis Sandys in 1796 to house the collections of the eccentric Earl Bishop of Derry. Few houses are less adaptable to modern living conditions than a large and uncompromising product of the Greek Revival, and very few are privately inhabited today. Scotland is especially rich in cold, grand, Greek Revival mansions: for example, Whittinghame, Kinmount and Newton Don, all by Smirke; Balbirnie, by Richard Crichton; Stracathro, by Archibald Simpson; Camperdown, by William Burn; Hopes, by James Burn; Broomhall, by Thomas Harrison; and Cairness, by James Playfair.

Especially remarkable is the contribution of the Wyatt family, above all Samuel Wyatt, in developing a recognisable family style dependent on shallow, segmental bows, smooth ashlar, and tripartite windows, as at Belmont, Bowden, Claverton, Dropmore, Goodwood, Phillips House, Shugborough and Tatton. Indeed, the phenomenon represented by the Wyatt dynasty is one of the dominating architectural features of the whole period. One constantly comes across James Wyatt, his brother Samuel, his son Benjamin Dean, and his nephews Jeffry (Wyatville) and Lewis William.

The Gothic Revival, as developed by architects like Wyatt, Nash, Atkinson, Wilkins, Burn and Salvin, flourished

Cairness House, Grampian Region, 1791–7; James Playfair. An unusual essay in rustication with eclectic interiors and an office wing in an advanced Neo-Classical style

Ickworth, Suffolk, 1796–1830; F. Sandys. South front. A unique example of the house as Temple of the Arts

Belsay Hall,
Northumberland,
1806–17; Sir
Charles Monck.
Above: General
view: uncompromi-
sing austerity

Left: The central
peristyle

Above near right: A
daunting Classical
box makes no
concessions to the
Picturesque in
either plan or
elevation

Above far right:
The superb
masonry portico
of the finest Greek
Revival mansion
in the country

Right: The
massively
columnar
chimney-piece in
the library

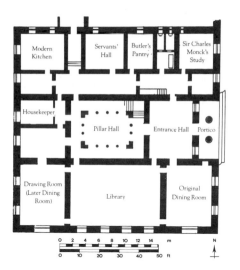

with especial vigour as an appropriate medium for the expression of Picturesque ideals. The stylistic contrasts of the period are nowhere better expressed than at Castle Goring, West Sussex, designed by J. B. Rebecca in c.1795–1815 for Sir Bysshe Shelley, Bt, the poet's grandfather. One façade is Greek Doric, the other Gothic, the same ambivalence being reflected internally. The romantic asymmetry of Horace Walpole's Strawberry Hill (1750 onwards) was raised to the Sublime by James Wyatt at Fonthill Abbey, which he built for William Beckford in 1796–1812. Something of this panache is discernible at Belvoir Castle as remodelled for the Duke of Rutland by Wyatt in 1801–13 and by the Rev. J. Thoroton in 1816–20, and at Ashridge, Hertfordshire, built by Wyatt in 1808–13 for the Earl of Bridgewater and further dramatised after 1813 by Wyatville. Thomas Hopper, one of the most stylistically diverse of all English architects, built Penrhyn Castle, Gwynedd, in c.1825–44 for G. H. Dawkins Pennant, a slate millionaire. This stupendous neo-Norman pile overlooking the Menai Straits gives us some sense of the Sublime drama of Fonthill before its demolition. Wales, poor in

Above: Bowden House, near Lacock, Wiltshire, 1796; J. Wyatt. Wyatt family style at its most perfect

Ashridge Park, Hertfordshire, 1808–17; J. Wyatt and Wyatville. *Above right*: Plan. Note the separation of family rooms, public rooms and servants' quarters. The detailed plan corresponds to sections 2 and 3 of the layout plan given in the inset

Right: General view

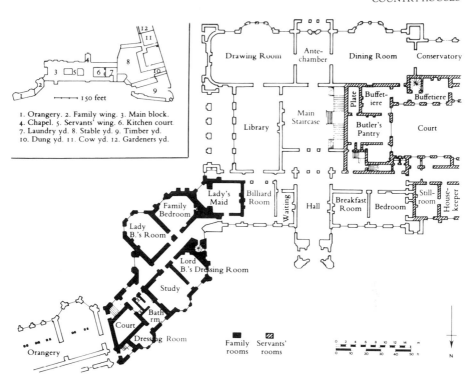

1. Orangery. 2. Family wing. 3. Main block.
4. Chapel. 5. Servants' wing. 6. Kitchen court.
7. Laundry yd. 8. Stable yd. 9. Timber yd.
10. Dung yd. 11. Cow yd. 12. Gardeners yd.

Drawing Room Ante-chamber Dining Room Conservatory

Library Main Staircase Plate Buffet-iere Buffetiere

Butler's Pantry Court

Lady's Maid Billiard Room Waiting Hall Breakfast Room Bedroom Still-room House-keeper

Family Bedroom

Lady B.'s Room

Lord B.'s Dressing Room

Study

Bath rm.

Court

Dressing Room

Orangery

Family rooms   Servants' rooms

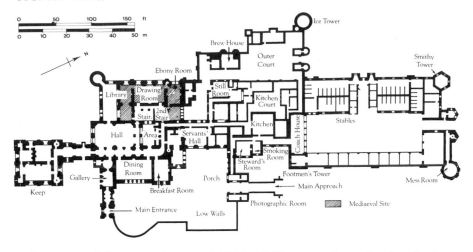

architecture of all types in the period 1790–1840, managed to produce a string of romantic castles – though none by Welsh architects – near the North Welsh coast: Hawarden, Halklyn, Gwrych, Bryn Bras and, by far the finest, Penrhyn.

The Picturesque castles of John Nash, stylistically dependent on Payne Knight's Downton Castle, have already been mentioned in the Introduction. Wilkins developed a

Penrhyn Castle, Bangor, Gwynedd, c.1825–c.44; T. Hopper. The dynamic Picturesque plan produces breathtaking surprises like the entrance into the corner of the vast vaulted Hall from the extremely narrow Gallery

Castle Goring, near Arundel, West Sussex, c.1795–1815; J. B. Rebecca. An astonishing split-personality house with a Classical south front (shown here) and a Gothic north front

more papery and symmetrical Gothic style as at Dalmeny House, Lothian Region (1814–17), for the Earl of Rosebery, and Tregothnan, Cornwall (1816–18), for Viscount Falmouth. Thin, too, was the work of the prolific William Atkinson, many of whose stucco castellated mansions can be seen in Scotland: Scone Palace (1803–12), Tulliallan Castle (1817–20), Abbotsford (1817–23) and Taymouth Castle (1818–28). At Abbotsford Atkinson revived the 'Baronial' style which had prevailed in Scotland between 1560 and 1660. Irregular compositions often of considerable height were characterised by crow-stepped gables, corbelled parapets and angle-turrets or tourelles inspired by the châteaux of the Loire. The Baronial style of Abbotsford was developed in Scotland by one of the most prolific country-house architects of all time, William Burn. Burn is also known for his contribution to the planning of the nineteenth-century country house with its careful segregation of private rooms for the owner and his family, public entertaining rooms, guests' rooms, and servants' quarters. Tyninghame House, Lothian Region (1829–30), for the Earl of Haddington, is a characteristic and well-preserved example. In 1838–53 Burn completed the astonishing neo-Jacobean Harlaxton Manor, Lincolnshire, begun in 1831 by Anthony Salvin. As a pupil of Nash, Salvin had learned how to relate a house Picturesquely to its setting, as is demonstrated in works of his like Mamhead, Devon; Scotney, Kent; and Peckforton Castle, Cheshire. Salvin became increasingly set

Gwrych Castle, Clwyd, c.1814; L. B. Hesketh *et al.* A superbly sited Regency Gothic castle with views across the Menai Straits

Taymouth Castle,
Tayside Region.
The breathtaking
Gothic staircase
hall, 1806–10; A.
& J. Elliot

Below:
Tyninghame
House, Lothian
Region, 1829–30;
W. Burn. A
textbook example
of the Scots
Baronial Revival

apart from the main currents in the period 1800–40 by his archaeological knowledge of medieval, especially fortified, architecture, which made him much in demand as a restorer of castles.

The emphasis on the role of associationism in the theory and practice of the Picturesque gave continuous encouragement to the cult of the exotic. The enchanting Sezincote, Gloucestershire, was built c.1805 in a glowing Cotswold stone by S. P. Cockerell for his brother, a retired Indian nabob. In an appropriately neo-Moghul style and with its long quadrant conservatory inspired by James Wyatt's at Dodington Park, it is one of the happiest products of the Regency passion for blending nature and architecture. Even more advanced in that respect was the now demolished Deepdene, Surrey, remodelled by the connoisseur, collector and designer Thomas Hope in 1818–23 in a bizarre combination of styles, and cleverly exploiting the irregularity of the site. The diagonal planning of Deepdene was perhaps inspired by Wyatville's Endsleigh, Devon, built for the Duke of Bedford in 1810. In a beautiful Repton setting, Endsleigh was an unusually lavish example of the characteristic cottage orné of the Regency period, a building type to which attention had been directed by the emphasis of Picturesque theorists on the charms of the rural scene. Robert Adam had made designs for Picturesque cottages, but in the 1790s a combination of sentimentality, nostalgia and Picturesque sensibility produced a flood of books of designs for cottages and villas which continued until well into the nineteenth century. Often these were illustrated with the new aquatint process which conveyed so perfectly the soft tints and shades of architecture blended with Picturesque landscape. A characteristic cottage orné is the lodge of c.1809 at Hinton Martell, Dorset, with its umbrella-like thatched roof, quaint Gothic windows and thatched porches supported on rustic tree-trunk columns.

John Soane, typically, needs separate consideration. His spectacular drawing room of 1791–3 at Wimpole Hall, Cambridgeshire, domed and T-shaped, represents an important step in the development of his personal style, and though no major house designed by him in this period survives in its entirety, his individual Classical hand can be recognised at Tyringham, Buckinghamshire; Aynho, Northamptonshire; Pitzhanger Manor, Ealing; Port Eliot, Cornwall; Moggerhanger, Bedfordshire; and Butterton Farm House and Pelwall, both in Staffordshire.

In landscape design Humphry Repton continued and developed the ideals of Capability Brown between 1790 and his death in 1818. Characteristic layouts by him survive at Attingham, Salop; Endsleigh, Devon; Port Eliot, Cornwall; Tatton, Cheshire; Tregothnan, Cornwall; Woburn, Bedfordshire; and Sheringham, Norfolk, in some ways the most perfect example, since the undulating parkland with views of the sea is offset by a chaste white-brick villa of 1813–18, designed to complement it by Repton's son, John Adey Repton. Surviving Picturesque parks and gardens from the Regency period by hands other than Repton's include Hawkstone, Salop; Swinton, North Yorkshire; Scotney, Kent; Elvaston, Derbyshire; Alton, Staffordshire; and Ash-

Below: Gaunt's House, near Hinton Martell, Dorset. Lodge, c.1809. A characteristic example of the cottage orné

Right: Wimpole Hall, Cambridgeshire. Drawing Room, 1791–3; Sir J. Soane.

Above: Alton Towers, Staffordshire. Conservatory, c.1824; R. Abraham. One of the several Regency buildings recalling Coleridge's 'stately pleasure dome'

Right: Pagoda, Alton Towers, c. 1824; R. Abraham

Above left: Nanteos, Dyfed. These stables, c.1839–49, by E. Haycock, are unusually impressive for their function

Left: Clytha Park, Gwent. Clytha Castle, 1790. An extensive Gothick folly by the young Nash

ridge, Hertfordshire. At the latter enough survives of Repton's ornamental gardens, laid out from 1814, for us to appreciate the revolution which he helped effect towards the end of his life by reintroducing flower gardens near the house. After Repton's death the Italianate Revival encouraged another kind of artificial or formal display near the house which blossomed into the elaborate terraced Italianate gardens of the Victorian period. One of the first of these was at Charles Barry's Trentham Park, Staffordshire, laid out between 1834 and 1841 for the 2nd Duke of Sutherland, whose fabulous wealth derived from agricultural rents, canals and coal.

The eighteenth-century passion for building follies on country estates continued unabated in the Regency period, ranging from modest cottages masquerading as castles, as at Strattenborough Castle Farm, Berkshire, to Nash's elaborately fanciful Clytha Castle in the grounds of Clytha Park, Gwent. To include in the present book anything like a representative selection of these countless charming if absurd buildings would be an impossible task, and the enthusiast is recommended to turn to Barbara Jones's admirable *Follies and Grottoes* (2nd edition 1974).

Swinton Park, North Yorkshire. Druids' Temple, c.1800. Follies of this kind are surprisingly numerous; a little-known one survives at Blenheim

4

CHURCHES

The wars of 1793–1815 had not merely slowed down building activity but also increased the pace of an entirely free-rein industrialisation so that new areas were growing up in manufacturing towns without the benefit of churches. It was believed that apart from their purely spiritual role, churches would have a stabilising influence on society by preventing the development of revolutionary ideas. It was against this background that Parliament passed the Church Building Act of 1818 which granted £1 million for the building of new churches mainly for the benefit of the new industrial towns. The development of Anglican church architecture in the Regency period was, of course, dominated by this Act which led to the building of six hundred new churches between 1818 and 1856.

The eighteenth century had not been rich in church architecture apart from the flurry of baroque building activity in the metropolis following the Act for Fifty New Churches of 1711. The Anglican Church was for the most part architecturally and spiritually moribund. Its ministry was also largely associated in both the eighteenth and the nineteenth centuries with the upper middle classes, a fact which tended to diminish its impact on the growing working-class population. Of the leading Neo-Classical architects of the eighteenth century, Chambers and Holland built effectively no churches, Adam and James Wyatt very few. A number of minor churches were built, often as the result of a landowner's whim, but in c.1790 came a small group of strikingly-planned parish churches paid for out of parochial rates. The first of these is All Saints, Newcastle, designed by David Stephenson in 1786 with a revolutionary elliptical nave. This was echoed by George

Steuart, in his no less unconventional St Chad's, Shrewsbury (1790), where a large circular nave is preceded first by a circular room under the tower and then by a beautiful elliptical vestibule with twin staircases leading to the gallery. The geometrically designed tower similarly has three stages of equal importance: a rusticated cube sporting an octagon in turn surmounted by a cylinder. In the same year came S. P. Cockerell's St Mary's, Banbury, Oxfordshire, with a square nave in which, as at Wren's St Stephen Walbrook, eight of the twelve free-standing columns are linked by arches to form a circle roofed in the form of a dome. In a slightly different tradition is the church built and paid for near the end of his life by the prolific architect Carr of York at his birthplace, Horbury, West Yorkshire. Built in 1791–3 in an Adamesque style, Horbury has an elegant, aisleless, tunnel-vaulted nave and a plan which is basically an octagon. John Plaw's St Mary's, Paddington (1788–91), another inventive design, is an elegant cube containing an octagonal gallery. Related to it is the much larger church of St John, Hackney (1792–7), by James Spiller, a friend and sometime collaborator of Soane. Its Greek-cross plan supports a shallow vault resting on segmental arches. Above its austere brick walls rises an astonishing

St Chad, Shrewsbury, 1790–2; G. Steuart. The east end of one of the most original churches in the country

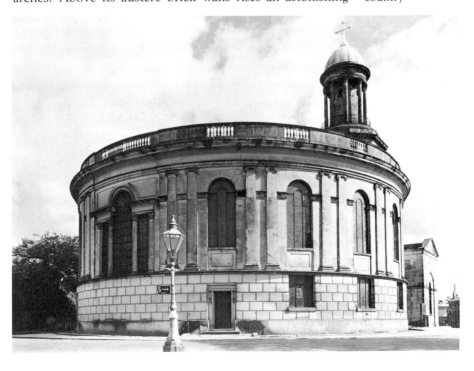

steeple of Portland stone added in 1812–13 from designs by Spiller in a style one can only describe as Soanean baroque.

The experimental planning of the churches by Stephenson, Steuart and Cockerell, which was taken up by non-conformist architects in the nineteenth century, was not echoed in the Commissioners' churches following the Act of 1818. In plan the Commissioners' churches were the simplest Protestant preaching boxes. This was not only for economical but also for liturgical reasons, since the churches from the first parliamentary grant just preceded the Catholic Revival in the Church of England. They compare unfavourably in this respect with the more ambitious and expensive churches associated with the Act of 1711 which reflected Laudian ideals as well as enthusiasms for baroque, antique and Early Christian architecture.

A new phase was opened with St Pancras New Church designed by the Inwoods in 1816. It precedes the 'Million' Act by two years and its cost of £70,000 was over four times as great as the most expensive of the Commissioners' churches which it superficially resembles. Not especially interesting in plan, it is memorable for the success with which the rich but taut ornamentation of the Erectheion in Athens is reproduced

St John, Hackney, London, 1792–7; J. Spiller. An essay in the Soane style with a tower of 1812–13, also by Spiller

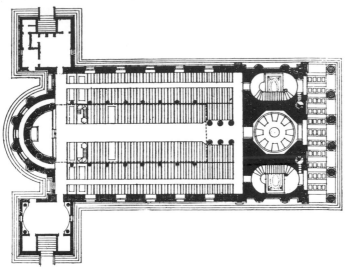

Left: St Pancras Church, Woburn Place, London, 1819–22; W. & H. W. Inwood. A principal function of the square projections at the east end is to house reproductions of the caryatid porch of the Erectheion in Athens

Below: The caryatid portico of St Pancras, the most elaborately Greek church in the country

in a new context. Reproduced is the right word, since some of the ornament, for example the architraves to the door in the portico, is made from casts sent specially from Athens. To some this literal approach to the Classical language of architecture was abhorrent. Thus C. R. Cockerell wrote of the church in his diary in July 1821: 'simple Greek, Greek, Greek – radiates bad taste thro the whole. it is anything but architecture'. While few today would go so far as Cockerell in condemning the St Pancras church, the Commissioners' churches are none the less generally considered deficient in imaginative architectural quality. A critic determined to be harsh could argue that Smirke, Porden, Hakewill, Bedford, Barry and the rest, tended to provide an institutional brick box lined internally with cast-iron galleries and tricked out externally with fashionable Greek or Gothic detail. However, the churches are well sited, and the porticos and bold towers of

St James, Bermondsey, London, 1827–9; J. Savage. The meticulously detailed tower

those in the Classical style have acted as valuable focus points in countless otherwise unmemorable urban areas. As Sir John Summerson neatly observed in *Georgian London*, Francis Bedford provided St John, Waterloo Road, London (1823-4), with 'a tower which does its best to be the *kind* of tower Ictinus *might* have put on the Parthenon *if* the Athenians had had the advantage of belonging to the Church of England'.

Nash, Soane and Smirke, as the three Crown architects retained by the Office of Works, were all invited to design Commissioners' churches. Soane's three executed churches, all surviving, were Holy Trinity, Marylebone Road; St Peter, Walworth; and St John, Bethnal Green, all in London. Even an architect of Soane's originality was defeated by the need to

St Mary (RC), Wigan, Greater Manchester, 1818. This gay Regency Gothic interior is in unexpected contrast to the church of St John further down the same street

St John (RC), Wigan, 1819, with an altar of 1834 by J. J. Scoles

produce large but economical structures, so that his churches, through exhibiting numerous curious details and arrestingly designed towers, have never been included amongst his most successful or powerful compositions. C. R. Cockerell, who was so censorious of St Pancras New Church, rejected the Commissioners' compromise planning and returned to first principles for the design of his Hanover Chapel in Regent Street in 1821. This was no rectangular box with a western tower riding incongruously above a portico, but a centrally-planned space lit by a remarkable glass and iron dome: a Wren theme in Neo-Classical dress. Outside, the Greek Ionic portico of Bath stone was most unusually flanked by twin towers, Picturesque features in the lively skyline of Regent Street. Both the Hanover Chapel and G. S. Repton's undistinguished St Philip's, Lower Regent Street, of 1819, have now been demolished, leaving Nash's All Souls', Langham Place (1822–5), with its fanciful circular portico and conical spire, as the only surviving church in Regent Street.

One of the most handsome of the early Commissioners' churches is St Thomas's, Stockport, Cheshire (1822), by George Basevi, a gifted pupil of Soane who became better

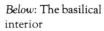

Everingham Park, Humberside. Catholic chapel, 1836–9; A. Giorgioli and J. Harper

Left: General view. A provocatively Italianate statement following Catholic Emancipation in 1829

Below: The basilical interior

known as the architect of the Fitzwilliam Museum at Cambridge. Like Inigo Jones's St Paul's, Covent Garden, and Cockerell's Hanover Chapel, it is approached through a portico placed at the east end so that one comes across the altar as soon as one enters. The portico is not solely an ornamental appendage but contains an open double-flight staircase of stone leading to the galleries.

St Thomas's, Stockport, is one of the few Classical churches built in the provinces with money from the first parliamentary grant. For reasons that are not entirely clear, the Gothic style was generally favoured in the provinces, though one of the most interesting Gothic churches was in London: James Savage's St Luke's, Chelsea (1820–4), with its celebrated and costly Bath-stone vault. Francis Goodwin built about a dozen churches in the Midlands and North-West, mainly in the Gothic style, though he was also a competent Greek Revivalist as his town halls of the early 1820s at Manchester and Macclesfield demonstrated. His Holy Trinity, Bordesley, Birmingham, has often been admired as an example of Regency Gothic at its prettiest. Thomas Rickman, who also worked extensively in the West Midlands, was a more accurate observer of medieval architecture than Goodwin, as is evident from St George's, Birmingham (1819, dem. 1960). However, the interior of his neo-Perpendicular St George, Everton, Liverpool (1813–14), is a dazzling and unarchaeological display of decorative and structural cast-iron, including tracery, galleries and even ceiling. His influential *Attempt to Discriminate the Styles of English Architecture from the Conquest to the Reformation* (1817) was a standard work throughout the nineteenth century. At Ombersley, in Hereford and Worcester, in 1825–9 he produced not a Commissioners' church but an estate church with an attractive spire for the Sandys family of Ombersley Court.

The story of Catholic and Nonconformist church building in this period is, of course, far less impressive architecturally. However, even before Catholic Emancipation in 1829, a number of architecturally quite substantial Catholic churches were put up. The Greek Revival was responsible for the best buildings: for example, Joseph Ireland's Catholic chapels at Walsall (1825–7) and Wolverhampton (1827–8); and, in the next decade, Charles Day's Catholic churches at Hereford and Bury St Edmunds, as well as the impressive St Bartholomew, Rainhill Stoops, Lancashire, a free-standing Ionic temple built by Joseph Dawson in

St Thomas (RC), Keith, Grampian Region, 1834; the Rev. W. Lovi. An unusual Italianate façade of a modified Gesù type

Below: Carver Street Methodist Church, Sheffield, 1804; the Rev. W. Jenkins. A good example of the standard type

St Giles, Elgin,
Grampian Region,
1827–8; A.
Simpson. One of
the most
impressive Greek
Revival churches
in Scotland

1838–40. These are the types of building against which Pugin
was to react so forcefully, though one can point to at least one
Catholic church of the 1830s which anticipates the kind of
historical accuracy which was to be increasingly characteristic
of the Gothic Revival: this is St Paulinus, Brough, North
Yorkshire, built in 1834–7 from designs by Sir William Lawson
and Ignatius Bonomi in imitation of the Early English Archbishop's Chapel (now library) at York.

The Wesleyan Methodists, who had been growing in
numbers and importance from the 1770s, were not interested
in lavish architectural display. In 1804 the Rev. W. Jenkins, a
Methodist minister, designed what was to be the characteristic
chapel of the early and mid nineteenth century: the Carver
Street Chapel, Sheffield, with its five-bay front, three-bay
pediment and round-headed first-floor windows.

The more muted liturgical flavour of Wales and Scotland makes those countries less rewarding for anyone in search of impressive ecclesiastical buildings in this period. Wales is singularly devoid of interest, but Scotland adopted the Greek Revival church with characteristic enthusiasm, as at North Church, Aberdeen, by J. Smith; St Mary, Edinburgh, by T. Brown; St Stephen, Edinburgh, by Playfair; St Giles, Elgin, by A. Simpson; St John's Free Church, Montrose, by W. Smith; North Leith church, by William Burn; and St Leonard, Perth, by Mackenzie. Gothic churches are far less successful. There are a number of modest country churches, often octagonal in plan, of which Glenorchy, by A. Elliot, is a good example. In Glasgow there is St David, by Rickman and Hutchinson, and St Andrew (RC), by J. G. Graham. The most attractive Gothic church in Edinburgh is St John, by Burn, with its pretty neo-Perpendicular vault.

5

ROYAL WORKS

The reigning monarchs in the Regency period were King George III (1760–1820); King George IV (1820–30), Prince Regent from 1811 to 1820; King William IV (1830–7); and, briefly, Queen Victoria (1837–1901). Of these the only one who seriously concerns us is George IV, for he is central to the whole story of architecture in Britain from 1800–30. Without his enthusiastic support it is unlikely that Nash's Regent Street and Regent's Park would ever have been created. One of his first acts as king in 1820 was to elevate Walter Scott to the baronetcy. Two years later it was Scott who stage-managed his visit to Edinburgh, the first to Scotland of any king since Charles II. It was on this visit that George IV in bogus tartan inaugurated the 'Highland' takeover of Scotland which was one of the lasting fantasies which the Victorian age was to inherit from the Regency.

The architectural output of the Office of Works in the period 1790–1840 is formidable. From these years date many of the buildings which to Englishmen and tourists express most forcefully the national identity. Nash gave us Buckingham Palace, Clarence House, the Marble Arch and the Brighton Pavilion; Wyatville (Jeffry Wyatt), the remodelled Windsor Castle, Fort Belvedere and the Virginia Water Ruins; Smirke, the British Museum, Royal Mint and (now demolished) the General Post Office; Wilkins, the National Gallery; Soane, the Board of Trade building in Whitehall (remodelled by Barry) and the Law Courts at Westminster (dem. 1883); and Barry, the Houses of Parliament, begun in 1840. In 1824–35 some £25,000 were also spent on a major repair of the Palace of Holyroodhouse in Edinburgh, following George IV's state visit in 1822.

The public buildings erected by Smirke and Wilkins are more appropriately included in a later chapter devoted to museums. The story in this chapter is largely that of the inordinate passion for building of King George IV for whom, as Summerson remarked in his *Life and Work of John Nash*, the pleasures of architecture were more in anticipation than in achievement. Nash, easy-going as a man and an architect, possessed a fatal attraction for the king. He switched

seductively from one style to another to suit the passing whims of his royal patron: Royal Lodge, Windsor, the most elaborate cottage orné of all, came in 1813–16; the fairy-tale orientalism of Brighton Pavilion in 1815–21; and, less successfully, the attempt to provide monumental Classicism at Buckingham Palace in 1825–30. Royal Lodge was subsequently remodelled by Wyatville, to whom is due much of what survives today. Nash's sumptuous remodelling of the ground floor of Carlton House in 1813 was lost when the building was demolished in 1827–8 following the transference of the king's affections to Buckingham Palace. In the summer of 1814 Nash devised a series of spectacular pavilions in the gardens of Carlton House and the parks of central London for a chain of national celebrations including the reception of the Allied Sovereigns in June. Extravaganzas such as the pagoda over the water in St James's Park have long since disappeared, but Nash's vast dodecagonal ballroom, a tent-like timber-frame construction, survives at Woolwich as the not inappropriate home of a military museum. Nearby are the Royal Military Academy, a castellated pile by James Wyatt of c.1800–6, and the Royal Artillery Barracks, one of the largest Neo-Classical buildings in the country, begun in 1775 but completed by Wyatt in 1802–8.

In 1800–14 King George III spent £150,000 in improvements at Windsor Castle which included much thin neo-Gothic work by Wyatt. Despite this, Parliament voted another £150,000 in 1824 to repair and remodel the castle. Those invited to submit designs were Jeffry Wyatt and the three attached architects of the Office of Works, Nash,

Left: Buckingham Palace, 1825–30; Nash. The scenically composed garden front

Below: Royal Artillery Barracks, Artillery Place, Greenwich, begun in 1775 and finished by J. Wyatt in 1808 on a scale worthy of St Petersburg

Smirke and Soane. The plans by Wyatt were chosen and work was carried out on remodelling the Upper Ward and Round Tower to his designs between 1824 and 1840. As a result, Windsor is effectively a nineteenth-century building, the image of what the Romantic movement thought a castle ought to look like with picturesquely disposed towers and machicolations, but with a comfortable, well-planned modern interior including a neo-Rococo ballroom, Gothic banqueting room and lushly Classical drawing rooms. By the end, more than £1 million of public money had been spent on the castle, though a committee of enquiry into the cost of completion, appointed in 1830, found no evidence of financial incaution on the architect's part. Two years earlier Nash had emerged with an almost equally unscathed reputation from a Select Committee of Enquiry of the House of Commons into the increasing and apparently uncontrolled expenditure on Buckingham Palace.

Jeffry Wyatt's other Picturesque contributions to Windsor included the remarkable arrangement of Roman columns brought to Virginia Water from Lepcis Magna to form an imaginary 'Temple of Augustus'; and the remodelling of the triangular Belvedere into the startling castellated folly known as Fort Belvedere. A specialist in Picturesque transformation, Jeffry Wyatt even went so far as to transform his own name in 1824, with the king's permission, into the more medieval-sounding Wyatville.

Windsor Castle: the east front, containing the Private Apartments, as remodelled by Wyatville from 1824.

6

MUNICIPAL BUILDINGS

I t should be remembered that English counties had no measure of self-government until 1888; that parish self-government was of negligible importance in the Regency period; that the Municipal Corporations Act, which set up municipal bodies elected by rate-payers, did not come until 1835, and that even after that date rural justice and rural administration were carried out by unpaid Justices of the Peace. Moreover, in Scotland there were no parliamentary or municipal representative institutions till 1832-3. A very different impression might, however, be formed from a glance at the numerous public buildings erected prior to 1835. The early nineteenth century saw the establishment in public architecture of a building type that was massive, plain, Doric, and marked with the unmistakeable stamp of authority. The gifted Chester architect Thomas Harrison played a leading role in establishing this style. Indeed, it is a field in which provincial architects especially flourished: for example, Edward Haycock in Salop, Blackburn in Gloucestershire, Kendall in Lincolnshire, Watson in Yorkshire, and Reid in Edinburgh.

One of the few metropolitan architects with an extensive provincial practice in this field was Robert Smirke: character-istic of his Grecian sobriety are his Shire Halls at Gloucester (1814), Hereford (1815) and Shrewsbury (1834), his County Buildings at Perth (1815-19), and his Council House at Bristol (1824). However, at Carlisle in 1810 and Lincoln in 1823 he provided Assize Courts in castellated Gothic. Since the provision of separate buildings for law courts had not begun before the eighteenth century, Smirke had few prece-dents to guide him. His choice of Gothic was prompted by the immediate proximity at Lincoln of the medieval castle and at

Left: Old Academy (now County Library), Perth, 1803–7; R. Reid. An admirable example of the Adam style which was shortly to be supplanted by the Greek Revival

Below left: County Buildings, Perth, 1815–19; Sir R. Smirke. Uncompromisingly Greek

Below: Sessions House, Knutsford, Cheshire, 1817–19; G. Moneypenny. An imposing façade long attributed to T. Harrison of Chester

Carlisle of the Tudor Citadel. Harrison had come to the same decision at Lancaster Castle which he reconstructed from 1786–99, providing a spectacular new Shire Hall (Crown Court), Grand Jury Room and Gaol. This work was completed by J. M. Gandy in 1802–23 to whom its design was until recently erroneously attributed.

In 1785–1822 Harrison rebuilt Chester Castle so as to create one of the most impressive Greek Revival public buildings in England with County Courts, Gaol (now demolished), Armoury, Barracks and Exchequer, approached through a monumental Doric gateway begun in 1810 and inspired by the Athenian propylaea. An early design by Harrison of c.1786 suggests that he had orginally considered adopting the Gothic style so as to be in keeping with the few surviving portions of the medieval castle. The Shire Hall was constructed behind the main Doric portico in 1791–1801. A coffered, top-lit semi-circle with a noble colonnade of ten free-standing Ionic columns, it was inspired by Gondoin's celebrated Ecole de Chirurgie in Paris (1771–6) and is one of the finest public interiors of the Neo-Classical period in the country. It makes an intriguing comparison with Harrison's contemporary Shire Hall, or civil court, at Lancaster Castle where a similar theme is given a Gothic treatment, incorporating a plan which consists of seven sides of a polygon in semi-circular formation.

In 1810 John Stokoe brought Harrison's chaste but monumental Neo-Classicism to Newcastle with his massively Greek design for the County Courts or Moot Hall, erected in Castle Garth in 1810–12. Exactly contemporary is the Glasgow Court House, Gaol and public offices by William Stark. This group, of which only the portico survives, is a possible rival to Smirke's Covent Garden Theatre as the first public building in Britain to boast a Greek Doric portico. Charles Watson adopted a similar manner in Yorkshire for his Court Houses at Beverley, Wakefield, Pontefract and Sheffield, all begun between 1804 and 1807. George Byfield's Sessions House at Canterbury (1806–10) is in a Greek Revival style, but his Assembly Room at Worcester Guildhall (1791) has an Adamesque mood which reminds us that he had almost certainly been a pupil of Robert Taylor.

The post-Harrison manner continues with Aikin's Wellington Assembly Rooms, Liverpool (1815–16), with their impressive windowless façade; Benjamin Wishlade's Town Hall at Kington, Hereford and Worcester (1820); Browning's Sessions House at Bourne, Lincolnshire (1821), enlivened externally with a pretty open staircase; Foulston's Devonport Town Hall (1821); Goodwin's Town Hall and Assembly Rooms at Macclesfield (1823–4) and at Manchester, of which the Ionic portico survives as a screen in Heaton Park; Richard Lane's town halls at Salford (1825–7) and Chorlton-on-Medlock, Manchester (1830); Lee's Barnstaple Guildhall (1826); and Thomas Cooper's Brighton Town Hall (1830–2). Then with the 1830s came the increasing grandeur, often of a Roman variety, which we associate with the Early Victorian period: Charles Day's Worcester Shire Hall (1834–8) owes something to Schinkel and Smirke, as does A. H. Wilds's Gravesend Town Hall (1836). Hansom and Welch's Birmingham Town Hall (1832–4, completed 1836 onwards by C. Edge) is an echo in Anglesey marble of the Temple of Castor and Pollux in the Forum at Rome. In Wales, Wyatt and Brandon's Shire Hall at Brecon, Powys (1839–43), is a late example of influence from Smirke, while D. Vaughan's Greek Doric Town Hall at Bridgend, Mid Glamorgan (1842), was unfortunately demolished in 1971. St George's Hall and Assize Courts at Liverpool is one of the finest Neo-Classical public buildings in Europe. Designed by Harvey Lonsdale Elmes in 1839–40 and completed after his death in 1847 by C. R. Cockerell, it is a combination of law courts, assembly hall and concert hall in a form inspired by the temples and baths of

Right: Sessions House (now Town Hall), Bourne, Lincolnshire, 1821; B. Browning. A novel and lively composition by a talented but little-known architect

Below right: Victoria Rooms, Bristol, 1839–41; C. Dyer. Civic dignity on an unusually opulent scale

ancient Rome. It is triumphant proof that revivalism can work.

The designs of hospitals and gaols in this period are closely related to each other. The crucifom and the radial plan both had a long history in Europe, the former reaching back to the late Middle Ages, the latter to the seventeenth century. However, the dominance of the country house as a building type in eighteenth-century England meant that buildings such as the Friends' Retreat of 1794–6 at Fulford, York, designed by John Bevans as an insane asylum run by Quakers, resembled a late Palladian country house. Similar in feel is the more modest Norfolk lunatic asylum, now St Andrew's Hospital, at Thorpe, Norwich, built in 1811–14 from designs by Francis Stone as probably the first public mental hospital in the country. More institutional in planning, though of considerable architectural refinement, is the Royal Naval (now St Nicholas) Hospital, Great Yarmouth. Built in 1809–11 from designs by William Pilkington or Edward Holl, it deploys four arcaded blocks, each twenty-nine bays long, approached through a triumphal arch. After c.1810 the Greek Revival dominates with its grand, correctly detailed stone

Infirmary, Carlisle, Cumbria, 1830–2; R. Tattersall. Subtle handling of rustication

Jesmond Road Cemetery Gateway, Newcastle, 1836; J. Dobson. An eloquent and novel composition

porticos: leading architects such as Smirke produced the Royal Salop Infirmary at Shrewsbury (1826–30) and Wilkins the St George's Hospital, London (1827). Scottish and provincial architects followed their lead: see, for example, W. Burn's hospital (now school) at Tranent, Lothian Region (1821–2), and his Murray Royal Asylum for the Insane at Kinnoull, near Perth (1827), the earliest surviving asylum in Scotland; as well as the infirmaries of 1829–32 by John Oates at Huddersfield, Richard Tattersall at Carlisle and Richard Lane at Stockport, John Whichcord's Oakwood Hospital, Maidstone (1830), and Henry Briant's Royal Berkshire Hospital, Reading (1837–9), a late and impressive example of the type.

The history of prison design in this period begins with the influential publications of John Howard, especially *The State of the Prisons* (1777) and *An Account of the Principal Lazarettos in Europe* (1789), in which he condemned the conditions in contemporary prisons and hospitals. What Howard admired was the Maison de Force at Ackerghem near Ghent, built on a radial plan in the 1770s as a house of correction for the whole of Flanders. The architect William Blackburn built nearly twenty prisons incorporating the ideas of his friend John Howard: for example, his County Gaol at Dorchester (1789–95), which has been largely demolished. More elaborate was the Millbank Penitentiary in London, begun in 1812 by Thomas Hardwick and also now demolished. It was an influential design in which each of the radiating arms formed a pentagon. An alternative to the radiating plan was the 'Panopticon' or 'all-seeing' plan proposed by Jeremy Bentham in 1791 which disposed the cells round the periphery of a circle with an observation post at the centre. Blackburn was once more the pioneer, and parts of his House of Correction at Northleach, Gloucestershire (1787–91), survive today as the Police Station. This was followed by the (now demolished) semi-circular Bridewell at Edinburgh, built in 1791–5 by Robert and James Adam of all people, and by the polygonal county gaol at Devizes, Wiltshire, by Richard Ingleman who specialised in asylum design. The Panopticon was an English speciality and nearly forty prisons were built on this principle in England and Wales between 1801 and 1833. Stylistically, prison design was still coloured by the Romantic tradition of 'architecture parlante', which meant that a prison should look grim and alarming. This tradition, which went back to Piranesi and Ledoux, had influenced Dance's celebrated Newgate Gaol (1770–85) and appeared even in minor buildings like Browning's House of Correction at Folkingham, Lincolnshire (1824–5), and the County Gaol at Canterbury (1806–10) by George Byfield, who designed similar gaols at Bury St Edmunds and Cambridge. The same theme can be detected at the well-preserved gaol at Beaumaris, Anglesey (1828–9), by Hansom and Welch, open to the public as a gripping museum of prison life.

Beaumaris Gaol, Anglesey, 1828–9; Hansom & Welch. The forbidding entrance

7

INSTITUTIONS OF LEARNING

The passion for collecting which had been so vital a part of the Neo-Classical movement of the eighteenth century flourished in the early nineteenth century in the provision throughout Europe of temples of art in the form of large public museums. In England Smirke led the way with his British Museum (1823–46), a solemn windowless temple with an uninterrupted Ionic colonnade which is remarkably close to the exactly contemporary Altes Museum in Berlin by Schinkel. In 1834 came the design of two more major museums: Basevi's Fitzwilliam Museum at Cambridge, and Wilkins's National Gallery. The Fitzwilliam Museum, completed internally after Basevi's death by Cockerell in 1845–7 and by E. M. Barry in 1870–5, is a monumental building with a Roman grandeur and richness which point to the Victorian future. Cockerell's Ashmolean Museum and Taylorian Institution at Oxford (1839–45) is one of the most arresting and original Classical buildings of its date anywhere in Europe. However, its masterly handling of a range of sources from Greek to baroque makes it more impressive as an aesthetic statement than as a functional museum. Cockerell had given little thought to techniques of picture display, unlike his German contemporaries Schinkel and Klenze, and unlike Soane, whose Dulwich Gallery (1811–14) was not only the first independent building erected as a picture gallery but was also important as an early example of top-lighting. W. H. Playfair's National Gallery of Scotland in Edinburgh (1850–7) is a late contribution to the tradition of Basevi and Smirke. A monumental composition, it yet retains a Schinkelesque sobriety.

One of the most characteristic building types in the provincial towns of Regency England was the Literary and Philosophical Institution. Like the museum, the 'Lit and Phil' was a consequence of the adoption by the educated middle class of the intellectual and literary pursuits associated in the eighteenth century with connoisseurs and dilettanti drawn from the nobility and gentry. The Greek Revival lent itself well to this new building type as can be seen from Cockerell's Literary and Philosophical Institution at Bristol (1821–3) and John Green's at Newcastle (1822–5), Barry's handsome Schinkelesque Royal Institution of Fine Arts (now City Art Gallery) at Manchester (1824–35), and T. G. Elger's Literary and Scientific Institute (now a public library) at Bedford (1834). The Philosophical Societies of York and of Scarborough commissioned handsome Greek Revival museums from, respectively, Wilkins in 1827–30 and Sharp in 1828–9.

Gentlemen's clubs underwent a similar social and architectural development in this period. The coffee houses and gambling houses of the eighteenth century were replaced by that note of professional sobriety which was such a feature

Fitzwilliam Museum, Cambridge, 1834–45; Basevi. One of the most splendid Classical buildings of its date in Britain

Yorkshire Museum, York, 1827–30; Wilkins. Wilkins claimed to have adopted the Grecian style so as not to compete with the nearby Gothic ruins of St Mary's Abbey

of the post-Waterloo years. The University Club (founded 1822), Athenaeum (founded 1824), Carlton (founded 1831) and Reform (founded 1836) are manifestly expressions of this new mood, while the United Service Club (founded 1815) and Travellers' (founded 1819) were even more direct products of the Napoleonic Wars. Indeed, the Travellers' is the quintessence of that spirit of Regency elegance and connoisseurship which grew out of the Georgian tradition of the Grand Tour, since it was founded by Castlereagh to promote friendship between Englishmen and foreigners at a time when the Continent was reopened to visitors after its virtual closure during the Napoleonic Wars.

In the architectural development of clubs Smirke is once more a dominant figure. His Junior United Service Club in Lower Regent Street (1817–19) has been demolished, but the Grecian façades of his Union Club (1822–7) survive as part of Canada House in Trafalgar Square. Facing each other across Waterloo Place are Decimus Burton's Athenaeum (1827–30) and Nash's United Service Club (1826–8), each designed round a magnificent staircase hall. The shift from the Greek Revival came as early as 1829 with Charles Barry's influential designs for the Travellers' Club in Pall Mall. He developed this theme with greater richness in the Reform Club (1837–41)

next door and, less impressively, at the Manchester Athenaeum (1837–9). The late Classical interiors of these clubs, in which an overall Greek austerity of line is offset by touches of succulent ornament such as lotus and acanthus leaves in plaster or mahogany, form a phase in interior design from c.1800–40 which is one of the happiest in English architecture. Below shallow coffered domes illuminated by elegant colza-oil lamps, gentlemen could relax in mahogany and leather armchairs, fitted with brass reading-stands, from which they could reach a nearby wine-table supported on a fluted Doric column – a pattern seemingly invented by Decimus Burton for the Athenaeum.

Athenaeum, Waterloo Place, London, 1827–30; D. Burton. (Attic storey added later.) A cast of the Parthenon frieze runs round the building below the cornice

This was not simply a style confined to a few fashionable London clubs but was a widespread Regency pattern found in provincial Reading Rooms and Mechanics Institutes. It is fortunate that an architect of the calibre of Thomas Harrison should have specialised in this field. His Lyceum at Liverpool, built in 1800–3, contains a News Room and a handsome domed Library founded in 1758 as the first gentlemen's subscription library in the country. His Portico Library at Manchester (1802–6) has a saucer-domed interior, and his News Room at Chester (1808) an elegant Ionic exterior. Thomas Johnson's Library at Leeds (1808) is similarly neo-Greek; Foulston's at Plymouth (1812, dem. 1941) is in a more Soanean manner; while Watson's at Wakefield (1820–1) is grandly Ionic. Rickman's Subscription News Room and

Library (demolished 1970) at Carlisle (1830) is untypically in a convincingly Gothic style. Arguably the most impressive Neo-Classical library in the country, after Smirke's King's Library at the British Museum, is the Signet Library in Parliament Square, Edinburgh. Lined with majestic Corinthian columns, the Upper and Lower Signet Libraries are of 1812–16 by William Stark, one of the ablest Scottish architects of his day. They are connected by a magnificent staircase by W. H. Playfair constructed in 1819–20 within façades by Robert Reid of 1810–12.

The medical and legal professions were quick to house themselves in premises of suitable Classical dignity. George Dance's Royal College of Surgeons in Lincoln's Inn Fields (1806–13, remodelled by Barry 1835–7) provided London with its first Greek Ionic portico. Smirke followed with the Royal College of Physicians in Trafalgar Square (1822–5), while Vulliamy built the Law Society's Hall in Chancery Lane (1828–32) in Smirke's Grecian style and, in 1838, the extraordinary frontage of the Royal Institution in Albemarle Street, consisting of a row of giant Corinthian half-columns. F. Long of Liverpool designed the Greek Ionic Royal Institution of South Wales at Swansea, West Glamorgan

Lyceum Club, Liverpool, 1800–3; T. Harrison. Reading Room

(1838–40), but in general only Edinburgh could provide professional buildings on the scale of those in London. W. H. Playfair built the imposingly Doric Royal Institution (now Royal Scottish Academy) in 1822–6 and 1832–5, as well as the Surgeons Hall, opposite the university, in 1830–2. To Thomas Hamilton is due one of the most arresting buildings of the whole period 1790–1840. This is the Royal College of Physicians in Queen Street, Edinburgh (1843–6), with a bold aedicular façade which skilfully evokes the work of Soane, Cockerell and Basevi: no mean achievement.

Royal Institution (now Scottish Academy), Edinburgh, 1822–6 and 1832–5; W. H. Playfair. Neo-Classical stylophily

Grammar schools and public schools as well as the universities of Oxford and Cambridge slumbered peacefully during the eighteenth century. The pattern of gradually-dropping numbers was sharply reversed during the Napoleonic Wars: for example, at Cambridge there were 150 matriculations in 1800, but 440 by 1830; at Oxford, 255 in 1800, 405 in 1830. This increase was reflected in a vast building campaign at Cambridge, though curiously not at Oxford.

The years 1790–1840 also saw important innovations in both the planning and the style of educational buildings. Gothic became established on associational grounds for Anglican schools and for the colleges of Oxford and Cambridge, while the Classical style survived in the chillier setting of Scotland, in dissenting academies, and in the public halls and libraries of great universities. A break was at last made in schools with the custom of teaching large numbers of boys in a single great chamber, Tite's Mill Hill School (originally Protestant Dissenters' Grammar School), of 1825–7, being an early instance of the provision of individual class-rooms for masters.

William Wilkins emerges as a leading architect in the field of educational architecture. His Greek Revival designs for Downing College, Cambridge (partially executed from 1807–20), and for the East India (now Haileybury) College, Hertfordshire (executed 1806–9), helped establish an undemonstratively Greek style for public buildings and institutions which was all too widely imitated: for example, at Tite's Mill Hill School, Middlesex. Wilkins himself soon deviated from it in his new buildings of the 1820s at Trinity, Corpus Christi and King's Colleges, Cambridge, for which he adopted a Tudor Gothic style of supposedly monastic association. Scotland, where educational standards had remained far higher during the eighteenth century than in England, took with her customary enthusiasm to the Greek Revival. Young boys were overwhelmed by Grecian templar magnificence in Playfair's Dollar Academy, Central Region (1818–20); W. Burn's Edinburgh Academy (1823–6); T. Hamilton's spectacularly composed Royal High School, Edinburgh (1825–9); the heavily elaborate Bathgate Academy, Lothian Region (1831), by R. & R. Dickson; and Angus's Dundee High School, Tayside Region (1832–4). In England the most impressive of all Greek Revival schools is William Flockton's Wesley Proprietary (now King Edward VII) Grammar School, Sheffield (1837–40). Its twenty-five-bay-long façade

Mill Hill School, Barnet, London, 1825–7; Sir W. Tite. Big bland composition in the Wilkins style

with a giant portico of eight Corinthian columns brought a touch of the aristocratic grandeur of a Wentworth Wood-house to the budding Methodists of the industrial West Riding.

Such schools were untypical. The characteristic school of the nineteenth century was to be Christian Gothic like its churches. The tone was set at Rugby School by the minor architect Henry Hakewill with his quadrangle, Headmaster's House and chapel (1809–21), forming an asymmetrical Tudor Gothic group. C. R. Cockerell worked in a similar style at Harrow School (1819–20) and at St David's College, Lampeter, Dyfed (1822–3). John Wilson's Elizabeth College, St Peter Port, Guernsey (1826–9) is a much larger Tudor Gothic pile comparable with Rickman and Hussey's New Court at St John's College, Cambridge, or with Wilkins's buildings in the same university. A closely related group of imposingly neo-Perpendicular buildings includes Christ's Hospital, Newgate Street, London (1820–32, dem. 1902), by the elder and younger John Shaw; Charles Barry's King Edward VI's Grammar School, Birmingham (1833–7, dem. 1936); and H. L. Elmes's Collegiate Institution, Everton, Liverpool (1840–3). The Sebright School at Wolverley, Hereford and Worcester (1829), probably by William Knight, is an early and curious example of a Pointed Gothic Revival.

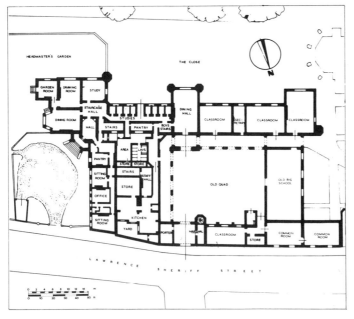

Rugby School, Warwickshire, 1809–16; H. Hakewill. An early example of the revival of the Tudor style for educational buildings

Dollar Academy, Central Region, 1818–20; W. H. Playfair. The Tuscan order is employed on an unusually monumental scale

Other prominent Gothic schools and colleges include Richard Lane's Blue Coat School at Oldham, Lancashire (1829–34); Blore's English School at Bedford (1833–7); the very pretty but now altered Sheffield Collegiate School (now City Training College) of 1835 by J. G. Weightman; J. Harper's St Peter's School, York (1838); and the Roman Catholic St Mary's College, New Oscott, Birmingham (1835–8) by Joseph Potter, with a chapel richly ornamented by Pugin in 1837–8.

One of the most originally planned schools of this date was the now demolished City of London School in Cheapside, erected in 1835–7 at the expense of the Corporation from designs by J. B. Bunning of Coal Exchange fame. The City of London School, which claimed to have been the first (1838) in England to give practical science lessons, was, like Mill Hill School, organised round separate class-rooms dedicated to specialist-subject masters. It also boasted a circular lecture theatre inspired by the 'Panopticon' principle proposed in Bentham's educational work, *Chrestomathia* (1816). A similar pattern seems to have been adopted for the lecture rooms at Hamilton's Edinburgh High School (1825).

This was not a major period for university buildings. However, Robert Adam's splendid university at Edinburgh, begun in 1789–93, was completed to a modified design in 1817–26 by W. H. Playfair, though the noble dome was not added till the 1880s by Rowand Anderson. Playfair also added the Upper Library with its coffered segmental vault resting on rows of fluted piers. C. R. Cockerell won a competition initiated in 1829 for replacing the Schools building at Cambridge with a mighty quadrangle of libraries and lecture rooms. Only the north range, now the Squire Law Library, was built (1837–40) on a scale suggesting that however brilliant its handling of the Classical language might be, the completed project would have been oppressive on so cramped a site. A commission of comparable importance, University College, London, fell not to Cockerell, who entered the competition, but to the far less talented Wilkins, whose designs, executed in 1827–8, provided an impressive portico and external staircase but nothing much else of practical or aesthetic consequence.

University Library (now Squire Law Library), Cambridge, 1836–7; C. R. Cockerell. (The book stacks are later.) The imposing barrel-vaulted vista is framed by Greek Ionic columns of the unique Bassae order

8

COMMERCIAL BUILDINGS

The great growth in banking and in life-insurance did not come until near the end of the Regency period. The establishment of note-issuing banking corporations outside the metropolis was not permitted until the Bank Act of 1826, which also enabled the Bank of England to establish branch offices for the first time. Such was the monopolistic power of the Bank of England that it was another seven years before note-issuing banking corporations were permitted in London itself. Our story, therefore, begins in London where Soane's Bank of England, perhaps the most architecturally distinguished bank premises of all time, was alas almost entirely destroyed in the 1920s. As banker to the Government, the Bank of England operated in a quite different way from the private banks. This was reflected in the monumental character of its columnar courts and domed halls as brilliantly remodelled by Soane in 1788–1833. The private banks in England tended to resemble private houses, with a central front door, business rooms on either side and accommodation for a resident manager above. Hoare's Bank, Fleet Street, by Charles Parker, of 1829–32, is a remarkable survival of this domestic tradition.

The most important commercial architect of the 1830s and 40s was C. R. Cockerell. It was he who helped establish the image of a bank in which the security of money is reflected in the security seemingly provided by the Doric order. His London and Westminster Bank in Lothbury (1837–9) has been demolished, but three of his branch Banks of England survive at Manchester, Bristol and Liverpool. Designed and executed in 1844–8, these fall chronologically though not stylistically outside the limits of this book. Admirable in their

brilliant handling of the orders, they are also interesting as being transitional in plan and appearance between the domestic and the public.

Covent Garden Market, London, 1828–30; C. Fowler. The west front as recently restored

In 1839 Cockerell prepared plans for the Royal Exchange which, had they been executed, would have given London a great masterpiece in that rich Classicism which marks the shift from Regency to Victorian. The Royal Exchange was eventually erected from designs by William Tite in a coarsely Classical style which is not aesthetically an improvement on David Hamilton's Royal Exchange (now Stirling's Library) in Glasgow of 1827–9. Though impressive in scale, the Glasgow Exchange is a somewhat disorganised Grecian variant on Gibbs's St Martin-in-the-Fields. Scottish architects played an important role in the design of banks and exchanges. We scarcely find outside Scotland banks on the scale of Crichton and Reid's Bank of Scotland in Edinburgh (1802–6), influenced stylistically by Adam; or Archibald Elliot's Bank of Scotland at Glasgow (1827), immediately west of Hamilton's Royal Exchange. With its giant Ionic portico, Elliot's bank vies in dignity with major public buildings in England.

In the eighteenth century life-insurance was largely unknown in Europe outside England. It developed in late eighteenth-century England as the consequence of the rise of a professional middle class with incomes only for life. Few companies provided themselves with architecturally significant premises before the later 1830s. The exceptions have not survived: for example, J. M. Gandy's Phoenix Fire and Pelican

Life Insurance Office, Charing Cross (1804–5); and Cockerell's stylistically more important Westminster Life and British Fire Office, Strand (1829–32).

In the 1820s and 30s England could boast one of the leading designers of markets in Europe, Charles Fowler. With its granite Tuscan columns and glass-roofed arcade, his Covent Garden Market (1828–30) combines the rationalist approach of Durand with the refinement of the best Regency tradition. It has recently been restored with great imagination and charm. His graceful glass and iron domed conservatory of 1827–30 at Syon House, Middlesex, also survives as does the Greek Doric Higher Market which he built at Exeter in 1835–8 from designs by George Dymond. However, his remarkable Hungerford Market, London (1831–3), and Lower Market, Exeter (1835–7), have both been demolished. Three other elegant markets with Grecian features survive in Cornwall: all built in the 1830s, they are at Helston and Bodmin, both by William Harris, and at Penzance, by J. J. Whitling. More fulsome is the imposing Market Hall at Bridgwater, Somerset, designed by John Bowen in 1826 and constructed in 1834. Its entrance façade with colonnaded rotunda and crowning cupola is curiously close to the Merchants Exchange in Philadelphia by William Strickland, of 1832–4. A more familiar English type is the Corn Exchange, often with a Tuscan portico. Characteristic examples are at Guildford (1818) by Henry Garling; Winchester (1836–8) by Owen Carter; and Sudbury (1841) by H. E.

Syon House, Hounslow, London. Conservatory, 1827–30; C. Fowler. An impressively architectural composition

Kendall. One of the most impressive of all markets is that at Newcastle constructed on a giant grid plan by Dobson in 1835–6 as the core of his scheme for revitalising the town. The choice of the Tuscan order for functional buildings such as markets was prompted by its modest place in the hierarchy of the orders. Renaissance theorists had considered it suitable for barns and simple country buildings.

A tradition related to that of the glazed market produced the shopping arcade or bazaar which enjoyed a great vogue in London and even more so in Paris in the period 1790–1840. They were especially popular with ladies who, free from the effects of inclement weather, could shop with greater leisure, comfort and elegance. The best surviving arcades are, in London, Nash's Royal Opera Arcade, with glazed domes over each bay, and Samuel Ware's Burlington Arcade, Piccadilly, both of c.1816; in Bristol, James Foster's Upper and Lower Arcades (1824–5); and in Glasgow, the less attractive Argyle Arcade (1827–8) by John Baird. Two of the finest examples have unfortunately been demolished: Nash's Lowther Arcade in the Strand, London (1830–2), and John Dobson's Royal Arcade, Newcastle (1831–2). In Motcomb Street, Belgravia, there is a bazaar and arcade of c.1830 by Joseph Jopling and opposite, by the same architect, the Pantechnicon (now Sotheby's Belgravia), designed as a furniture repository for the

Below: Market Hall, Bridgwater, Somerset, 1826 and 1834; J. Bowen. This forms a lively group with the spire of the parish church

Right: Royal Opera Arcade, Pall Mall, London, 1816–18; Nash. Less altered than the better-known Burlington Arcade in Piccadilly

local residents. With its stucco façade adorned with ten engaged Greek Doric columns, the Pantechnicon is a perfect statement of the flashy side of Regency taste.

Despite the ephemeral nature of shops, a surprising number of Regency shop fronts survive in the towns and villages of England. There are, for example, several in Stamford, Lincolnshire, though the best-known is probably Fribourg and Treyer in the Haymarket, London. At Woburn Walk, designed by Cubitt in 1822, a whole street of such shops survives within a stone's throw of Euston Station.

The halls of the city companies form a category of their own. Of those surviving from this period, three give an attractive and instructive picture of the styles through which English architecture was passing: Mylne's façade of Stationers' Hall (1800–1) is a tautly elegant composition reminiscent of Samuel Wyatt; Fishmongers' Hall (1831–5), smoothly Greek Revival in style, is by Henry Roberts who had been trained by Charles Fowler and Robert Smirke; while Goldsmiths' Hall (1829–35) is an astonishing neo-baroque essay by Philip Hardwick. Outside London the cutlers of Sheffield were in a position to erect a noble Corinthian pile in 1832 from designs by Worth and Taylor. Now the Chamber of Commerce, Cutlers' Hall was much enlarged in 1867 and 1881.

Few Regency theatres have survived, spectacular exceptions being Benjamin Wyatt's Theatre Royal, Drury Lane (1810–12), with its enchanting vestibules and staircases; and the Corinthian façade of Nash's Haymarket Theatre (1820–1).

Theatre Royal, Drury Lane, London, 1810–11; B. D. Wyatt. The elegant lobbies and staircases still survive but the auditorium, semi-circular in imitation of antique theatres, has been remodelled

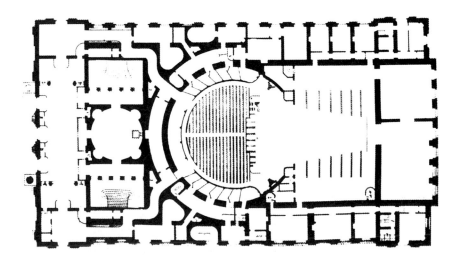

The auditoria of both these theatres have been rebuilt in recent times, but Wilkins's theatre at Bury St Edmunds (1819) is a well-preserved example both inside and out of the small provincial theatres of Late Georgian England.

If Regency theatres are rare, hotels are prolific. Indeed, no European country seems to have been more generous in its provision of hotels in this period than England. Indulgence in travelling, as a legacy of the Grand Tour; the stage-coach boom of the early nineteenth century; the relative shortness of distances in England; and the growing popularity of spas and seaside resorts, are all factors related to the rise of the hotel.

From the late eighteenth century there is Henry Holland's Swan Hotel at Bedford; the George Hotel at Lichfield; and the White Hart at Salisbury, aggrandised in the early nineteenth century with a tall Ionic portico. A new monumentality arrived in the nineteenth century which is especially associated

Stamford Hotel, Stamford, Lincolnshire, c.1810–29; J. L. Bond. Built on a lavish scale by the Tory Sir Gerard Noel of Exton Park, largely as a political gesture in an attempt to attract support for his campaign against the Whig influence of the Cecils of Burghley

Bedford Hotel, King's Road, Brighton, 1829; T. Cooper. The impressive two-storeyed colonnaded central hall

with the incorporation of hotels into large-scale town-planning schemes. At North Shields, Tyne and Wear, David Stephenson designed the New Quay and Market Place in 1806–17, incorporating a hotel as part of a monumental composition. John Linnell Bond's impressive Stamford Hotel, Lincolnshire (c.1810–29), with its engaged Corinthian columns rising through the two upper storeys, was an important step in the transformation and modernisation of the old coaching-inn. Even more unusual in conception was John Foulston's Royal Hotel, Athenaeum, Assembly Rooms and Theatre at Plymouth (1811–13). Never fully executed and now demolished, this was a single complex of buildings round a courtyard, close in conception to Weinbrenner's Badischer Hof at Baden-Baden (1807–9) and an influence on Robert Wallace's Greek Revival group of Royal Hotel, Athenaeum, Bank and Post Office at Derby of 1837–9.

Elegant hotels arrived along the south coast in the 1820s

by Thomas Cooper at Brighton; by James Burton at St Leonards-on-Sea; and by J. B. Rebecca at Worthing. Hotels were no less important at spas: for example, the Clifton Hotel and Assembly Rooms built in 1806–11 as part of an elegant town-planning scheme by F. H. Greenway; the Regent Hotel of 1819 by Charles Smith, and the Clarendon Hotel (1830), both at Leamington Spa, Warwickshire; the Hastings (now Royal) Hotel of 1826 at Ashby-de-la-Zouche, Leicestershire, by Robert Chaplin who also designed the striking Greek Revival Ivanhoe Baths (1822, dem. 1962) in the same town; and, grandest of all, the Queen's Hotel at Cheltenham (1836–8) by R. W. Jearrad, an immense four-storeyed pile of thirteen bays dominated by a six-columned Corinthian portico. This seems to have influenced the Royal Western Hotel (now offices) at Bristol, which also has thirteen bays and four storeys. It was built in 1837–8 from designs by R. S. Pope who had worked for both Smirke and C. R. Cockerell. Following an idea by Brunel, it was especially intended for passengers on the newly founded Atlantic steamship services, but it closed in 1855. The great railway hotels date from after 1840 and so find no place in the present book.

9

TRANSPORT AND INDUSTRY

The pattern of English life and landscape was transformed between 1760 and 1830 by the adoption of the machine, factory methods and new forms of transport. The architecture of transport and industry reached perhaps its highest points of sophistication in the period 1790–1840, thanks to the genius of designers like Telford, Rennie, Harrison and Brunel. The 1790s were the decade in which bridge building largely passed from the hands of architects to those of engineers. The expansion of trade had promoted the growth of cheap, bulk, water transport from 1761 in a countryside generally lacking metalled roads. To this long established tradition of canal engineering Telford and Rennie brought a new sense of Classical architectural dignity which makes their achievements especially worthy of note here.

It was the two Scots, Thomas Telford and John Loudon Macadam, who transformed the somewhat random network of turnpike or toll roads into a coherent system of finely gravelled hard roads which was the envy of Europe by the 1840s. In 1803 Telford became surveyor and engineer to the newly appointed Commission for Highland Roads and Bridges. During the next eighteen years he created nearly a thousand miles of new road and over a thousand bridges. Amongst the finest bridges are Tongland, Dumfries and Galloway Region (1805–6); Dunkeld, Tayside Region (1806–9); and Dean Bridge, Edinburgh (1829–31). Telford's other major road-building operation, initiated in 1815, was the road from London to Holyhead via Shrewsbury. Two natural obstacles on this route were overcome with a breathtaking skill which resulted in the celebrated Menai Suspension Bridge (1819–26), the first on such a scale in the world, and the graceful suspension bridge at Conwy (1821–6). The bridge over the Menai Straits inspired the suspension bridge at Hutton, Borders Region (1820), by Samuel Brown, and also the awe-inspiring Clifton Suspension Bridge (1829–64) by the great Isambard Kingdom Brunel.

No less distinguished than Telford as a bridge builder was his fellow Scott, John Rennie. Unlike Telford, however, Rennie's interest in roads was confined to carrying them over rivers. His first major bridge at Kelso, Borders Region (1800–3), with its level roadway and elliptical arches separated by coupled Doric columns, set the pattern which he was to follow in numerous bridges in Scotland and England and, above all, in his three great bridges over the Thames in London. Of these, Waterloo Bridge (1811–17) was one of the finest Greek Revival buildings of its date in the country, so that its demolition in the 1930s was a major architectural loss.

Rennie's principal canal works were the Kennet and Avon Canal, and the Lancaster Canal. For these he built the noble Classical aqueducts of stone over the Lune at Lancaster (1794–7), and over the Avon at Limpley Stoke, near Bath

Conwy Suspension Bridge, Gwynedd, 1821–6; Telford

(1795–1800), with coupled Doric pilasters separating its three arches. Telford, who was appointed architect, engineer and surveyor to the Ellesmere Canal in 1793, established the feasibility of water-tight iron aqueducts. He included two of these in the canal from Llangollen to Ellesmere, one at Chirk

Left: Kelso Bridge, Borders Region, 1800–3; J. Rennie

Left below: Pont Cysyllte Aqueduct, Clwyd, 1794–1805; Telford

Below: St Katharine's Docks, London, 1825–8; Telford and P. Hardwick. Before alteration

(1798–1801), and the more splendid Pont Cysyllte (1795–1805) which, crossing the Dee Valley below Llangollen in nineteen noble arches, has always been regarded as the supreme achievement of British canal engineering. In Scotland Hugh Baird followed his example with the impressive Avon Aqueduct on the Union Canal, Central Region, in 1818–22. In designing the Gloucester-Berkeley Ship Canal, opened in 1827, Telford and Mylne provided an attractive series of lock-keepers' houses like miniature Greek temples.

Amongst the best-known monuments of the functional tradition tempered by the Greek Revival are the great warehouses and offices by Telford and Philip Hardwick at St Katharine's Docks, Stepney (1827–9), and, on a scale worthy of Ledoux, the Albert Dock at Liverpool (c.1841–5) by Philip Hardwick and Jesse Hartley. Hardwick was again responsible for the most celebrated of all monuments raised in the heroic early days of rail transport, the Euston Arch (1836–40), a noble Doric portico, the demolition of which in 1962 was a national scandal. The great booking-hall at Euston of 1846–9 by Hardwick's son, P. C. Hardwick, was, alas, demolished at the same time. The earliest surviving station of importance of

this period is Philip Hardwick's Curzon Street Station at Birmingham (1838–42), with a tall entrance block adorned with four free-standing Ionic columns. Brunel's two surviving stations, the Great Western at Bath (1840) and Temple Meads Station at Bristol (1839–41), are both approached through neo-Tudor entrance façades: a striking foretaste of the future

Curzon Street Goods Station, Birmingham, 1838; P. Hardwick. A triumphal arch lends its authority to the railway age

The growth of trade accompanying the Industrial Revolution and England's rise to imperial dignity was reflected in the expansion of the cotton industry in South and Central Lancashire, following the switch from water-power to steam engines. However, the architectural interest of mills and factories is much less than that of the other building types discussed in this chapter. The former silk mill (now card factory) in Chester Road, Macclesfield, is a bold example of a standard later eighteenth-century type, of seventeen bays and four storeys with a pediment and small cupola. An important change came with the employment of iron at the end of the century. Marshall, Benyon and Bage's flour mill (now Allied Breweries) at Ditherington, Shrewsbury (1796–7), has been claimed as the first iron-frame structure ever. Brick jack arches connect the span between cast-iron beams resting on cast-iron columns, but though it is a fireproof structure it is not technically a fully iron-framed one, since the walls carry part of the load and there are no longitudinal beams. The numerous cotton mills owned by the Strutt family at Belper, Derbyshire, were mostly demolished in the 1960s, but the North Mill (1804) survives as one of the earliest fireproof buildings with an iron frame and segmentally arched ceilings of hollow pot construction. Of the cloth mills in the Stroud Valley, Gloucestershire, that at King's Stanley (1812–13), with Venetian windows and prominent quoins, was amongst the earliest fully fireproof buildings in the country: of iron construction within and brick and stone without, it completely ·avoided the use of timber. Early nineteenth-century Leeds was given much of its character by the buildings erected for Benjamin Gott, the leading manufacturer in the town. Note here not only Burley Mills and Armley Mills but also Armley House, the Greek Revival mansion in Gott's Park which Smirke elaborately remodelled for him in c.1818.

New Lanark, Strathclyde Region. General view of Robert Owen's early nineteenth-century industrial town

Of exceptional interest are the New Lanark Mills, Strathclyde Region, founded by Richard Arkwright in 1785 and managed by the philanthropist and manufacturer Robert Owen from 1799 till 1824, when he left for America to establish New Harmony, Indiana. Owen's New Lanark was a

Above: Dixon's Mills, Junction Street, Carlisle, 1835–6; R. Tattersall

Left: Marshall's Mills, Marshall Street, Leeds, 1842; J. Bonomi junior

planned industrial community in which the giant cotton mills were integrated with schools, shops, church and workers' model dwellings. It began a tradition which was still being reflected in the garden cities of the early twentieth century.

In Norwich two former yarn mills have a dignity on account of their sheer size: the five-storeyed factory in Cowgate (now Jarrold's works), begun in 1834–5 from designs by John Brown and subsequently much extended, has a small dome at one corner; and the smaller Albion Mills in King Street of 1836–7, which has been less altered. Of the same date is the massive Dixon's Mills in Junction Street, Carlisle, designed by Richard Tattersall. Seven storeys high and twenty-two bays long, with a single chimney three hundred feet high, it was the largest cotton mill of its day in the country. Totally different was the prestigious Marshall's Mills at Leeds of 1842 by Joseph Bonomi junior. Functionally up-to-date with its internal iron columns hollow for drainage and its modern flax-spinning machines, it is clothed with a solemn array of massive Egyptian columns inspired by the Typhonium at Denderah. For reasons which are not entirely clear neo-Egyptian buildings of this type – especially prisons, court-houses, reservoirs, cemeteries and masonic temples – were far more popular in North America than in Great Britain.

CONCLUSION

The imagination and dynamism of architects and engineers during the Regency period created much of the world we live in and which foreign visitors come to see. The national identity is given expression for many by the conjunction in central London of buildings and places designed or remodelled at this time: Buckingham Palace and St James's Park; Trafalgar Square and the National Gallery; Piccadilly Circus and Regent Street; the Houses of Parliament.

Country-house life as a lazy succession of house parties in luxuriously appointed and sun-filled apartments is an image often associated today with Edwardian England, although its roots lie, as we have seen, in the Regency period. The urban elegance of Regency England has, alas, found no parallel or successor in later times; on the other hand, the Regency development of the moderate-sized house with windows opening on to a garden has persisted as an ideal, as has the romantic nostalgia for the country cottage. Of even greater significance was the stylistic pluralism which the Regency period raised to such a pitch. This allowed the adoption of totally different styles according to the function and situation of different buildings. After its long burial beneath the stifling orthodoxy of the Modern movement this concept is being revived today with striking effect.

GAZETTEER

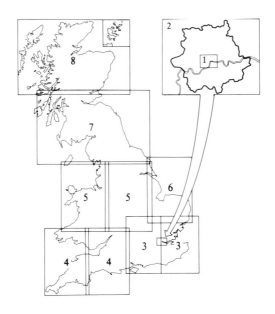

Key to Symbols

⊙ town or village with various good buildings of the period

○ large modern town

⌂ house

⚲ park or garden

□ terrace, square or street

⛩ palace or very large house

✠ church

⛫ town hall or government institution

▢ college, school or library

▣ hospital or almshouse, etc.

◩ theatre or place of entertainment

▲ industrial or commercial building

⌒ bridge

■ other building or monument

MAPS

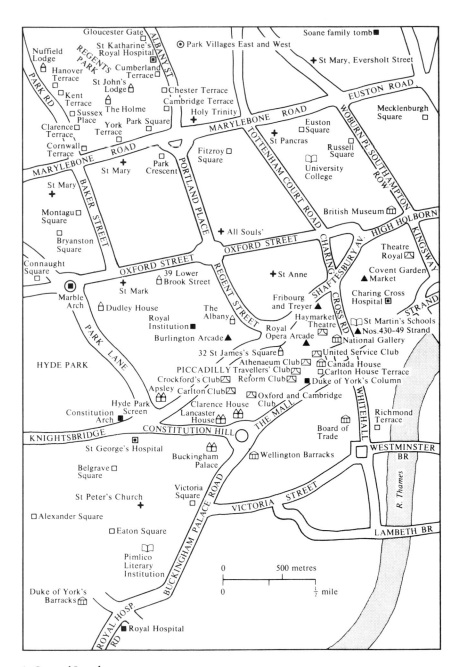

1 Central London

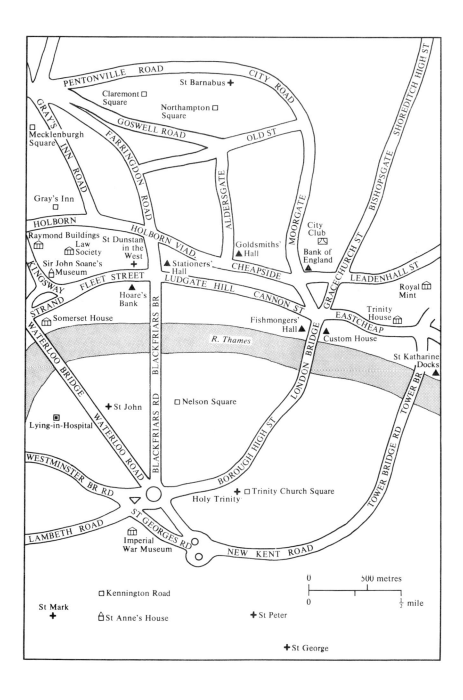

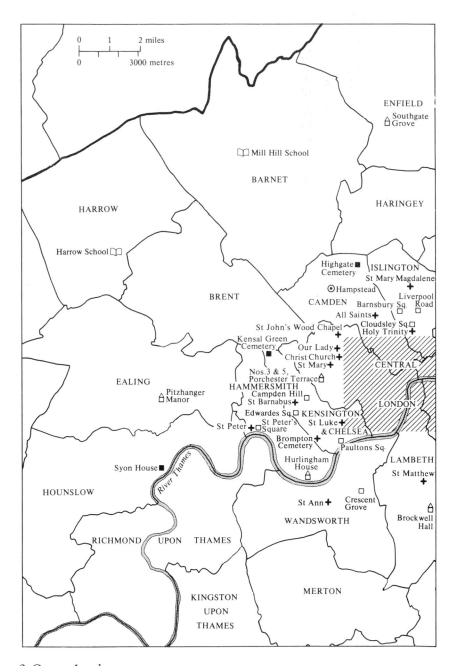

2 Greater London

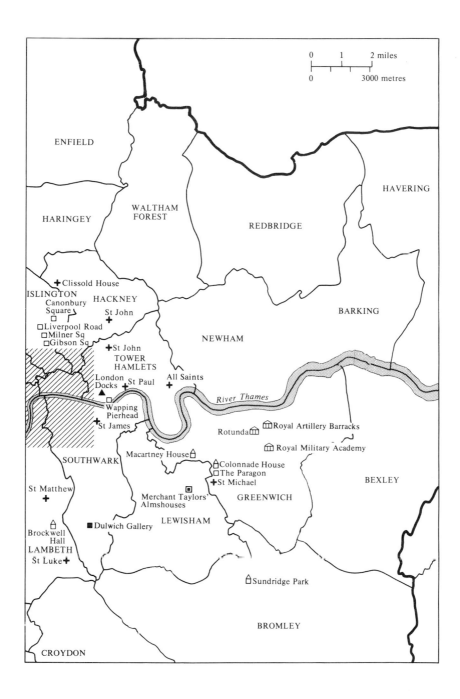

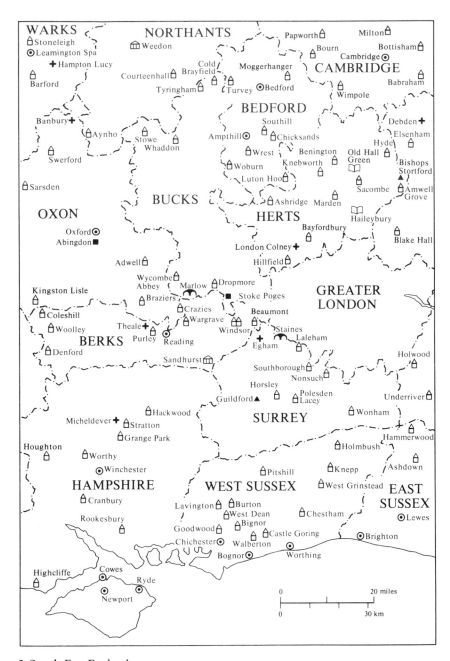

3 South-East England

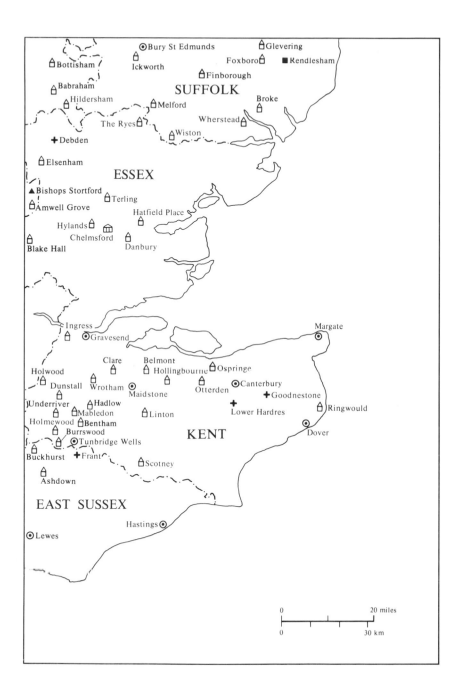

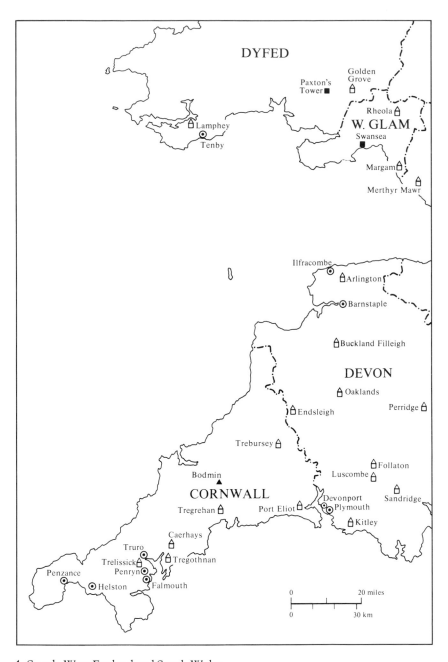

4 South-West England and South Wales

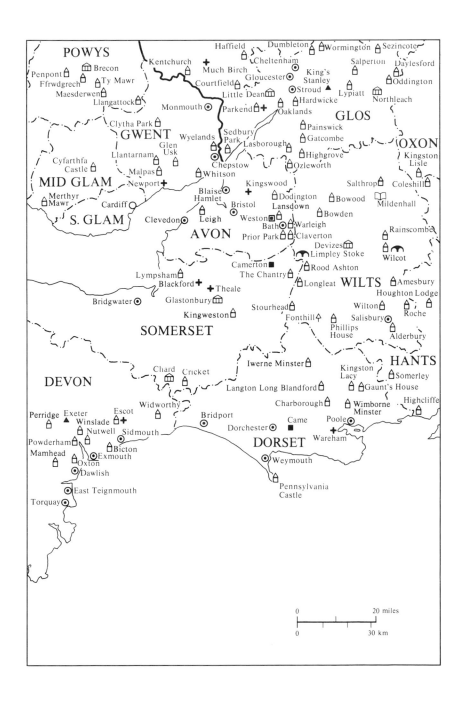

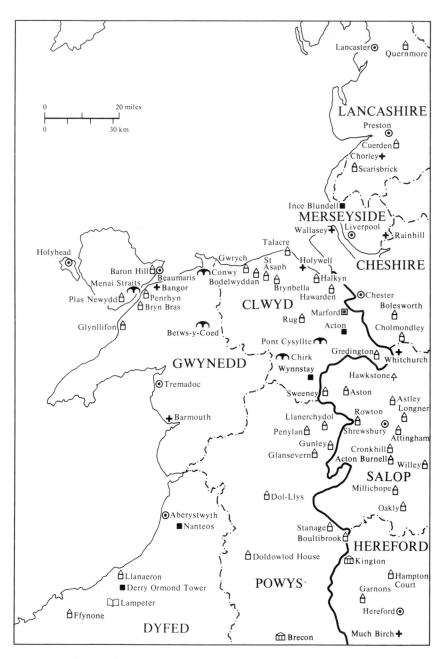

5 North and Central Wales and Central England

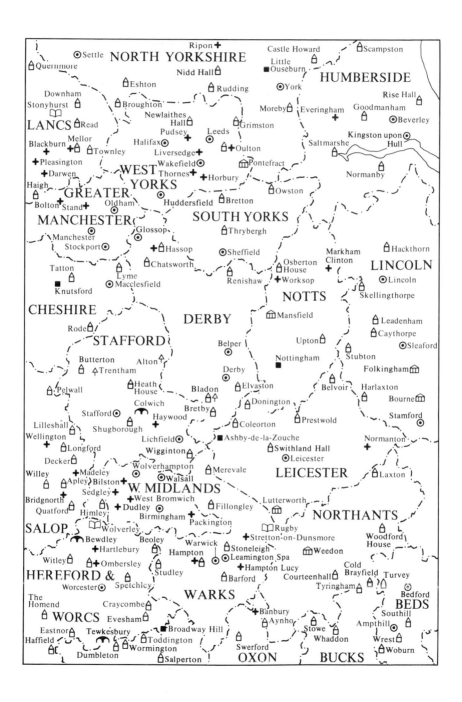

6 East Anglia

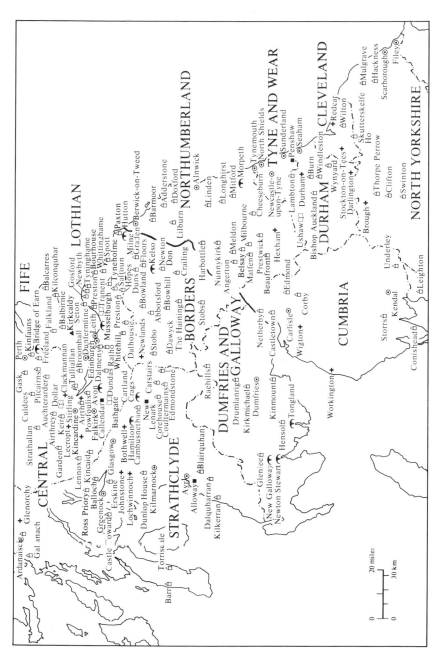

7 Northern England and Southern Scotland

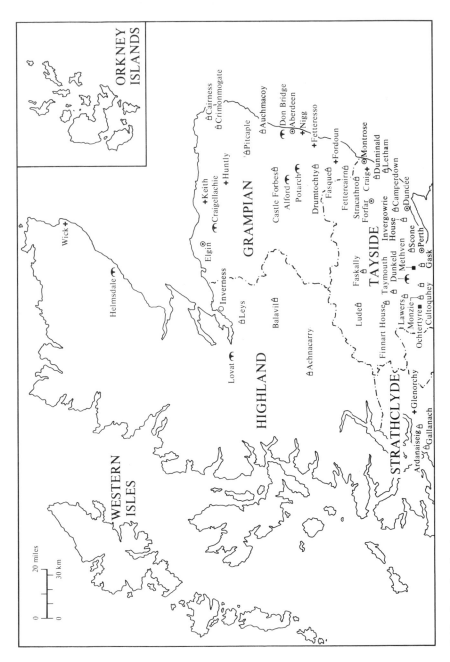

8 Northern Scotland

GAZETTEER

Where specific buildings are referred to in the preceding part of this book, relevant page numbers are given in brackets; italicised page numbers indicate illustrations.

Abbotsford, *Borders Region*. (29, 57.) By W. Atkinson, 1816–23, for Sir Walter Scott, Bt. Influential early example of Scots Baronial style. Irregular skyline with crow-stepped gables and tourelles. Armour in entrance hall; original fitted shelves and ceiling with pendant bosses in library; gallery with cast-iron railings in study.
Aberdeen, *Grampian Region*. *St Andrew* (now Cathedral), King Street, by A. Simpson, 1816–17, Gothic. (Later additions.) *South Church*, by J. Smith, 1830–1, Gothic. *North Church* (76), by J. Smith, 1830–1, with tetrastyle unpedimented Ionic portico and tall tower crowned with imitation of Lysicrates Monument. *St Nicholas East*, by A. Simpson, 1835–7, Gothic, with galleried interior. *County Assembly Rooms*, by A. Simpson, 1820–2, Greek Revival, with portico. *Athenaeum Reading Room*, Union Street, 1822–3. Good Regency granite façades in *Union Street*.
Aberystwyth, *Dyfed*. Several late C18 & early C19 houses and terraces, e.g. *Laura Place*, c. 1800, which also contains the *Assembly Rooms* (now Students' Union), by G. S. Repton, 1820.
Abingdon, *Oxfordshire*. Gaol, by Wyatville, 1805–11, typical plan with octagonal centre block and 3 radiating wings.

Achnacarry, *Highland Region*. Unimpressive house in the Adam/Paterson castle-style, by J. G. Graham, 1802–37, for D. Cameron.
Acton Burnell, *Salop*. House remodelled by J. Tasker, 1814, for Sir J. Smythe, Bt. Greek Ionic portico. (Interior remodelled after fire in 1914.)
Acton Park, *near Wrexham, Clwyd*. The house by J. Wyatt now demolished, but handsome Greek Doric entrance screen of c. 1810 survives on main road.
Adderstone Hall, *near Belford, Northumberland*. By W. Burn, 1819, for T. Forster. Greek Revival, with domed hall with columnar screens.
Adwell House, *Oxfordshire*. Very plain late C18 5-bay stuccoed front with Doric porch. Inside, handsome staircase, c. 1820, top-lit with dome flanked by ribbed half-domes.
Airth, *Central Region*. *North Church*, by W. Stirling, 1818, impressive neo-Perp.
Airth Castle, *Central Region*. L-shaped C15 & C16 castle made triangular with new entrance front by D. Hamilton, 1807–9, for T. G. Stirling. Castellated symmetrical façade with round angle towers, Gothic entrance hall, other interiors Classical.
Airthrey Castle, *Central Region*. By R. Adam, 1790–1, for R. Haldane. Unusual D-shaped mansion in Adam's vigorous but symmetrical castle-style. (Enlarged 1891.)
Alderbury, *Wiltshire*. *St Marie's Grange*, small asymmetrical house of 1835 by Pugin for himself (altered in 1870s), a landmark in history of the Gothic Revival.
Alford Bridge, *Grampian Region*. By T. Telford, 1810–11.
Alloway, *Strathclyde Region*. *Burns Monument*, by T. Hamilton, 1820–3.
Alnwick, *Northumberland*. *Northumberland Hall*, Market Place, 1826, Grecian. *Percy Tenantry Column*, by D. Stephenson, 1816, Greek Doric. *Swansfield House, S of Alnwick*, plain 5 bay Classical house by J. Dobson, 1823, for H. C. Selby. In the grounds the *Peace Column*, erected 1814 to commemorate the Peace of 1814.
Alton Towers, *Staffordshire*. (60, 63.) Fanciful castellated pile of c. 1810–52 by many architects including Pugin. (Now a ruin.) The astonishing garden for 15th Earl of Shrewsbury survives with bridge and temples by Papworth, 1818–22;

conservatory, prospect tower and pagoda in lake, by Abraham; iron bridge, Choragic Monument of Lysicrates, and a stonehenge.

Amesbury House, *Wiltshire.* (*134.*) House of c. 1660 by Webb was completely rebuilt by T. Hopper, 1834–40, for Sir E. Antrobus, Bt. Giant portico and daunting arcaded staircase hall.

Ampthill, *Bedfordshire. Avenue House*, Church Street, c. 1780 with chaste red-brick extension, 1792–5, for J. Morris, brewer, probably by J. Wing. *Woburn Road*, pairs of thatched cottages ornés, 1812–16.

Amwell Grove, *Great Amwell, Hertfordshire.* By R. Mylne for himself, 1794–7. Plain 3-bay Georgian block flanked by 1-storey set-back wings. Centre and wings now have tactfully added C19 top storey.

Angerton Hall, *Northumberland.* Symmetrical Tudor Gothic house by Dobson, 1823, for R. Atkinson.

Apley Park, *Salop.* By J. Webb, 1811, for T. Whitmore. Large castellated Gothick house with symmetrical 9-bay S front with angle towers, Gothic interiors, e.g. fan-vaulted stair hall with glazed octagonal lantern. Described, and illustrated, as 'Arley' in *First Childhood* (1934) by Lord Berners.

Ardanaiseig House, *Loch Awe, Strathclyde Region.* By W. Burn, 1833, for A. Campbell. Asymmetrical Jacobethan. (Interiors altered.)

Arlington Court, *Devon.* By T. Lee, 1820–3, for Col. J. P. Chichester. Fine stone Greek Revival mansion with something of the austere authority of Belsay (q.v.). Entrance front with coupled antae at corners and semi-circular Greek Doric porch. Interiors, by contrast, are richer and more elaborate, e.g. splendid entrance hall and painted Music Room. (National Trust.)

Ashby-de-la-Zouche, *Leicestershire.* (*107.*) *Royal Hotel*, by R. Chaplin, 1826, Grecian exterior and central columnar hall inside.

Ashdown House, *near Forest Row, East Sussex.* By B. H. Latrobe, 1793, for T. Fuller. Elegant ashlared villa with 3-bay front, the flanking ground-floor windows

Amesbury House, Wiltshire, 1834–40; T. Hopper. South front. A powerful and unusual composition inspired by the house by Webb of the 1660s which previously stood on the site

set in blank arches. Semi-circular porch of 4 Erectheion Ionic columns related to semi-circular space within so as to produce a circular porch with coffered vault. Staircase with iron balustrade of unusual design, heavy Greek key frieze and columns with lotus-leaf capitals on the landing.

Ashman's Hall, *Barsham, Suffolk*. White-brick house, c. 1810, in Wyatt style. Tripartite entrance front with Ionic colonnade; quadrant office wing; 9-bay W front with domed bow; fine staircase.

Ashridge Park, *Hertfordshire*. (54, 55, 64.) Begun by J. Wyatt, 1808–13, for 7th Earl of Bridgewater; completed and extended by Wyatville, 1813 onwards. Perhaps most impressive and best preserved of the Regency Gothic extravaganzas, vast, asymmetrical, castellated and spired. Sublime staircase, rich chapel, and elaborate flower gardens laid out by Repton.

Astley House, *Salop*. 3-bay Late Georgian with neo-Greek enrichments.

Aston Hall, *near Oswestry, Salop*. By J. Wyatt, 1789–93, for the Rev. J. R. Lloyd. Elegant stone mansion with Louis XVI details, e.g. carved swags.

Attingham Hall, *Salop*. (60.) House of 1780s by Steuart to which Nash added important picture gallery, 1807–10, with glazed coved cast-iron roof made by the Coalbrookdale Company. (National Trust.)

Auchmacoy House, *Logie Buchan, Grampian Region*. By W. Burn, 1831–3, for J. Buchan. Jacobethan exterior with Classical interiors.

Auchterarder House, *Tayside Region*. By W. Burn, 1832–3, for J. Hunter. Picturesque Scots-Jacobean. (Alterations 1886–9.)

Avon Aqueduct, *Union Canal, Central Region*. (111.) By H. Baird, 1818–22.

Aynho Park, *Northamptonshire*. (59.) Substantial C17 & C18 house mainly by Thomas Archer, remodelled and extended by Soane, 1799–1804, for W. R. Cartwright. Soane added the 2 triumphal arches which link house with the previously unattached service wings flanking the entrance court. Inside, his groin-vaulted and apsed garden hall, dining room, library, and white staircase, survive. Capability Brown park.

Ayr, *Strathclyde Region*. *Town Hall*, by T. Hamilton, 1828–30, Classical. (Enlarged 1880.) *Wallace Tower*, by T. Hamilton,

1831–4, Gothic.

Babraham Hall, *Cambridgeshire*. By P. Hardwick, 1829–32, for H. J. Adeane. Early and ugly example of the Jacobean Revival. (Enlarged 1864.)

Balavil House (formerly Belleville House), *near Kingussie, Highland Region*. By R. Adam, 1790–6, for James Macpherson of the Ossian hoax. 7-bay Classical front with 3 tripartite windows and end bays treated as towers.

Balbirnie House, *Fife Region*. (50, 136.) By R. Crichton, 1815–19, for Gen. R. Balfour. Large and early Greek Revival mansion. Bleak 5-bay entrance front with hexastyle Doric portico; 11-bay S front with tripartite windows and Diocletian windows in attic. Best interior is the long gallery with 4 shallow saucer domes lit only by high side lunettes.

Balcarres House, *Fife Region*. By W. Burn, 1836–8, for Col. J. Lindsay. Baronial style. (Extended 1863–7.)

Balloch Castle, *Strathclyde Region*. By R. Lugar, 1809, for J. Buchanan. Castellated and asymmetrical with octagonal tower and canted service wing. Important early example of Picturesque influence in Scotland, inspired by Nash and Downton Castle.

Banbury, *Oxfordshire*. (66.) *St Mary*, by S. P. Cockerell, 1792–7, unusual centrally-planned church à la Wren with shallow dome carried on 8 Ionic columns. Cylindrical tower and semi-circular Doric portico by C. R. Cockerell, 1818–22: a form ultimately inspired by Archer's St Paul, Deptford (1713–30), but here given heavily rusticated Neo-Classical dress.

Bangor, *Gwynedd*. *Our Lady* (RC), High Street, Classical church of 1834–44. (Much altered.)

Barford House, *Barford, Warwickshire*. Stuccoed Regency house with imposing 9-bay entrance front with engaged Ionic order.

Barmoor Castle, *Northumberland*. By J. Paterson, 1801, for F. Sitwell. Elegant castellated villa with several oval rooms and unusual palm-leaf balustrade on staircase.

Barmouth, *Gwynedd*. *St David*, by E. Haycock, 1830, cruciform Gothic church.

Barnstaple, *Devon*. *Guildhall* (84), High Street, by T. Lee, 1826–8, modest pedimented building with Ionic pilasters over rusticated ground floor. Some good

Balbirnie House, Fife Region, 1815–19; R. Crichton. The Long Gallery, a powerful neo-antique space

Regency houses, e.g. *Trafalgar Lawn*, c. 1805.

Baron Hill, *near Beaumaris, Anglesey, Gwynedd*. House built 1776 by S. Wyatt, rebuilt in modified form after fire in 1836. (Now a ruin.)

Barr House (formerly Glenbarr Abbey), *Kintyre, Strathclyde Region*. Built c. 1815 for Col. M. MacAlister, probably by J. G. Graham whose Ross Priory it closely resembles.

Bath, *Avon*. (36.) *Lansdown Crescent* (35), by J. Palmer, 1789–93, spectacularly undulating. Interior of No. 19 remodelled for William Beckford by H. E. Goodridge, 1835. Leading architect after 1800 was J. Pinch who built terraces below Lansdown Crescent, e.g. *Cavendish Place* and *Crescent*, and *Sion Hill Place*. In Sion Hill is *Doric House*, memorable Grecian essay by J. M. Gandy, c. 1810–18. *York Street*, Grecian terrace with *Friends' Meeting House* (former Masonic Hall), by Wilkins, 1819, with Greek Ionic portico. In London Road, *Walcot Methodist Chapel*, by W. Jenkins, 1815–16, round-headed windows and Greek Doric porch. *Bathwick* extensively developed 1790–1820, e.g. *Sydney Gardens*, hexagonal layout by C. H. Masters who built as its climax the impressive *Sydney Hotel*, 1796–7 (altered 1836 and 1915 and now the Holburne of Menstrie Museum). J. Pinch built terraces at Bathwick, 1805–25, e.g. *New Sydney Place*, *Daniel Street* and *Raby Place*.

In Raby Place, *St Mary*, by J. Pinch, 1814–20, Gothic. (Chancel 1873.) Higher up *Bathwick Hill* terraces give way to villas, the best by Goodridge, e.g. asymmetrical Italianate *Montebello*, 1828. *Station* (112), 1840, by Brunel, neo-Tudor entrance front. *Theatre Royal*, Beaufort Square, by G. Dance and J. Palmer, 1804–5, 5-bay façade with panel-led pilasters; later interior.

Bathgate, *Lothian Region*. (95.) *Bathgate Academy*, Marjoribanks Street, by R. & R. Dickson, 1831–3, vast Greek Revival composition, centre with wings, all very templar.

Bayfordbury, *Hertfordshire*. Elaborate and impressive Greek Revival mansion of 1809–12 for W. Baker, incorporating a mid-Georgian house with 25-bay front. Good park.

Beaufront Castle, *Northumberland*. By J. Dobson, 1837–41, for W. Cuthbert. Brilliantly Picturesque composition in domestic castellated style of C15, central sky-lit vaulted hall with cloister on 3 sides and impressive staircase. Beautifully situated in fine park.

Beaumaris, *Anglesey, Gwynedd*. Regency-style terraces, e.g. *Edge of Green*, by J. Hall, 1824–5, and *Victoria Terrace*, by Hansom & Welch, 1830–5. *Bulkeley Arms Hotel*, by Hansom & Welch, 1835 (extended 1873). *Gaol*, (88, 88) by Hansom & Welch, 1828–9, small but well-preserved example of the forbidding Neo-Classical type.

Beaumont Lodge, *Berkshire*. By H. Emlyn, c. 1790, for H. Griffiths. Columns in the portico have capitals of the 'British' order invented by Emlyn.

Bedford. *Swan Hotel* (105), by H. Holland, 1792, for 5th Duke of Bedford, elegant 3-bay pedimented front with round-headed tripartite windows. Nearby, 5-arched *Bridge*, by J. Wing, 1811–13 (widened later). *General Hospital*, Kimbolton Road, includes former House of Industry, by J. Wing, 1795–6. *Gaol*, Dame Alice Street, by J. Wing, 1801, (later additions). *Bedford Modern School* (97), Harpur Street, by Blore, 1833–7, neo-Tudor. *Public Library* (formerly Literary and Scientific Institute) (90), Harpur Street, by T. G. Elger, 1834, stuccoed Grecian front.

Belmont Park, *Kent*. (50.) By S. Wyatt, 1787–92, for 1st Lord Harris. Perfect Late Classical house with characteristic Wyatt domed bows, faced with mathematical tiles, and linked by Ionic colonnade. Impressive staircase hall; library and drawing room both with bowed ends.

Belper, *Derbyshire*. (112.) Late C18 & early C19 cotton-spinning town developed by Strutt family. *North Mill*, 1804, fire-proof with iron framing. *George Brettle's Warehouse*, Chapel Street, 1834–5, 19 bays, with pediments. *Lion Inn*, Bridge Street, early C19. *Bridge* and *Weir*, begun 1796–8 by T. Sykes. Workers' housing of 1790s off *Bridge Street. St Peter's Church*, by M. Habershon, 1824, neo-Perp.

Belsay, *Northumberland*. (50, 52, 53.) By Sir C. Monck, Bt., for himself, 1806–17. Arguably the most distinguished Greek Revival house in the country. Austere stone façades of great weight and authority adorned only with antae and massive Greek Doric portico, distyle in antis; windows cut into the stone without mouldings; interior organised round imposing neo-antique peristyle, colonnaded and 2-storeyed. Picturesque gardens cleverly contrived to incorporate the quarry hewn to provide stone for the house. Similar expedient was adopted at Millichope (q.v.).

Belvoir Castle, *Leicestershire*. (54.) Medieval castle remodelled in C17 and even more completely in 1801–c. 30 for 5th Duke of Rutland, by James Wyatt and the Rev. J. Thoroton who employed Wyatt's sons, B. D. Wyatt and M. C. Wyatt, to decorate interiors. The result, expecially when viewed from a distance, is one of the most romantically impressive of English castles, with its towers, turrets and machicolation, now neo-Norman, now neo-Gothic. Sumptuous interiors, often Classical, e.g. Regent's Gallery, Dining Room, Picture Gallery and Elizabethan Saloon, important early example of the French Rococo Revival.

Benington, *Hertfordshire*. *The Lordship*, sham neo-Norman castle, 1832.

Bentham Hill, *Southborough, Kent*. By D. Burton, 1832–3, for A. Pott. L-shaped neo-Tudor mansion.

Beoley Hall, *Hereford and Worcester*. House, c. 1700, remodelled 1791 for T. Holmes by J. Sanders, a pupil of Soane. Tripartite windows, Tuscan porch and good interiors.

Berwick-on-Tweed, *Northumberland*. *Custom House*, Quay Walls, late C18, round-headed windows. *Lions House,* Windmill Hill, exceptionally plain Late Georgian. *Ravensdowne,* long street lined with elegant early C19 houses. *Wellington Terrace,* 3 houses of c. 1820–5.

Bessingby Hall, *Humberside.* By T. Cundy senior, 1807, for H. Hudson. Chaste understated white-brick house of 5 bays and 2 storeys. On entrance front the central bay is recessed slightly and boasts a segmental balustraded porch with Greek Doric columns and segment-headed window over. Good staircase.

Betws-y-Coed, *Gwynedd. Waterloo Bridge,* by T. Telford, 1815, with prettily decorated iron spandrels.

Beverley, *Humberside.* (84.) *Beverley Arms Hotel,* North Bar Within, by W. Middleton, 1794. *Sessions House,* North Bar Without, by C. Watson, 1804–14, dull despite large Ionic portico. *County Record Office,* Cross Street, c. 1831, built as a club, simple Grecian. *Guildhall,* Register Square, Greek Doric portico added by C. Mountain, 1832. Early C19 houses include *No. 11 Cross Street,* c. 1830, with Tuscan eaves, by E. Page for himself.

Bewdley, *Hereford and Worcester. Bridge,* by T. Telford, 1795–9.

Bicton House, *Devon.* By J. Wyatt, c. 1800, for 1st Lord Rolle. Classical. (Remodelled 1908.) Early C19 glasshouses, fine gardens and trees. (Mausoleum by Pugin, 1850.)

Bignor Park, *West Sussex.* By H. Harrison, 1826–8, for J. Dawkins. Plain and stuccoed Grecian villa in style of R. Smirke, tripartite entrance front, handsome library with contemporary shelving.

Bilston, *West Midlands. St Leonard,* by F. Goodwin, 1826, Classical (later alterations). *St Mary,* Oxford Street, by F. Goodwin, 1829–30, Commissioners' Gothic with polygonal apse.

Birmingham, *West Midlands.* (96.) *Town Hall,* by Hansom & Welch, 1832–4, completed 1835–61 by C. Edge. Splendid Anglesey-marble echo of the Temple of Castor and Pollux, Rome. Interior much remodelled. *St Peter,* St Peter's Place, simple late C18 & early C19 RC church. *Midland Bank,* Waterloo Street, by Rickman & Hutchinson, 1830, elaborate Corinthian design. *Curzon Street Goods Station* (112, 113), by P. Hardwick, 1838, Ionic, one of the earliest surviving stations in the

country. *Bordesley: Holy Trinity* (73), Camp Hill, by F. Goodwin, 1820–3, pretty neo-Perp. *The Retreat,* Warner Street, 1831, almshouses forming 3-sided court. *Perry Barr: St Mary's College* (RC) (97), New Oscott, by J. Potter, 1835–8, Tudor Gothic. Chapel elaborately decorated by Pugin, 1838–40.

Bishop Auckland Castle, *Co. Durham.* Partly medieval but now largely a Gothicisation by J. Wyatt, c. 1795, including a screen wall, gateway and principal interiors.

Bishops Stortford, *Hertfordshire. Corn Exchange,* by L. Vulliamy, 1828, stuccoed Greek Revival.

Blackburn, *Lancashire. St Peter,* St Peter's Street, by J. Palmer, 1819–21, Gothic, expensive Commissioners' church. *St Mark,* Buncer Lane, by E. Sharpe, 1836–8, Romanesque with tower.

Blackford, *Somerset. Holy Trinity,* by R. Carver, 1823, octagonal Gothic church.

Bladon Castle, *near Newton Solney, Derbyshire.* Villa by Wyatville, 1799, for A. Hoskins. Enlarged into castellated towered house 1801–5.

Blairquhan, *Straiton, Strathclyde Region.* By W. Burn, 1820–4, for Sir D. Hunter Blair. Tudor Gothic inspired by Wilkins's Dalmeny (q.v.). Symmetrical entrance front with porte-cochère; high tower rising from centre of house; interiors in featureless Classical style except for 2-storeyed Gothic saloon.

Blaise Castle House, *Henbury, near Bristol, Avon.* By W. Paty, c. 1795, for J. S. Harford. Top-lit picture gallery added 1832 by C. R. Cockerell. Curved orangery and thatched dairy. Triangular castellated tower (1766) by R. Mylne.

Blaise Hamlet, *Henbury, near Bristol, Avon.* (15.) By Nash, 1810–11, for J. S. Harford. Almshouses in the form of cottages ornés picturesquely grouped.

Blake Hall, *Bobbingworth, Essex.* Stuccoed early C18 mansion with 7-bay main front to which Basevi added Greek Doric porch and 2 lower wings with round-headed windows in 1822 for Capel Cure.

Blickling Park, *Norfolk.* Pyramidal mausoleum for 2nd Earl of Buckinghamshire, by J. Bonomi, 1794. (National Trust.)

Bodelwyddan Hall, *Clwyd.* By Hansom & Welch, c. 1830–40, for Sir J.

Williams, Bt. Castellated.

Bodmin, *Cornwall*. (101.) *Assize Court*, Mount Folly, by H. Burt, 1837–8, granite, Classical. *Market House*, Fore Street, by W. Harris, 1839–40, granite, with large carved bulls' heads in the frieze inspired by antique building in Island of Delos.

Bognor, *West Sussex*. Some Regency houses and terraces, e.g. *Waterloo Place*, *Carlton Hotel* and *Steyne*. *Sudley Lodge*, High Street, Italianate villa, by J. Shaw, 1827.

Bolesworth Castle, *Cheshire*. By W. Cole, 1829, for G. Walmsley. Castellated asymmetrical Gothic. (Interiors Classicised 1920 by C. Williams-Ellis.)

Bolton, *Greater Manchester*. Holy Trinity, Trinity Street, by T. Hardwick, 1823–5, elaborate Commissioners' church, neo-Perp and more accurate than most.

Bonaly Tower, *Edinburgh*. Peel tower built by W. H. Playfair, 1836–8, for Lord Cockburn. (Wings added in 1870s and 80s.)

Bothwell, *Strathclyde Region*. Church, by D. Hamilton, c. 1825–33, adjacent to ruined collegiate church, Gothic with tower. (Interior altered.)

Bottisham Hall, *Cambridgeshire*. Elegant 3-bay white-brick house of 1797 for the Rev. G. L. Jenyns. Entrance front with semi-circular bow; oval entrance hall; D-shaped stair hall with 1st-floor screen of 2 unfluted Ionic columns.

Boultibrook, *Presteigne, Powys*. By R. Smirke, 1812–15, for Sir H. J. Brydges. Stuccoed house with broadly projecting eaves and octagonal top-lit library at the back.

Bourhouse, *near Dunbar, Lothian Region*. By Bryce and Burn, 1835–6, for Col. J. Carfrae. Jacobethan mansion.

Bourn Hall, *Cambridgeshire*. Rebuilt by J. A. Repton, 1817–19, for 5th Earl De La Warr, as an early example of Elizabethan Revival.

Bourne, *Lincolnshire*. *Sessions House* (84, 85), by B. Browning, 1821, interesting façade with open staircase behind columnar screen.

Bowden House, *near Lacock, Wiltshire*. (50, 54.) By J. Wyatt, 1796, for B. Dickinson. Ashlar-faced S front of exceptional elegance with semi-circular bow ringed with free-standing Ionic columns and flanked by tripartite windows with blank segmental tympana; over these in 1st floor are long panels of carved rinceaux. Excellent interiors,

especially drawing room with numerous Classical reliefs in panels on the walls.

Bowhill, *near Selkirk, Borders Region*. Undemonstrative Classical house for 5th Duke of Buccleuch, by W. Atkinson, 1812–17, and W. Burn, 1831 onwards. Long disjointed composition extended further in 1870s. Magnificent contents.

Bowland House, *Stow, Borders Region*. Probably by J. G. Graham, c. 1811, for Gen. A. Walker. Castellated Tudor Gothic. (Additions in 1890 and 1926.)

Bowood House, *Wiltshire*. (47.) Chapel, library and breakfast room by C. R. Cockerell, 1822–4, for 3rd Marquess of Lansdowne.

Braziers Park, *near Ipsden, Oxfordshire*. By D. Harris, 1799, castellated Gothic rebuilding of late C17 house.

Brecon, *Powys*. (84.) *Shire Hall* (now Brecknock Museum), Glamorgan Street, by Wyatt & Brandon, 1839–43, with big Greek Doric portico, a late example of Smirke's influence.

Bretby Hall, *Derbyshire*. Extensive castellated pile by Wyatville, c. 1813–15, for 5th Earl of Chesterfield. Never completed; interiors mainly Classical.

Bretton Hall, *South Yorkshire*. C18 house remodelled and extended c. 1815 by Wyatville for Col. T. R. Beaumont. Greek Doric portico on E front, spectacular staircase with high domed vestibule which is Soanean in detail but painted with huge Roman ruin compositions by A. Aglio. Other impressive interiors, e.g. Library and Music Room, sadly stripped of contents.

Bridge of Earn, *Tayside Region*. *Bridge*, by J. Rennie, 1819–21.

Bridgnorth, *Salop*. St Mary Magdalene, by T. Telford, 1792–4, grave design inspired by French Neo-Classical churches. (Chancel 1876.)

Bridgwater, *Somerset*. (101.) *Holy Trinity*, by R. Carver, 1839, in his usual archaeologically inaccurate Commissioners' Gothic style. *Baptist Church*, St Mary Street, by R. Down, 1837, Ionic portico in antis. *Market Hall* (102), designed in 1826 by J. Bowen and executed in 1834, with eye-catching semi-circular entrance colonnade of Ionic columns surmounted by dome and cupola.

Bridport, *Dorset*. St Swithin, Allington, by C. Wallis, 1826–7, stuccoed pedimented façade with Tuscan portico and cupola. *Unitarian Chapel*, 1794, with Ionic porch. *Literary and Scientific Institute*, 1834, rusticated stone façade with Greek Doric doorway.

Brighton, *East Sussex*. (43, 107.) With Cheltenham, the best Regency town in England. *Royal Crescent*, 1798–1807, first terrace to be built facing the sea. The following all by C. Busby, c. 1823–50: *Kemp Town* (i.e. *Sussex Square, Lewes Crescent*, the magnificent *Arundel Terrace* and *Chichester Terrace*); and *Brunswick Town*, Hove (i.e. *Brunswick Square, Terrace* and *Place, Lansdowne Place* and *Square*). Other leading architect was A. H. Wilds who built, 1825–9, *Oriental Place* and *Terrace, Sillwood Place, Western Terrace, Hanover Crescent, Park Crescent*, and *Montpelier Crescent* (1843–7). *Adelaide Crescent*, by D. Burton, 1830–4. *St Peter* (26), Victoria Gardens, by Barry, 1824–8, charming Regency Gothick church. *St Andrew*, Waterloo Road, Hove, by Barry, 1827–8, modest but early example of Quattrocento Revival. *Congregational Chapel*, Union Street, by A. Wilds, 1820, Grecian. *Town Hall* (84), Market Place, by T. Cooper, 1830–2, tall Greek Revival building. *Bedford Hotel* (106, 107), by T. Cooper, 1829, original Grecian composition with 2-storeyed domed central hall and staircase. *Royal Pavilion* (6, 7, 15, 77, 79), Holland's elegant Classical villa of 1780s for the Prince of Wales, transformed for same patron by Nash in 1815–21 into an onion-domed oriental extravaganza with exotic interiors to match.

Bristol, *Avon*. (43, 112.) *St George, Great George Street*, by R. Smirke, 1821–3, Greek Revival. *Holy Trinity*, Hotwell Road, by C. R. Cockerell, 1829–30, Neo-Classical with baroque elements. *St Mary-on-the-Quay* (RC), by R. S. Pope, 1839–40, with impressive Corinthian portico. *Commercial Rooms*, Corn Street, by C. A. Busby, 1810–11, with Soanean interior. *Arcade* (102), Horsefair, by J. Foster, 1824–5. *Old Council House* (81), Broad Street, by Smirke, 1824–7, with distinguished Grecian façade. *Custom House*, Queen Square, by Smirke, 1826. *Court of Justice*, by R. S. Pope, 1827–8. *Victoria Rooms* (now part of Bristol University) (85), by C. Dyer, 1839–41, unusual Beaux-Arts composition with vast Corinthian portico. *Bank of England* (26, 99), Broad

Street, Doric masterpiece by C. R. Cockerell, 1844–7. (Former) *Royal Western Hotel* (now offices) (107), St George's Road, by R. S. Pope, 1837–8, eye-catching façade with Ionic colonnade and engaged Corinthian order. *Temple Meads Station*, 1839–40, neo-Tudor entrance front by Brunel. *Clifton* (7) was charmingly laid out in the 1820s and 30s on a sloping site with terraces, crescents, passages, trees and villas. See especially *Bellevue; Cornwallis Crescent*, by W. Paty, 1790; *Windsor Terrace*, probably by J. Eveleigh, 1793, with Corinthian pilasters; the *Paragon*, 1809–13, elegantly curved; *Royal York Crescent; Saville Place; Prince's Buildings; Harley Place; Vyvyan Terrace*; and the *Mall* with *Hotel* and *Assembly Rooms* by Greenway and Kay, 1806–11, the latter on rusticated arched basement with 5-bay pediment and engaged Ionic order. Former RC *Pro Cathedral*, Park Place, Clifton, begun 1834 by H. E. Goodridge as French Neo-Classical temple but completed 1847–8 by C. Hansom in Italian Romanesque style. *Clifton Vale* (41), *Caledonia Place*, and *New Mall*, c. 1840–3, by J. Foster. *Clifton Suspension Bridge* (32, 32, 109), designed 1829 by Brunel, built 1836–40 and 1861–4, in position and design the finest suspension bridge in the country.

Broadway Hill, *Hereford and Worcester*. *Broadway Tower*, by J. Wyatt, 1794, for 6th Earl of Coventry, unusual triangular neo-Norman folly.

Broke Hall, *Nacton, Suffolk*. C16 house Gothicised by J. Wyatt, 1791–2, for P. Broke.

Broomhall, *Fife Region*. (50.) By T. Harrison, 1796–9, for 7th Earl of Elgin (of the Elgin Marbles). Chaste segmental bow in garden front but generally dull. (Completed 1865.)

Brough Hall, *North Yorkshire*. (75.) *St Paulinus Chapel* (RC), by Sir W. Lawson and I. Bonomi, 1834–7, inspired by C13 Archbishop's Chapel at York.

Broughton Hall, *North Yorkshire*. By W. Atkinson, mainly 1809–11, for S. Tempest. Superb Regency drawing rooms with original Gillow furniture; Italianate wings added by G. Webster, 1838–41; conservatory and Italian gardens by W. A. Nesfield, c. 1855.

Brynbella, *Tremeirchion, Clwyd*. By J. C. Mead, 1794, for G. Piozzi, Mrs Thrale's dancing master. Elegant villa with 2 3-bay segmental bows, in attractive park.

Bryn Bras Castle, *Gwynedd*. (56.) Early C19, cement-rendered, neo-Norman, perhaps by S. Beazley.

Buckhurst Park, *Withyham, East Sussex*. By J. A. Repton, c. 1830–5, for 5th Earl De La Warr. Neo-Elizabethan.

Buckland Filleigh House, *Devon*. By J. Green, 1810, for J. I. Fortescue. Greek Revival with impressive interiors.

Burn Hall, *Co. Durham*. By I. Bonomi, 1821–34, for B. J. Salvin. Large stone mansion with Ionic portico.

Burrswood, *near Groombridge, Kent*. By D. Burton, 1831–8, for D. Salomons. Muddled neo-Tudor.

Burton Park, *near Petworth, West Sussex*. By H. Bassett, 1831, for J. Biddulph. Large Greek Revival mansion with 3-storeyed front dominated by unusual screen of 4 Greek Ionic columns rising through 1st and 2nd storeys. Most spectacular feature is the cast- and wrought-bronze staircase, c. 1800, apparently brought from Michel Grove, Sussex, with alternate greyhounds and leaf patterns in the banisters. Monumental 2-storeyed hall like something strayed from British Museum.

Bury St Edmunds, *Suffolk*. (88.) *St Edmund* (RC) (73), Westgate Street, by C. Day, Ionic portico in antis; interior altered. *Athenaeum*, Angel Hill, by F. Sandys, 1804, modest Classical front. *Theatre* (105), Westgate Street, by Wilkins, 1819, with Doric portico and wel-restored interior.

Butterton, *Staffordshire*. (59.) *Butterton Farm House*, by Soane, 1815, for T. Swinnerton, striking red-brick composition with canted pilasters.

Caerhays Castle, *Cornwall*. (46.) By Nash, c. 1808, for J. B. Trevanion. Impressive castellated asymmetrical pile well placed in woods near the sea. Interesting planning with characteristic Nash feature of a long wide gallery.

Cairness House, *Grampian Region*. (50, 51.) By James Playfair, 1791–7, for C. Gordon, completed by Soane. Unusual and sharply detailed Neo-Classical design. 7-bay entrance front with 2-storeyed centre, marked by 1-storeyed pedimented Greek Doric portico, flanked by 3-storeyed wings with tripartite windows. Egyptian billiard room, Doric dining room, and Ionic drawing room. Most arresting feature is the office courtyard in a great hemi-cycle

at rear of house in style of Ledoux or Gilly with stunted Doric columns in massive arches.

Callendar House. Central REgion. *Mausoleum*, by A. Elliot, 1816, handsome Greek Doric tholos.

Cambridge. (88, 94, 98.) *Corpus Christi College* (29, 95), New Court, by Wilkins, 1823–7, neo-Perp, with chapel, hall, library and Master's Lodge. *Downing College* (22, 95), begun 1807 from designs by Wilkins which were an early and influential Greek Revival statement. *King's College* (29, 95), new buildings and entrance screen with pinnacled Porter's Lodge, 1824–8, by Wilkins, neo-Perp to blend with chapel; bridge, 1819, also by Wilkins, Classical. *Peterhouse*, Gisborne Court, by W. M. Brookes, 1825–6, modest Gothic. *St John's College* (96), New Court, by Rickman & Hutchinson, 1825–31, romantic Gothic, approached by Bridge of Sighs. *Trinity College* (29, 95), New Court, by Wilkins, 1821–3, Tudor Gothic. *Observatory*, Madingley Road, by J. C. Mead, 1822–3, with Greek Doric portico. *University Press*, Trumpington Street, by Blore, 1831–3, Tudor Gothic. *Fitzwilliam Museum* (73, 89, 90), Trumpington Street, by Basevi, 1834–45, magnificent Roman temple of the arts (staircase by E. M. Barry, 1870–5); attached to museum on the S, *Grove Lodge*, Classical villa by W. Custance, c. 1800. *Squire Law Library* (26, 98, 98), Old Schools, by C. R. Cockerell, 1837–42, N range of projected new University Library; masterly Classical pile with noble tunnel-vaulted 1st-floor library. *Bene't Place*, terraced houses, c. 1820. *Fitzwilliam Street*, complete domestic street of 1821–2. *The Grove*, Huntingdon Road, Classical villa by W. Custance, 1814. *Maid's Causeway*, Jesus Lane, 6 substantial houses related to smaller houses in *Willow Walk, Short Street* and *Fair Street*, all by C. Humfrey, 1815–26. *Downing Terrace*, Lensfield Road, 1819. *Scroope Terrace*, Trumpington Street, 1839–64.

Cambusnethan Priory, *Wishaw, Strathclyde Region*. Gothic extravaganza by J. G. Graham, 1816–19, for R. Lockhart.

Came House, *Winterbourne Came, Dorset*. *Camelia House*, c. 1840, one of the most elegant of early C19 cast-iron and glass conservatories.

Camerton Court, *Somerset*. By G. S. Repton, 1838–40, for J. Jarrett. Late Classical.

Camperdown House, *Dundee, Tayside Region*. (50.) By W. Burn, 1824–6, for 1st Earl of Camperdown. Massive Greek Ionic exterior inspired by Wilkins's Grange Park (q.v.), with typical Burn plan with family rooms separate from state rooms and guests' rooms.

Canterbury, *Kent*. *County Gaol and Sessions House* (84, 88), Longport, by G. Byfield, 1806–10, Greek Doric. *Methodist Church*, St Peter's Street, by W. Jenkins, 1811, with usual round-headed windows.

Carlisle, *Cumbria*. *Holy Trinity*, Wigton Road, by Rickman & Hutchinson, 1828–30, Commissioners' church in solid Gothic style. *Assize Courts* (81), Court Square, by R. Smirke, 1810–12, large towered Gothic pile. *Infirmary* (86, 87), Newton Road, by R. Tattersall, ambitious Greek Revival design (extended 1870s). *Dixon's Mills* (114, 115), Junction Street, by R. Tattersall, 1835–6, vast functional block with iron-beamed interiors. *Savings Bank* (formerly Athenaeum), Lowther Street, by A. & G. Williams, 1840. Regency-style houses in *Lowther Street*, *Victoria Place* and *Lonsdale Street*.

Carstairs House, *Strathclyde Region*. By W. Burn, 1822–4, for H. Monteith. Neo-Tudor, inspired by Wilkins's Dalmeny, with 80ft-long vaulted corridor.

Cartland Crags Bridge, *Strathclyde Region*. By T. Telford, 1821–2.

Castle Forbes, *Grampian Region*. By A. Simpson, 1814–15, for 17th Lord Forbes. Massive granite pile in not specially Picturesque castellated style.

Castle Goring, *near Arundel, West Sussex*. (54, 56.) Remarkable split-personality house, half Greek Revival, half Gothic, by J. B. Rebecca, c. 1795–1815, for Sir B. Shelley, Bt.

Castle Howard, *North Yorkshire*. Sculpture Gallery and Museum created in W range by C. H. Tatham, 1800–1, for 5th Earl of Carlisle. Influential on museum design.

Castle Toward, *Toward Point, Cowal, Strathclyde Region*. By D. Hamilton, 1820–1, for K. Finlay. Multi-towered Picturesque composition.

Castletown House, *near Rockcliffe, Cumbria*. By P. Nicholson & W. Reid, 1811, for R. Mounsey. Greek Revival

house, ashlar-faced, with Soanean details (e.g. pilaster strips) and good interiors.

Caythorpe Hall, *Lincolnshire*. By W. Parsons, 1824–7, for Col. G. H. Packe. Chaste 4-bay Classical block.

The Chantry, *near Nunney, Somerset*. Stylish ashlar-faced villa built c. 1825 for J. Fussell, an ironmaster. Delicate recessions on 3-bay N entrance front culminating in semi-circular Greek Doric porch. Built on sloping site so that S front, looking towards the lake, is half a storey higher than the N; it has a curved bow in the centre.

Charborough Park, *Dorset*. C17 house, extended in C18 and c. 1810 by Nash for R. Erle Drax Grosvenor. 11-bay front with 5-bay pedimented Ionic centre by Nash. Fine park. *Peacock Lodge*, 1837, ashlar-faced elliptical arch flanked by entrance lodges. *Tower*, 1790, 5-storeyed octagonal Gothick folly, rebuilt 1839.

Chard, *Somerset*. Town hall, 1834, Tuscan.

Chatsworth House, *Derbyshire*. Baroque palace extended with long wing to N by Wyatville, 1820–41, who also remodelled interiors, e.g. sumptuous library. His N wing for 6th Duke of Devonshire contains fine dining room, sculpture gallery, orangery, and theatre capped by prominent belvedere, a Picturesque Italianate feature. By Wyatville, also, the entrance lodges and gateway to forecourt.

Cheeseburn Grange, *Northumberland*. By Dobson, 1813 and 1819, for R. Riddell. Plain Classical house. (Gothic chapel by Hansom, 1860.)

Chelmsford, *Essex*. *Shire Hall*, by J. Johnson, 1789–91, Adamish in style. *County Gaol*, Springfield, by T. Hopper, 1822–6 and 1845–8, Tuscan.

Cheltenham, *Gloucestershire*. (7, 43.) Developed from 1824 by J. B. Papworth and the Jearrads with enchanting Greek Revival and Italianate terraces and villas in tree-lined streets. Especially rewarding terraces include: the *Promenade, Lansdowne Place, Terrace, Court, Crescent* and *Parade*; *Montpelier Terrace* and *Parade*; *Oriel Terrace* and *Parade*; *Wolseley Terrace*; *Royal Well Terrace*; *Royal Parade*; *St George's Terrace*; *Royal Crescent*; *St Margaret's Terrace*; *Segrave Place*; *Park Place* (villas); also numerous villas in *Pittville* and the *Park*. Typical of more substantial Greek Revival villas, both in Thirlestaine Road, are *College House* (formerly Lake House), and the grander

Thirlestaine Hall, in style of Wilkins with tetrastyle Ionic portico. *Pittville Pump Room* (42), by J. B. Forbes, 1825–30, with Ionic colonnades and superb coffered, domed and galleried interior. *Montpellier Spa*, by G. A. Underwood, 1817, with remarkable dome by Papworth, 1825–6. *Masonic Hall*, Portland Street, by G. A. Underwood, 1818–23. *Queen's Hotel* (107), 1837–8, immense Classical pile by the Jearrads. *St James*, Suffolk Square, by E. Jenkins, 1825, Gothic. *St Paul*, St Paul's Road, by J. B. Forbes, 1829–31, Greek Ionic. *Christ Church*, Malvern Road, by R. W. & C. Jearrad, 1838–40, Gothic.

Chepstow, *Gwent. Iron bridge*, by J. Rennie, 1815–16. *Piercefield*, by Soane, 1785–93, for G. Smith. Completed by J. Bonomi, 1797. (Now a ruin.)

Chester. Pre-eminently the town of the Neo-Classical architect Thomas Harrison. The following all by him: *Chester Castle* (22, 23, 24, 83), 1788–1822, distinguished Neo-Classical complex of which the highlights are the Greek Doric entrance gateway, inspired by the Athenian propylaea, and the semi-circular Shire Hall with its coffered semi-dome. (Former) *News Room* (92), Northgate Street, 1808. *North Gate*, 1808–10. *St Martin's Lodge*, c. 1820, for himself. *Watergate House*, Watergate Street, 1820, elegant Classical house on the angle of two streets, with circular entrance vestibule. *Grosvenor Bridge*, 1827–33.

Chestham Park, *near Henfield, West Sussex*. Greek Revival house, c. 1830, perhaps by A. H. Wilds.

Chichester, *West Sussex. St John*, St John's Street, by J. Elmes, 1812–14, neo-Greek, though oddly with elongated octagonal plan. *Market House*, North Street, by Nash, 1807–8, Greek Doric.

Chicksands Priory, *Bedfordshire*. Georgianised remains of medieval priory, remodelled by J. Wyatt, 1813, for Sir G Osborn, Bt. Symmetrical 7-bay Gothic E front. Gothic interiors include entrance hall and staircase.

Chirk, *Clwyd*. (110.) *Aqueduct*, by T. Telford, 1796–1801. *Bridge*, by T. Telford, 1831.

Cholmondley Castle, *Cheshire*. Simple Gothic house of 1801–4 by 2nd Marquess of Cholmondley for himself, extended with Picturesque towers by Smirke, 1817 and c. 1829. Interiors behind this impressive and extensive pile

are unexceptional apart from 2-storeyed arcaded Gothic hall.

Chorley, *Lancashire. St George*, St George's Street, by Rickman & Hutchinson, 1822–5, expensive Commissioners' church, Gothic, with W tower and cast-iron galleries.

Clackmannan, *Central Region. Church*, by J. G. Graham, 1815, Gothic with tower.

Claverton Manor, *near Bath, Avon*. (50.) By Wyatville, c. 1820, for J. Vivian. Elegant if rather old-fashioned Anglo-Palladian villa with 5-bay pedimented W front and longer S front enlivened with 2 segmental bows separated by centrepiece with 2 engaged Ionic columns. Interiors now largely masked by C17–19 interiors brought from N America.

Clevedon, *Avon. Christ Church*, Chapel Hill, by T. Rickman, 1838–9, large Gothic church with impressive SW tower. Some Regency domestic architecture survives on the sea-front.

Clifton Castle, *near Masham, North Yorkshire*. By J. Foss, 1802–10, for T. Hutton. Not castellated, despite its name, but a fine ashlared composition with Ionic portico, fine staircase and bowed drawing room similar to that (by Foss and Wyatt) at Swinton Park (q.v.).

Clytha Park, *Gwent*. (2, 50, 62, 64.) By E. Haycock, c. 1830, for W. Herbert. Impressive Greek Revival mansion of Bath stone with hexastyle Erectheion Ionic portico on SW front shielding pretty iron and glass curved porch. Side elevation has curved bow with Greek Doric colonnade. Circular entrance hall with engaged Tuscan columns and ribbed ceiling, stair hall with octagonal lantern and screen of Greek Doric columns. In park, *Clytha Castle*, 1790, early work of Nash, remarkably festive and attractive Gothick folly.

Cold Brayfield House, *Buckinghamshire*. By C. Humfrey, 1809, for S. Farrer. Ashlared and chastely Classical 2-storeyed entrance front of 3 bays, the central bay recessed, ground-floor windows in flanking bays set in blank round-headed recesses, porch by Detmar Blow. Long 2-storeyed S front of 9 bays, the central 3 forming a curved bow over which the façade rises to form a pedimented 3rd storey or attic. Attractive iron verandah along the length of this front. (Portions of the earlier gabled house survive.)

Coleorton Hall, *Leicestershire*. By G. Dance, 1804–8, for the collector Sir G. Beaumont, Bt. Joyless building in grey stone but interesting example of Dance's stripped Gothic style (spoilt with additions by S. P. Cockerell, 1862). Inside, central Gothic tribune, tall, galleried and vaulted, on 12-sided plan.

Coleshill, *Berkshire*. *Strattenborough Castle Farm*, c. 1792, false Gothick façade added to farmhouse to act as eye-catcher from Coleshill House.

Colinton House, *Edinburgh*. By R. Crichton, 1801, for Sir W. Forbes, Bt.

Colwich, *Staffordshire*. *Wolseley Bridge*, by J. Rennie, 1798–1800.

Conishead Priory, *Cumbria*. By P. W. Wyatt, 1821–36, for T. R. Gale, whom it all but bankrupted. Extravagant neo-Perp mansion, L-shaped, asymmetrical and unarchaeological in detail; elaborate Gothic and Jacobean interiors.

Conwy, *Gwynedd*. (*109*, 109.) *Suspension Bridge*, by T. Telford, 1821–6, hung from stone supports built in the form of medieval towers modelled on those of Conwy Castle.

Corby Castle, *Cumbria*. By P. Nicholson, 1812–17, for H. Howard. Incorporates peel tower with C17 & C18 additions. Imposing Greek Revival pile with features derived from Smirke and Soane. 5-bay S entrance front of 3 storeys with central tripartite window and Diocletian window over; hexastyle Greek Doric entrance porch flanked by 1-storeyed loggia with round-headed windows; 7-bay W front with central 3 bays recessed and connected on ground floor by open Greek Doric loggia. (Interiors partly of 1730s.)

Corehouse, *Strathclyde Region*. By Blore, 1824–7, for Lord Corehouse. Manorial house with stepped façades.

Coultermains, *Strathclyde Region*. By W. Spence, 1838, for A. Sim.

Courteenhall, *Northamptonshire*. By S. Saxon, 1791–4, for Sir W. Wake, Bt. Exceptionally reticent Classical house of 7 bays and 3 storeys; ground-floor windows set in blank segmental arches. Dining room with screen of columns and fine plasterwork in style of Chambers of whom Saxon was a pupil; exquisite library with apsed end containing 2 exedras screened by columns with Tower of the Winds lotus-capitals. Park by Repton.

Courtfield, *Welsh Bicknor, Hereford and Worcester*. 7-bay Regency stuccoed front with semi-circular porch of Greek Doric columns. Seat of the Catholic family of Vaughan since 1575 and now a school run by the Mill Hill Fathers.

Craig, *Tayside Region*. *Church*, perhaps by R. Crichton, 1799, Gothic, with W tower.

Craigellachie, *Grampian Region*. *Bridge*, by T. Telford, 1812–15, iron with Gothic towers.

Crailing House, *Borders Region*. By W. Elliot, 1803, for W. Paton. Simple 5-bay front with central 3 bays pedimented and divided by Doric pilasters.

Cramond, *Edinburgh*. *Craigcrook Castle*, by W. H. Playfair, 1835, for Lord Jeffrey, Baronial style. *Bridge*, by J. Rennie, 1819–23.

Cranbury Park, *Hampshire*. (*44*.) Curious Classical house of 1780s, by G. Dance for T. Dummer, with superb Neo-Classical vaulted ballroom. Additions of 1830s by J. B. Papworth for T. Chamberlayne including handsome library with rosewood bookshelves and screen of scagliola Tuscan columns, and the Tent Room, an Empire Style confection with pink silk brocade hangings.

Craycombe House, *Fladbury, Hereford and Worcester*. By G. Byfield, 1791, for G. Perrot of the East India Co. Chaste ashlar-faced villa with 5-bay entrance front with ground-floor windows set in blank round-headed arches. Tripartite entrance doorway with Corinthian pilasters beneath giant lunette with fan glazing.

Crazies, *Crazies Hill, Berkshire*. Freak house of 1899 incorporating Tuscan porticos and cupola from former town hall at Henley, by W. Bradshaw, 1795–6.

Cricket Court, *Cricket Malherbie, Somerset*. Bizarre Greek Revival house, c. 1820, for and perhaps designed by Admiral Pitt. Ground-floor windows have heavy Doric triglyph friezes above which is a continuous iron balcony. 4-bay 2-storeyed entrance front on high basement; porch of 4 unfluted Greek-Doric columns with pediment crowned by an oddly canted roof – indeed, the ungainly mansard roofs seem in general to be a later remodelling. Entrance hall with oval dome on unbelievably eccentric curved vaulting. Best interior is the circular library with delicately Soanean ribbing in domed ceiling. Interesting and attractive grounds with ice house.

Cricket House, *Cricket St Thomas, Somerset.* Plain Late Georgian block of 7 by 6 bays with Tuscan porch and colonnades. Alterations by Soane for 1st Viscount Bridport in 1786 and, more importantly, 1801–4. Further alterations since, e.g. handsome imperial staircase.

Crimonmogate, *Lonmay, Grampian Region.* By A. Simpson, c. 1825, for Sir A. Bannerman. Greek Revival. (Mansard roof a later addition.)

Cronkhill, *near Shrewsbury, Salop.* By Nash, c. 1802, for F. Walford. Earliest and most attractive of Picturesque Italianate villas, its asymmetrical composition perhaps inspired by building in background of Claude's 'Landscape with the Ponte Molle'. Round tower with conical roof and broadly projecting eaves; L-shaped loggia of round-headed arches.

Cuerden Hall, *Lancashire.* Remodelled by L. W. Wyatt, 1815, for R. T. Parker. Curious Classical style with corner towers and central belvedere forming a clerestory over the staircase. This attempt to create a Picturesque Vanbrughian skyline derives from the theories of Uvedale Price.

Culdees Castle, *Tayside Region.* By J. G. Graham, c. 1810, for Gen. A. Drummond. Symmetrical castle-style with 1 round tower. (Burnt 1887, restored 1910.)

Cultoquhey House, *Tayside Region.* By R. Smirke, for A. Maxtone. Designed 1818 and built from c. 1822 in simplified manorial style.

Cyfarthfa Castle, *near Merthyr Tydfil, Mid Glamorgan.* By R. Lugar, 1825, for W. Crawshay. Picturesque castellated pile.

Dalhousie Castle, *Lothian Region.* Remodelled and extended by W. Burn, 1826–8, for 9th Earl of Dalhousie.

Dalmeny House, *Lothian Region.* (30, 31, 57.) By Wilkins, 1814–17, for 4th Earl of Rosebery. Large and stylistically influential Tudor Gothic mansion.

Dalquharran Castle, *Strathclyde Region.* Designed by R. Adam, 1782–5, for T. Kennedy, built 1790. Castle-style with projecting tower in centre of garden front. (Wings added 1881.) (Now a ruin.)

Danbury Place, *Essex.* By T. Hopper, 1832, for J. Round. Elaborate, irregular,

red-brick house in Tudor Gothic style.

Darlington, *Co. Durham. Methodist Church*, Bondgate, by W. Jenkins, 1812, large but simple Classical building.

Darwen, *Lancashire. Holy Trinity*, by Rickman & Hutchinson, 1827–9, neo-Perp.

Dawlish, *Devon.* Simple early C19 terraces. *Stonelands*, c. 1818, villa with porch of 4 Greek Doric columns and staircase hall with Erectheion Ionic columns.

Dawyck House (formerly Posso House), *Borders Region.* By W. Burn, 1832–3, for Sir J. Nasmyth of Posso, Bt. Baronial style. (Enlarged 1898.)

Daylesford House, *Gloucestershire.* (17.) By S. P. Cockerell, 1788–93, for Warren Hastings. Neo-Classical mansion in golden ashlar with French details, but a disjointed composition with 3 markedly different façades. 7-bay 3-storey entrance front with Doric portico flanked by lower projecting wings; long S elevation with canted bays at each end and central Doric portico opening at semi-basement level on to terrace; W front with segmental bow surmounted by dome with a faintly Muslim cap. Below this on 1st floor, enchanting circular boudoir with lotus-capital colonnettes and cloud-painted ceiling. Good Classical interiors, e.g. morning room with superb chimney-piece by Banks (1792) showing Indian women returning from the Ganges. Exceptionally pretty Gothick conservatory, presumably also by Cockerell, pedimented with bowed ends. Fine park with lake.

Debden Church, *Essex.* Octagonal Gothic chapel and monument added 1792–3 by the antiquary John Carter, for R. M. T. Chiswell.

Decker Hall, *Shifnal, Salop.* Stuccoed house c. 1810 with striking 5-bay entrance front dominated by 2 giant Ionic columns in antis.

Denford House, *Berkshire.* By Wyatville, c. 1815, for W. Hallett. Compact Classical villa with semi-circular domed bay in centre of S front. Alterations by J.B. Papworth, 1827–8. (Wings added 1939.)

Derby. (106.) *Gaol.* Vernon Street, by F. Goodwin, 1823–7, Greek Doric. (Altered 1880.) *Royal Hotel* and *National Westminster Bank*, Cornmarket, by R. Wallace, 1837–9, Greek Ionic. *Arboretum*, Osmaston Road, laid out by

J. C. Loudon, 1839–40, as 1st of the C19 public parks in English towns. *Allestree Hall*, Allestree, by J. Wyatt, 1795, for B. Thornhill, 5-bay Classical villa with bow.

Derry Ormond Tower, *Dyfed*. Perhaps by C. R. Cockerell, 1821–4, landmark on the hill above Cockerell's now demolished Derry Ormond House.

Devizes, *Wiltshire*. (88.) *Town Hall*, by T. Baldwin, 1806–8, in Adam style. *Assize Court*, Northgate Street, by T. H. Wyatt, 1835, with Greek Ionic portico.

Dinton House. See under Phillips House.

Dodington Park, *Avon*. (59.) By J. Wyatt, 1798–1813, for C. Codrington. Impressive Neo-Classical house with noble Corinthian portico, rich interiors and quadrant conservatory leading to Greek Doric domed chapel. Set in lovely Capability Brown park.

Doldowlod House, *Rhayader, Powys*. By R. W. Mylne, 1827, for J. Watt, son of the inventor. Neo-Elizabethan 4-bay block inspired by Aston Hall, Birmingham (Additions 1878.)

Dollar, *Central Region*. (95, 97.) *Academy*, by W. H. Playfair, 1818–20, ambitious pile with hexastyle Tuscan portico and flanking wings. (Later additions).

Dol-Llys, *Llanidloes, Powys*. Picturesque stuccoed Gothic villa, c. 1820.

Don Bridge, *near Aberdeen, Grampian Region*. By T. Telford, 1826–9.

Donington Hall, *Leicestershire*. By Wilkins senior, 1790–3, for 2nd Earl of Moira. Symmetrical 11-bay castellated Gothic front with turreted central tower containing massive open arch with curious glazing. Classical interiors.

Dorchester, *Dorset*. *Shire Hall*, High West Street, by T. Hardwick, 1795–7, with simple 7-bay pedimented front. *Antelope Hotel*, South Street, c. 1815, with shallow segmental 2-storey bows.

Dover, *Kent*. *Waterloo Crescent*, by P. Hardwick, 1834–8, stuccoed and eye-catching.

Downham Hall, *Clitheroe, Lancashire*. By G. Webster, 1834–5, for W. Assheton, 9-bay Classical front.

Doxford Hall, *Northumberland*. By Dobson, 1818, for W. Taylor. 5-bay Grecian house. (Since altered.)

Dropmore, *Buckinghamshire*. (50.) Long, low Regency house with curved bows by S. Wyatt, 1792–4, for Lord Grenville, George III's Prime Minister.

Extended to N and S, 1806–9, by Tatham who perhaps added the remarkable Doric trellis-work pergolas, iron aviary, etc. Good interiors.

Drumlanrig Castle, *Dumfries and Galloway Region*. Massive late C17 castle provided with impressive forecourt wings, c. 1830–4, probably by W. Burn, for 5th Duke of Buccleuch.

Drumtochty Castle, *Grampian Region*. By J. G. Graham, c. 1815, for G. H. Drummond. Romantic towers inspired by Warwick Castle.

Dudley, *West Midlands*. *St Thomas*, High Street, by W. Brooks, 1816–17, very original Gothic church with canted aisle walls.

Dumbleton Hall, *near Evesham, Gloucestershire*. By G. S. Repton, c. 1830, for E. Holland. Symmetrical Tudor Gothic.

Dumfries, *Dumfries and Galloway Region*. *Burns Mausoleum*, St Michael's churchyard, by T. F. Hunt, 1815, Ionic with dome. *Old Episcopal (now Wesleyan) Church*, Buccleuch Street, by T. F. Hunt, c. 1815.

Dundas Castle, *Lothian Region*. By W. Burn, 1818, for J. Dundas. Like R. Smirke's Lowther Castle, one façade is castellated, the other ecclesiastical Gothic.

Dundee, *Tayside Region*. *St David's Church*, by D. Neave, 1822–4. *St Andrew (RC)*, Nethergate, by G. Mathewson, 1836, Gothic. *Thistle Hall*, Union Street, 1826–9, by Neave who also laid out *Union Street, Dock Street, Exchange Street* and *Tay Street*, c. 1818–28. *Nos. 8–11 Exchange Street* (formerly Exchange Coffee Room), by G. Smith, 1828–30. *Commercial Street, Lindsay Street* and *Panmure Street* laid out 1828 and 1839 by J. Black who also built houses in *Magdalen Place, Douglas Terrace* and *Union Street*, 1836–40. *High School* (95), by G. Angus, 1832–4, Greek Revival, inspired stylistically by T. Hamilton; its portico closes *Reform Street* which Angus laid out in 1833. *Watt Institution* (now YMCA), by Angus, 1838–9. *Custom House*, by J. Leslie and J. Taylor, 1839–40, fine Classical design.

Dunfermline, *Fife Region*. New *Abbey Church*, by W. Burn, 1818–21, neo-Perp. *County Buildings*, High Street, by A. Elliot, 1809 and 1811.

Dunkeld Bridge, *Tayside Region*. (108.) By T. Telford, 1806–9, in centre of town, high semi-circular arches separated by semi-cylindrical piers adorned with blind arrow slits.

Dunlop House, *Strathclyde Region*. By D. Hamilton, 1831–4, for Sir J. Dunlop, Bt. Tall composition in Scots-Jacobean style.

Dunninald House, *Craig, Tayside Region*. By J. G. Graham, 1823–4, for P. Arkly. Nearly symmetrical castellated front with large round corner tower inspired by Lugar's Tullichewan Castle (1808). Attractive sequence of Gothic hall, stairs and cloister.

Duns Castle, *Borders Region*. By J. G. Graham, 1818–22, for W. Hay. Imaginative composition in the castle-style, high and towering.

Dunstall Priory (formerly Gold Hill), *near Shoreham, Kent*. By R. Lugar, 1806. Early example of asymmetrical Italianate villa with round tower at one end surrounded by verandah. Inspired by Nash's Cronkhill (q.v.), though not so well composed.

Durham. *St Cuthbert* (RC), Court Lane, by I. Bonomi, 1827–7, Gothic. (Later alterations.)

East Malling, *Kent*. (*47*.) *Clare House*, by M. Searles, 1793, for J. Larking, surprising villa with circular, oval and octagonal rooms.

Eastnor Castle, *Hereford and Worcester*. By R. Smirke, 1812–20, for 2nd Lord Somers. Large, symmetrical, neo-Norman and castellated mansion in beautiful setting. (Sumptuous Gothic drawing room by Crace and Pugin, 1849.)

East Teignmouth, *Devon*. *St Michael*, by A. Patey, 1822–3, neo-Norman. *Den Crescent*, by A. Patey, 1826, with colonnaded Public Rooms (later cinema) as its central feature.

Edinburgh, *Lothian Region*. (7, 37, 95, 97, 108.) The *New Town* is stylistically dependent on, and follows chronologically, the Woods' work at Bath. *Charlotte Square* (37, *39*), by R. Adam, 1791. *Second New Town* (*39*), built from 1802 by Reid and Sibbald, e.g. *Royal Circus. Moray Estate* (*39*), by J. G. Graham, 1822: *Randolph Crescent* (*39*), *Ainslie Place* (*39*), and *Moray Place* (*39*, *40*). Terraces N of Calton Hill (*39*) by W. H. Playfair, from 1819, e.g. *Regent Terrace* and *Hillside Crescent*. *Waterloo Place*, by A. Elliot, 1819. *St George*, Charlotte Square, by R. Reid, 1811–14, with high dome on colonnaded drum. *St Mary* (RC) (now Cathedral), Broughton Street, by J. G. Graham, 1813–14, Gothic. (Later alterations.) *St John* (76), Princes Street, by W. Burn, 1816–18, neo-Perp with pretty fan-vault. (Apse 1879.)*St Mary* (76), Bellevue Crescent, by T. Brown, 1823–6, Corinthian portico and tall 3-tiered tower. *St Stephen* (76), St Vincent Street, by W. H. Playfair, 1827–8, Classical church with remarkable octagonal plan. (Interior altered.) *St Mark's Unitarian Chapel*, Castle Terrace, by D. Bryce, 1834–5, astonishingly Italianate façade. *St Margaret's Convent Chapel*, by J. G. Graham, 1835, Romanesque. *University* (97), begun by R. Adam, 1789–93, continued by W. H. Playfair, 1817–26; Adam's most impressive public building. (Dome 1887.) *Bank of Scotland* (100), The Mound, by Reid & Crichton, 1802–6, in Adam style. *New Law Courts*, Parliament Square, by R. Reid, 1804–10 and 1825–40. *Upper and Lower Signet Library* (93), by Reid, Stark, Playfair and Burn, 1810–26; superb Classical interiors. *Register House*, begun by Adam, 1774–92; rear wing in similar style by R. Reid, 1822–30. *Royal Institution* (now Scottish Academy) (*94*, 94), by W. H. Playfair, 1822–6 and 1832–5, Greek Doric. *Edinburgh Academy* (95), Henderson Row, by W. Burn, 1823–6, 1-storeyed with Greek Doric portico and oval assembly room. *Royal High School* (*22*, 95), Regent Road, by T. Hamilton, 1825–9, one of the finest Greek Revival buildings in Britain. *John Watson's Hospital School*, Belford Road, by W. Burn, 1825–8, 21-bay front with hexastyle Greek Doric portico. *Surgeons' Hall*, Nicolson Street, by W. H. Playfair, 1832, Grecian. *Royal College of Physicians* (94), Queen Street, by T. Hamilton, 1844–6, stylishly Classical. Buildings on *Calton Hill:Nelson Monument*, by R. Burn and T. Bonnar, 1807–16, circular castellated tower; *City Observatory*, by W. H. Playfair, 1818, Greek-cross plan with central dome and 4 Roman Doric porticos; *National Monument*, 1824–9, unfinished version of the Parthenon by C. R. Cockerell and W. H. Playfair; *Burns Monument*, by T. Hamilton, 1830–2, circular temple; *Dugald Stewart Monument*, by W. H. Playfair, 1831, circular temple.

Edmond Castle, *Hayton, Cumbria*. By R.

Smirke, 1824, for T. Graham. Modest Tudor.

Edmonstone Castle, *Strathclyde Region*. By J. G. Graham, 1815, for J. Brown. Modest essay in the castle-style.

Egham, *Surrey*. *St John the Baptist*, by H. Rhodes, 1817–20, strange and austere stock-brick church inspired by Soane's stripped Classicism, e.g. at Dulwich Gallery. Lacking Soane's nervous grace, Rhodes produced something verging on ugliness. Oddly detailed W tower surmounted by small tempietto, high and blank E end. Interior, less altered than many of this date, has galleries and segmental chancel arch.

Elgin, *Grampian Region*. *St Giles* (75, 76), by A. Simpson, 1827–8, on an island site in centre of High Street. Massive hexastyle Greek Doric portico with wreaths in frieze, and tower crowned by imitation of Lysicrates Monument. *Court House and Public Offices*, by W. Robertson, 1837 (rebuilt c. 1930). *Episcopal Church and parsonage*, North Street, by W. Robertson, 1825. *Anderson Institution*, by A. Simpson, 1830–3.

Elsenham Hall, *Essex*. Symmetrical castellated Late Georgian mansion of red brick, with 5-bay entrance front, the central 3 bays recessed and linked at ground-floor level by attractive 3-bay stuccoed Tudor porch.

Elvaston Castle, *Derbyshire*. (60.) Early C17 house extensively remodelled by R. Walker, c. 1815–19 (from designs by J. Wyatt), for 3rd Earl of Harrington. Fine Gothic entrance hall and library, Classical staircase, 9-bay E front probably by L. N. Cottingham, 1830–40. Important park laid out 1830–50 by W. Barron of Edinburgh with arboretum, lake, grottoes, Moorish temple, arch, Alhambra, etc.

Ely, *Cambridgeshire*. *Shire Hall and Gaol*, Lynn Road, by C. Humfrey, 1820–2, modest white-brick building with impressive tetrastyle Greek Doric portico.

Endsleigh, *near Milton Abbot, Devon*. (59, 60.) By Wyatville, 1810–11, for 6th Duke of Bedford. Setting by Repton. The most elaborate cottage orné of the Regency period with asymmetrical diagonal planning which was revolutionary and influential.

Erskine House, *Strathclyde Region*. By R. Smirke, 1828, for 11th Lord Blantyre. Gothic.

Escot House, *Devon*. By H. Roberts, a pupil of Smirke, 1838, for Sir J. Kennaway, Bt. Greek Revival. Escot *church*, 1839–40, by same architect for same patron, Gothic.

Eshton Hall, *North Yorkshire*. By G. Webster, 1825–7, for M. Wilson. Early example of Jacobean Revival.

Everingham Park, *Humberside*. (72.) Catholic *chapel*, 1836–9, for W. Constable-Maxwell, by A. Giorgioli of Rome, executed by J. Harper of York. Striking Italianate basilica with rich interior, coffered tunnel vault and apse.

Evesham, *Hereford and Worcester*. *Abbey Manor*, quite impressive square castellated Gothic house, c. 1840, in style reminiscent of Blore's Pitt Press, Cambridge. 5-bay 3-storeyed front with end bays slightly projecting.

Exeter, *Devon*. (101.) *Higher Market*, by G. Dymond and C. Fowler, 1835–8, with Greek Doric porticos in antis.

Exmouth, *Devon*. Early C19 *terraces*. *A la Ronde*, 1795, for the Misses Parminter, remarkable 16-sided cottage orné with central octagonal hall 60ft high. Also built for the Parminters, higher up the hill, *Point-in-View*, 1811, a chapel, almshouses and schoolroom.

Falkirk, *Central Region*. *Town Steeple*, by D. Hamilton, 1813–14, square tower with Neo-Classical lower stages adorned with Greek Doric columns but surmounted by Gibbsian spire.

Falkland House, *Fife Region*. By W. Burn, 1839–44, for O. Tyndall Bruce. Elaborate and expensive Jacobethan house with rich interiors.

Falmouth, *Cornwall*. *Custom House*; *Royal Cornwall Polytechnic*, Church Street, 1833; and (former) *Classical and Mathematical School*, Killigrew Road, 1824: all Greek Doric. *Marlborough House*, Marlborough Avenue, 1805–15, provincial Neo-Classical villa with curved Ionic colonnade. Several minor Regency terraces.

Faskally, *Tayside Region*. By W. Burn, 1829, for A. Nutter. Characteristic example of Burn's Scots-Jacobethan style.

Fasque, *Grampian Region*. Symmetrical castellated front of 9 bays flanked by 2 3-bay lower wings. Elegant elliptical stair hall, Classical but with sparing Gothic details.

Fettercairn, *Laurencekirk, Grampian Region*. Picturesque neo-Jacobean mansion with numerous shaped gables by W. Burn, 1826, for Sir W. Forbes.

Fetteresso, *Grampian Region*. Octagonal Gothic *church* by J. Paterson, 1810–12, with curved wings leading to W tower.

Ffrwdgrech, *Llanfaes, Powys*. Greek Revival *villa* of 1828.

Ffynone, *Dyfed*. By Nash, 1792–6, for J. Colby. Simple 5-bay villa with pedimented entrance front. (Altered 1904.)

Filey, *North Yorkshire*. *The Crescent*, by C. Edge, 1835–8, 6 stuccoed terraces, not notably crescent-shaped in layout.

Fillongley Hall, *Warwickshire*. Stone mansion of 1824–5 which has rightly been compared to Dobson's houses in Northumberland. 5-bay entrance front with central loggia formed by 2 Ionic columns in antis, impressive columnar entrance hall with glazed dome.

Finborough Hall, *Suffolk*. By F. Sandys, the architect of Ickworth, 1795, for R. Pettiward. S front with bow window flanked by Tuscan colonnade, large staircase hall.

Finnart House, *Loch Rannoch, Tayside Region*. By W. Burn, 1838, for D. McLaren. Jacobethan.

Floors Castle, *Kelso, Borders Region*. Vast house of 1720s by W. Adam dramatically remodelled in Jacobethan style by W. H. Playfair. 1837–45, for 6th Duke of Roxburgh. Romantic skyline was inspired by Heriot's Hospital, Edinburgh. Interiors mostly Edwardian though Playfair's dining room survives.

Folkingham, *Lincolnshire*. (88.) *House of Correction*, by B. Browning, 1824–5, powerful 3-bay Classical façade with echoes of Ledoux.

Follaton House, *near Totnes, Devon*. By G. S. Repton, c. 1826–9, for S. Cary. 9-bay front with Ionic portico.

Fonthill Abbey, *Fonthill Gifford, Wiltshire*. (29, 54.) The fragmentary survival of Wyatt's Gothic extravaganza for Beckford of 1796–1812 is part of N wing including Lancaster Tower, Sanctuary and Oratory. More extensive souvenir of Beckford is his rich and exotic planting in the steep and beautiful valleys of Fonthill Gifford.

Fordoun Church, *Grampian Region*. By J. Smith, 1828–9. Gothic with elaborate tower.

Forfar, *Tayside Region*. *Academy*, by D. Logan, 1815, Greek Doric. *County Buildings*, by D. Neave, 1823–4.

Foxboro Hall, *Melton, Suffolk*. Perfect Regency villa with festive faintly colonial mood. White-brick 3-bay S entrance front with 1-bay flanking wings and shuttered windows, semi-circular portico with giant Ionic columns over which the façade rises half a storey and is crowned by a pediment.

Frant, *East Sussex*. *St Alban*, by J. Montier, 1819–22, neo-Perp, ashlared with W tower; iron piers.

Freeland House, *Tayside Region*. By Blore and Burn, 1825–6, for 6th Lord Ruthven. Freely asymmetrical neo-Tudor vernacular. (Later additions.)

Gallanach House, *Strathclyde Region*. By W. Burn, 1814–17, for D. MacDougall. An early work and still symmetrical though castellated; good Classical interiors. (Enlarged c. 1903.)

Garden House, *Central Region*. New E front by W. Stirling, 1830, for J. Stirling. 5 bays with Greek Doric porch.

Garnons, *Hereford and Worcester*. By W. Atkinson, 1815–c. 30, for Sir J. G. Cotterell, Bt. (Substantial additions c. 1855; truncated 1958.) Superb Repton park of 1791.

Gask House, *Tayside Region*. By R. Crichton, 1801, for L. Oliphant. Classical style inspired by Adam, with high centre and flanking wings.

Gatcombe Park, *Gloucestershire*. Late C18 stone house with wings added by Basevi, c. 1820, for D. Ricardo, MP, incorporating library and conservatory. Good landscaped park. Home of HRH the Princess Anne and Captain Mark Phillips.

Gaunt's House, *near Hinton Martell, Dorset*. By W. Evans, 1809, for Sir R. C. Glyn, Bt. Elegant villa now engulfed in additions of 1880s. Remarkable lodge (60) on B3078 in the form of a cottage orné, doubtless also designed by Evans.

Glansevern Hall, *Berriew, Powys*. By J. Bromfield, c. 1805, for Sir R. Vaughan, Bt. Austere stone Greek Revival house.

Glasgow, *Central Region*. *St George*, Buchanan Street, by W. Stark, 1807–8, with Tuscan columns and spire. *St David* (76), Ingram Street (Ramshorn church), by Rickman & Hutchinson, 1824–6, decorated Gothic (later alterations). *St Andrew's Chapel* (RC) (now Cathedral) (76), Great Clyde Street, by J. G. Graham, Gothic with impressive W front. (Later alterations.) *Royal Exchange*

(100), Queen Street, by D. Hamilton, 1827–9, extensive Grecian pile with tower and portico. *Argyle Arcade* (102), Argyle Street, by J. Baird, 1827–8. 34 *Buchanan Street* and *Princes Square*, by J. Baird, 1840.

Glastonbury, *Somerset*. *Town Hall*, Magdalene Street, designed 1813 by J. B. Beard, built 1818, Palladian 5-bay 2-storeyed front with pedimented centre over rusticated round-arched ground floor.

Glen Usk, *Gwent*. Greek Revival house, c. 1820.

Glenlee, *Dumfries and Galloway Region*. *Villa*, by R. Lugar, 1823, for Lady Ashburton.

Glenorchy church, *Strathclyde Region*. (76.) By A. Elliot, 1808–11, octagonal Gothic nave with square tower.

Glevering Hall, *Suffolk*. By J. White, 1792–4, with additions of 1834–5 by D. Burton for A. Arcedeckne. 7- by 5-bay block with tripartite windows, S front with pilasters and pediment. Elegant orangery, presumably by Burton, 7 bays long with dome carried on palm-tree columns. Park by Repton.

Glossop, *Derbyshire*. *All Saints* (RC), Church Terrace, by M. E. Hadfield, 1834–7, Greek Revival. *Town Hall*, Norfolk Square, by Weightman & Hadfield, 1838, Classical.

Gloucester. *Gaol*, by W. Blackburn, 1788–91, enlarged 1845–55 *Shire Hall* (81), Westgate Street, by R. Smirke, 1814–16, with Ionic portico in antis. (Later alterations.) *Horton Road Hospital* (formerly lunatic asylum), by W. Star and J. Collingwood, 1813–23, in the form of a large stuccoed crescent. *Over Bridge*, by T. Telford, 1825. Near the spa Regency terraces and villas, e.g. *Ribston Hall*, *Sherborne House*, *Somerset House* (now Judge's Lodgings), by R. Smirke, c. 1816, *Beaufort Buildings* and *Brunswick Square*.

Gloucester-Berkeley Ship Canal, *Gloucestershire*. (111.) Greek Revival lock-keepers' houses, by Mylne and Telford, c. 1827, e.g. Frampton-on-Severn, Gloucester, Hardwicke, Moreton Valance, Quedgeley and Whitminster.

Glynllifon Park, *Llandwrog, Gwynedd*. (11.) Probably by E. Haycock, 1836–40, for 3rd Lord Newborough. Arguably the largest Neo-Classical mansion in Wales, with stuccoed 13-bay front boasting portico of 6 marble Ionic columns and

rich Classical interiors, e.g. 1st-floor drawing room.

Golden Grove, *Dyfed*. By Wyatville, 1826–37, for 1st Earl of Cawdor. Neo-Elizabethan mansion similar to Wyatville's Lilleshall (q.v.). Canted plan but dull interiors.

Goodmanham, *Humberside*. *Hall Garth* (formerly Rectory), by C. Mountain, 1823–4, for the Rev. W. Blow. Simple 5-bay W entrance front of white brick, S front with central curved bow; fine entrance hall approached through Ionic screen and boasting Ionic colonnades on 1st floor.

Goodnestone, *Kent*. *Holy Cross*, early English nave and chancel in flint and Caen stone added by Rickman & Hussey, 1838–41.

Goodwood House, *West Sussex*. (50.) By J. Wyatt, 1787, for 3rd Duke of Richmond. Incorporates S wing of 1750s by W. Chambers into a bizarre domed octagonal house of which only 3 sides were completed. 2-storeyed hexastyle portico on SW front. Numerous buildings by Wyatt in park including the *Dower House*, Molecombe, c. 1790–1806.

Gosford House, *Lothian Region*. By R. Adam, 1790–c. 1800, for 7th Earl of Wemyss. Neo-Classical palace rivalling Stowe (q.v.) in splendour, main W front with 3 vast round-headed windows, applied Corinthian order and central dome. (Remodelled and extended 1883–91 by W. Young, largely gutted 1940, but S wing rehabilitated 1951 and now inhabited by the Wemyss family.)

Grange Park, *Hampshire* (22, 50.) C17 red-brick house remodelled in cement by W. Wilkins, 1809, for H. Drummond. Perhaps the most thorough-going Greek Revival mansion in the country. Greek Doric portico modelled on the Theseion and centrepieces of side elevations modelled on the Choragic Monument of Thrasyllus. (Deliberately gutted by its owner in 1972 and now a ruin in the care of the DoE.) Beautiful park.

Gravesend, *Kent*. (84.) *Town Hall*, High Street, refronted by A. H. Wilds, 1836, with Greek Doric portico. *Cemetery*, Old Road West, by A. H. Wilds, 1838–41, with Grecian entrance lodges and chapel. Milton Park Estate, e.g. *Berkeley Crescent*, laid out by A. H. Wilds, c. 1830.

Great Yarmouth, *Norfolk.* (86.) *Royal Naval (now St Nicholas) Hospital*, by W. Pilkington or E. Holl, 1809–11, 4 29-bay-long blocks with round-arched colonnades approached through triumphal arch. *Nelson Column*, by W. Wilkins, 1817–20, 145ft-high Greek Doric column oddly surmounted by a drum surrounded by Victories and crowned by gilt statue of Britannia.

Gredington, *near Hanmer, Clwyd.* House by T. Harrison, 1810–15, for 2nd Lord Kenyon.

Greenock, *Strathclyde Region. Custom House*, by W. Burn, 1817–18. *George Square Congregational Church*, by J. Baird, 1839–40, Gothic.

Grimston Park, *North Yorkshire.* By D. Burton, 1840–50, for 2nd Lord Howden. Flashly Italianate palazzo with formal Italianate gardens by W. A. Nesfield.

Guildford, *Surrey.* (101.) (Former) *Corn Exchange*, High Street, by H. Garling, 1818, giant Tuscan portico.

Gunley Hall, *Forden, Powys.* 5-bay Neo-Classical front by J. H. Haycock, 1810, for R. Pryce.

Gwrych Castle, *Clwyd.* (56, 57.) Extravagantly Picturesque fantasy, c. 1814, by its owner, L. B. Hesketh, with assistance from numerous architects.

Hackness Hall, *near Scarborough, North Yorkshire.* By P. Atkinson senior, 1797, for Sir R. V. B. Johnstone, Bt. Old-fashioned Palladian mansion of local stone, 7-bay W front with 3-bay pedimented centre divided by fluted Ionic pilasters, shorter S front with central canted bow. Interior reinstated after fire in 1910. Good U-shaped stableyard also by Atkinson.

Hackthorn House, *Lincolnshire.* By J. Lewis, c. 1798, for J. Cracroft. Restrained Classical house of Yorkshire stone with oval top-lit staircase.

Hackwood Park, *Hampshire.* House of 1680s completely rebuilt by S. & L. W. Wyatt, 1806–25, for 1st and 2nd Lords Bolton. L. W. Wyatt designed the rendered S front with its impressive Ionic centrepiece, and the interiors, e.g. Neo-Classical dining room, screened, apsed and segmentally vaulted; library, with unusual Grinling Gibbons revival ceiling; and entrance hall, with carvings in same style by E. Wyatt, 1815. *London lodge*, a Greek Doric screen.

Hadlow Castle, *Kent.* What survives is the fantastic 170ft-high Gothic tower,

inspired by Fonthill, built c. 1838–40 by G. L. Taylor, for W. B. May.

Haffield House, *near Donnington, Hereford and Worcester.* By R. Smirke, 1817–18, for W. Gordon. Hexastyle Greek Doric portico.

Haigh, *Lancashire. St David*, by Rickman & Hutchinson, 1830, modest Gothic Commissioners' church. (Chancel 1886.)

Haigh Hall, *Lancashire.* Built 1827–40 for, and apparently designed by, 24th Earl of Crawford and Balcarres. Large, 3-storeyed, ashlar-faced house with 11-bay entrance front and Tuscan porch, side façade with 3 3-storeyed canted bay windows looking towards Wigan. Fine domed staircase hall.

Haileybury College, *Hertfordshire.* (22, 95.) By Wilkins, 1806–9. Influential Greek Revival building. (Later additions.)

The Haining, *Borders Region.* Remodelled with Erectheion Ionic loggia by A. Elliot, c. 1820, for J. Pringle.

Halifax, *West Yorkshire. Holy Trinity*, Harrison Road, by T. Johnson, 1795–8, classical with domed tower. *Zion Congregational Church*, Wade Street, 1819, Greek Doric.

Halkyn Castle, *Clwyd* (56.) By J. Buckler, 1824–7, for 2nd Earl Grosvenor. Tudor Gothic. (Enlarged 1886.)

Hamilton, *Strathclyde Region. Bridge over Avon*, by T. Telford, 1825.

Hammerwood Lodge, *East Sussex.* (50.) By Latrobe, 1790–2, for J. Sperling. Important and earnestly self-conscious monument of early Greek Revival. Odd N entrance front of 3 storeys and 3 bays with unmoulded tripartite windows; adjacent to the W is an asymmetrical wing with Greek Doric porte-cochère inscribed *Pax intrantibus. Exeuntibus Pax.* Showpiece is S front consisting of 5-bay centre with giant Doric pilasters linked by lower wings to 1-bay pavilions adorned with tetrastyle pedimented porticos of unfluted Paestum Doric columns, a primitivist gesture. SE portico bears Greek inscription and is dated 1792; both contain Classical reliefs in Coade stone.

Hampton Court, *Hereford and Worcester.* Medieval house repeatedly remodelled but most extensively and romantically in 1835–41 by C. Hanbury Tracy for J. Arkwright.

Hampton Lucy, *Warwickshire*. *St Peter*, by Rickman & Hutchinson, 1822–6, the best of their many Gothic churches, paid for by the Lucy family. Tall W tower, high arcades and plaster vault. (Apse 1856.)

Hampton-on-the-Hill, *Warwickshire*. *St Charles* (RC), T-shaped Gothic church of 1819 and 1830. *Grove Park*, by C. S. Smith, 1833–8, for 11th Lord Dormer, large, plain and Gothic.

Harbottle, *Northumberland*. *Castle House*, by Dobson, 1829, for T. F. Clennell, plain Classical villa incorporating C17 core.

Hardwicke Court, *Gloucestershire*. By R. Smirke, 1817–19, for T. J. Lloyd Baker. Almost featureless Late Georgian E entrance front with 3-storey 5-bay centre flanked by lower 1-bay wings. Similarly restrained interiors.

Harlaxton Manor, *Lincolnshire*. (30, 57.) Begun 1831–7, by Salvin, for G. de Ligne Gregory, completed by Burn from 1838. Spectacular Elizabethan pile with remarkable neo-baroque staircase.

Hartlebury, *Hereford and Worcester*. *St James*, broad Gothic nave added by Rickman, 1836–7.

Hassop, *Derbyshire*. *All Saints* (RC), by J. Ireland, 1816–18, Greek Revival chapel for Eyre family. *Hassop Hall*, remodelled 1827–33, for T. Eyre, Classical.

Hastings, *Sussex*. *Pelham Crescent* (42.) by J. Kay, 1824–8, for 1st Earl of Chichester. Exceptionally vivacious crescent of houses below cliffs with curved bow windows and Diocletian windows. Dramatically broken in centre by Ionic portico of Kay's church of *St Mary-in-the-Castle* (42), with a highly original plan consisting of D-shaped auditorium-type nave and rectangular chancel hewn out of the living rock. *St Leonards-on-Sea* was developed from 1828 by J.Burton with Ionic terraces along sea-front, broken in centre by *St Leonards* (later *Royal Victoria*) *Hotel* with giant Corinthian order. (Remodelled 1903.) Also by Burton the Greek Doric *Assembly Rooms* (now Masonic Hall), and *St Leonards Gardens*, with Greek Doric South Lodge and Picturesque villas, the whole layout inspired by Nash's Regent's Park.

Hatfield Place, *Hatfield Peverel, Essex*. Elegant 3-bay villa, 1792–4, for Col. J. Tyrell.

Hawarden Castle, *Clwyd*. (56.) Mid C18 house extended and remodelled by T. Cundy, 1809–10, for Sir S. Glynne, Bt. Based on designs by Nash; asymmetrical castellated composition with elegant Classical interiors, e.g. library and dining room.

Hawkstone Park, *Salop*. (60.) Early C18 house restored and extended for Sir R. Hill, Bt., 1832–4, by L. W. Wyatt who provided a range of eclectic interiors including Louis XIV-style drawing room and Empire Style dining room. Hawkstone is best known for its astonishing late C18 Picturesque park, containing a *hotel* built c. 1790 to house visitors to the park, and the *Citadel*, castellated house of 1824–5 by T. Harrison.

Haywood, *Staffordshire*. *St John Baptist* (RC), built 1828 at Tixall by J. Ireland, re-erected at Haywood, 1845. Elaborate neo-Perp.

Heath House, *Tean, Staffordshire*. By T. Johnson, 1836–40, for J. B. Philips, owner of Tean Hall Mills. Impressive Tudor mansion of stone with tower, porte-cochère, mullioned bay windows and elaborate staircase.

Heaton Hall, *Prestwich, Greater Manchester*. Rebuilt by J. Wyatt for 1st Earl of Wilton, c. 1772, altered by S. Wyatt, 1790 (e.g. Music Room), and by L. W. Wyatt, 1806–24, who designed N front, library, Picturesque chimneystacks, orangery and lodges.

Helmsdale Bridge, *Highland Region*. By T. Telford, 1811–12.

Helston, *Cornwall*. (101.) *Market Hall*, Coinagehall Street, by W. Harris, 1837–8, with 4 engaged Greek Doric columns on 1st floor: distinguished design influenced by C. R. Cockerell. Other austerely Neo-Classical buildings in granite, e.g. in *Coinagehall Street* and *Cross Street*.

Hensol, *near Castle Douglas, Dumfries and Galloway Region*. By R. Lugar, c. 1825, for J. Cunningham. Mullioned windows and ogee-capped corner towers.

Hereford, *Hereford and Worcester*. *St Francis Xavier* (RC) (73), Broad Street, by C. Day, 1837–8, Greek Revival, i.e. before the impact of Pugin. Narrow but arresting façade with Doric portico in antis; good largely unaltered interior. *Shire Hall* (81), St Peter Street, by R. Smirke, 1814–16, classic example of Greek Revival at its most commanding and austere: hexastyle Theseion Doric

portico set between massive square bays
of largely unadorned masonry. *City Arms
Hotel*, Broad Street, built c. 1790 as Duke
of Norfolk's townhouse. *Nelson Column*,
Castle Green, by T. Hardwick and T.
Wood, 1806–9, Tuscan with swags and
urn.
Hexham, *Northumberland*. *St Mary the
Virgin* (RC), 1828–30, pretty Gothick
plasterwork in shallow canted chancel.
Highcliffe Castle, *Hampshire*.
Remodelled by W. Donthorn, 1830–4,
for Lord Stuart de Rothesay. Romantic
Gothic extravaganza incorporating
features from the medieval Hôtel des
Andelys, Normandy. (Now a ruin.)
Highgrove, *Doughton, Gloucestershire*. 5-
by 3-bay 3-storeyed block of 1796–8 for
J. P. Paul. Pilasters on upper storeys.
Restored 1894 after extensive fire. Home
of the Prince and Princess of Wales.
Hildersham Hall, *Cambridgeshire*. By E.
Lapidge, 1814, for T. Fassett. Attractive
park and lake of c. 1811. Stuccoed 5-bay
entrance front with Ionic portico in antis,
elegant stair hall with glazed lantern.
Hillfield Lodge, *Aldenham,
Hertfordshire*. By Wyatville, c. 1800–5,
for the Hon. G. Villiers. Cemented
castellated villa with separate gate-house
furnished with portcullis.
Himley Hall, *Staffordshire*. Early C18
house remodelled in ineloquent Classical
style with Ionic portico by W. Atkinson,
1824–7, for 4th Viscount Dudley.
Hollingbourne House, *near Maidstone,
Kent*. 1799–1800, for B. D. Duppa, by C.
Beazley, a pupil of Sir R. Taylor. Long
low villa with broad-spreading eaves and
shuttered windows, curious 10-bay 2-
storeyed garden front with pedimented
centre only 2 windows wide flanked by
very narrow bays with blank round-
headed niches.
Holmbush, *near Cuckfield, West Sussex*.
By F. Edwards, 1829, for T. Broadwood.
Asymmetrical castellated Gothic, with
large angle tower in fine setting.
Holmewood (formerly Mitchells),
Langton Green, Kent. By D. Burton, 1827.
Late Classical with 7-bay front of
sandstone.
Holwood House, *Kent*. By D. Burton,
1823–6, for J. Ward. Ambitious 15-bay
garden front with central bow ringed
with giant Ionic columns, Greek Doric
loggias in the wings. (Interiors altered.)
Repton park, c. 1791.
Holyhead, *Anglesey, Gwynedd*. *Admiralty*

Pier, by J. Rennie, 1821. *Custom House*
and *Harbour Office*, 1830, Classical.
Doric Memorial Arch, by T. Harrison,
1824, to commemorate George IV's visit
in 1821.
Holywell, *Clwyd*. *Catholic church*, by J. J.
Scoles, 1833, Italianate. (Extended
1895.)
The Homend, *Stretton Grandison,
Hereford and Worcester*. C17 house with
5-bay entrance front by R. Smirke,
1814–21, for E. Poole. Restrained
Classical design. Fine park.
Hopes, *near Gifford, Lothian Region*.
(50.) By J. Burn, c. 1825, for Capt. Hay.
Square Greek Revival house, elegant
entrance hall and staircase.
Horbury, *West Yorkshire*. (66.) *SS Peter
and Leonard*, by J. Carr, 1791–3, built at
his own expense in his birthplace.
Attractive and unusual church with Ionic
portico, tower and spire, and Adamesque
interior, segmentally vaulted.
Horsley Place (now **Towers**), *Surrey*. By
Barry, 1834, for W. Currie. Dull Tudor
style in flint. (Dramatic additions in
1840s and 50s include bizarre entrance
tunnel, cloisters and chapel.)
Houghton Lodge, *Hampshire*.
Ambitious cottage orné, c. 1800, in the
style of Nash's Royal Lodge, Windsor.
Gothick windows, twisted chimneys,
steep (originally thatched) roofs, and
bow on E front containing circular
drawing room with sky-painted ceiling.
Huddersfield, *West Yorkshire*. *Holy
Trinity*, Trinity Street, by T. Taylor,
1816–19, Gothic with tower and
galleried interior. *Methodist church*,
Queen Street, 1819, Classical. *Infirmary*
(87), New North Road, by J. Oates,
1831, with Greek Doric portico. (Later
additions.)
Hull, *Humberside*. *Neptune Inn* (later
Custom House Buildings), Whitefriar
Gate, by G. Pycock, 1794–6, elegant with
good interiors. *Whitefriar Gate*, S side, by
C. Mountain, 1829–31. *Trinity
Almshouse*, Posterngate, by C. Mountain,
1828, 13-bay façade. (Portico destroyed
1941.) *Assembly Rooms* (now New
Theatre), Kingston Square, by R. H.
Sharp, 1830–4, Grecian.
Huntly, *Grampian Region*. *St Margaret*
(RC), Chapel Street, 1834, octagonal
church with portico and tower, designed
by Bishop Kyle.
Hutton, *Borders Region*. (109.)
Suspension Bridge, by S. Brown, 1820.

Hyde Hall, *Hertfordshire*. Tudor courtyard house completely remodelled by Wyatville, 1803–7, for 2nd Earl of Roden. Façades have curious Soanean pilaster-strips with palm-leaf capitals; inside, impressive domed staircase hall, Greek Doric with Soanean touches. Greek Doric entrance lodges with wide Tuscan eaves.

Hylands, *near Chelmsford, Essex*. By W. Atkinson, 1819–25, for P. C. Labouchère. Ionic portico and good interiors.

Ickworth, *Suffolk*. (50, 51.) Remarkable domed rotunda built for Earl Bishop of Derry, 1796, by F. Sandys from designs by M. Asprucci, completed c. 1825–30 by J. Field. Adorned with terracotta friezes based on Flaxman's illustrations to Homer, the stuccoed rotunda is linked by quadrant wings to 2 9-bay pavilions intended to house the bishop's collections. Finest interior is the library with segmental outer wall, 2 screens of Ionic columns and chimney-piece by Canova. (National Trust.)

Ilfracombe, *Devon*. Some *terraces* of 1830s. Also *Tunnel Baths*, 1836, with Greek Doric entrance.

Ince Blundell, *Merseyside*. *Pantheon*, built 1802 for H. Blundell, to house his collection of antique sculpture. With its tall coffered dome, this remarkable Neo-Classical monument (now lacking its contents) is adjacent to the Early Georgian Ince Blundell Hall.

Ingress Abbey, *Greenhithe, Kent*. By C. Moreing, c. 1832–4, for J. Harmer. Symmetrical Tudor mansion of Portland stone supposedly brought from Old London Bridge.

Invergowrie House, *Tayside Region*. Remodelled by W. Burn, 1837, for A. Clayhills. Scots-Jacobean style.

Johnstone Church, *Strathclyde Region*. 1792, Gothic with octagonal tower.

Keir, *Central Region*. C18 house enlarged by D. Hamilton, 1829–34, for A. Stirling. Sumptuous Classical drawing room and barrel-vaulted gallery. (Edwardian remodelling.) Unusual Greek Doric entrance lodges by Hamilton, 1820.

Keith, *Grampian Region*. (74.) St Thomas (RC), by the Rev. W. Lovi, 1834, Greek-cross plan with 2-storeyed Roman baroque façade.

Kelso Bridge, *Borders Region*. (109, 110.) By J. Rennie, 1800–3.

Kendal, *Cumbria*. 3 churches by G. Webster: *Holy Trinity* (RC), 1835–7, with canted Gothick chancel; *St Thomas*, Stricklandgate, Gothic; *St George*, Castle Street, 1839–41, Early English W front. (Later alterations.) *Stramongate Bridge*, by T. Harrison, 1793–4.

Kentchurch Court, *Hereford and Worcester*. Partly medieval house remodelled by Nash, c. 1795, for J. Scudamore. Picturesque castellated style.

Keswick Hall, *Norfolk*. By Wilkins, 1817–19 and 1837, for H. Gurney. Simple Classical house, enlarged 1951 for present use of Training College.

Kilconquhar Castle, *Fife Region*. Rebuilt by W. Burn, 1831–9, for Sir H. Bethune, Bt. Baronial with corbelled angle turrets.

Kilkerran House, *Dailly, Strathclyde Region*. Classical wings added by J. G. Graham, c. 1815, for Sir J. Fergusson, Bt.

Kilmarnock, *Strathclyde Region*. *King Street UP Church*, by R. Johnston, 1831, Gothic with spire. *St Kilmarnock Church*, by J. Ingram, 1836, Gothic with tower.

Kincaid Castle, *Central Region*. Remodelled by D. Hamilton, c. 1812. Symmetrical entrance front in old-fashioned minimal Gothic with round corner towers, but pretty semi-circular Greek Doric porch.

Kincardine-in-Menteith Church, *Central Region*. By R. Crichton, 1814, Gothic with W tower.

Kinfauns Castle, *Tayside Region*. (155.) By R. Smirke, 1820–2, for 15th Lord Gray. Vast symmetrical pink stone castle with details inspired by Fonthill.

King's Stanley, *Gloucestershire*. (112.) *Stanley Mill*, 1812–13.

Kingston Lacy, *Dorset*. Important house by Pratt of 1660s, remodelled inside and out by C. Barry, 1835–9, for W. J. Bankes, MP. Impressive Barry staircase. (National Trust.)

Kingston Lisle, *Oxfordshire*. Mid C18 house remodelled in early C19 with extravagant coffered tunnel-vaulted entrance hall and, at right angles to this, vaulted corridor with large caryatids on top of fluted Doric columns framing the approach to a dramatic flying staircase: a provincial reaction to Soane and Cockerell.

Kingswood, *near Bristol, Avon*. *Holy Trinity*, 1819–21, by J. Foster, Gothic, ashlar-faced, with castellated W tower.

Kington, *Hereford and Worcester*. (84.)

Town Hall, by B. Wishlade, 1820, Grecian.

Kingweston House, *Somerset*. Simple Late Georgian house with Greek Doric portico added by Wilkins for W. Dickinson before 1828.

Kinmount, *Dumfries and Galloway Region*. (50.) By R. Smirke, 1812, for 5th Marquess of Queensbury. Vast neo-Greek pile.

Kirkcaldy, *Fife Region. Bank of Scotland*, High Street, by W. Burn, 1833.

Kirkmichael House, *Dumfries and Galloway Region*. By W. Burn, 1832–3, for J. S. Lyon. Scots-Jacobean.

Kitley House, *Devon*. Remodelled in Elizabethan style by G. S. Repton, c. 1820–5, for E. P. Bastard. Fine Regency library, beautiful setting by lake.

Knebworth House, *Hertfordshire*. Confused romantic Gothic extravaganza in rendered cement by J. B. Rebecca, 1813, for Mrs Bulwer Lytton. Remodelled by H. E. Kendall, 1844, for the novelist Bulwer Lytton, and by J. Lee in 1878–83.

Knepp Castle, *West Grinstead, West Sussex*. By Nash, c. 1809, for Sir C. Burrell, Bt. Castellated with round tower. (Burnt 1904.)

Knutsford, *Cheshire*. (*83.*) *Sessions House and House of Correction*, Toft Road, by G. Moneypenny, 1817–19, eloquently grim

Neo-Classical composition in style of George Dance with Ionic centrepiece flanked by bare side pavilions featuring heavily rusticated doorways.

Laleham Park, *Surrey*. By J. B. Papworth, 1803–6, for 2nd Earl of Lucan. Greek Doric porch and further additions by Papworth, 1827–9 and 1839.

Lambton Castle, *Durham*. Picturesque and asymmetrical castellated Gothic, by J. Bonomi, c. 1796–7, and more especially by I. Bonomi, c. 1820–8, for Earl of Durham.

Lampeter, *Dyfed*. (*96.*) *St David's University College*, by C. R. Cockerell, 1822–7, Tudor Gothic quadrangle in rendered brick with cast-iron Tudor windows, preserving the staircase-plan of Oxford and Cambridge colleges. Hall and chapel have been altered but attractive library survives.

Lamphey Court, *near Pembroke, Dyfed*. Greek Revival mansion, c. 1820, with 7-bay 2-storeyed stone front and tetrastyle Ionic portico: an unusual type for Wales.

Lancaster. (*83, 109.*) *Castle*, reconstructed by T. Harrison, 1788–1822, and by J. M. Gandy, 1802–23, including the Shire Hall, one of the most arresting interiors of the early Gothic Revival: ribbed Gothic vault shoots up from what is in plan the 7-

Kinfauns Castle, Tayside Region, 1820–2; Sir R. Smirke. Even when handling the romantically asymmetrical castellated style Smirke shows his love of geometry and intersecting cubes.

sided half of a polygon. Gothick
furniture and rich Gothic canopies along
the straight E wall. *Lune Aqueduct*, Caton
Road, by J. Rennie and A. Stevens,
1794–7.

Langton Long Blandford, *Dorset*. C. R.
Cockerell's *Langton House* of 1827–33
now demolished except for superb
octagonal stableyard (*156*) approached
through massive archway.

Lansdown, *near Bath, Avon*. *Lansdown
Tower*, by H. E. Goodridge, 1824, for
William Beckford. Obsessed by towers,
Beckford here built one 154ft high,
crowned by cast-iron lantern inspired by
the Choragic Monument of Lysicrates in
Athens. At its foot Beckford's
Picturesque Italianate house.

Lasborough Park, *near Tetbury,
Gloucestershire*. By J. Wyatt, 1794, for E.
Estcourt. Symmetrical castellated house
with towers at the corners and
Adamesque Classical interiors.

Lauriston Castle, *Edinburgh*. Old
tower-house enlarged in Jacobean style
by W. Burn, 1827, for T. Allan.

Lavington House, *East Lavington, West
Sussex*. By J. Lewis, 1790–4, for J.
Sargent. Restrained Classical 5-bay block
now embedded in Edwardian additions.

Lawers House, *Tayside Region*. By W.
Adam, 1720s and 30s, remodelled by R.
Crichton, c. 1810, for D. R. W. Ewart.
Long Tuscan colonnades on S front
flanked by pavilions with broad curved
ends, glazed like greenhouses. Adjacent
on the W are Crichton's handsome

stables, Grecian but plain.

Laxton Hall, *Northamptonshire*. Glum
Classical house by J. A. Repton,
1805–11, for G. F. Evans, with interiors
by G. Dance, c. 1812, especially the
domed entrance hall with its screen of 4
Ionic columns carried on semi-circular
arch cut into horizontally rusticated wall:
unusual Neo-Classical device, perhaps
inspired by Dubut's *Architecture Civile*
(1803).

Leadenham House, *Lincolnshire*. By C.
Staveley, 1790–6, for W. Reeve. Massive
7-bay 3-storey entrance front, the centre
bay very wide and containing tripartite
windows, otherwise unadorned.
Additions by Vulliamy, 1829. Plain
interiors.

Leamington Spa, *Warwickshire*. (43,
107.) Pleasant not specially distinguished
terraces, hotels and *villas* of c. 1820–40.
*County Library, Reading Rooms and Royal
Assembly Rooms*, Bath Street, by S.
Beazley, 1820–1.

Lecropt Church, *Central Region*. By W.
Stirling, 1824–6. Large Gothic building.

Leeds, *West Yorkshire*. (112.) St Mary,
Quarry Hill, by T. Taylor, 1823–6,
Commissioners' church, built to a
Gothic hall-church plan. *Brunswick
Methodist Church*, Brunswick Street, by J.
Simpson, 1824–5, with rich neo-Greek
façade. *St George*, Great George Street, by
J. Clark, 1836–8, Gothic with cast-iron
galleries. (Apse 1900.) *Leeds Library*
(92), Commercial Street, by T. Johnson,
1808, Greek Revival. *Marshall's Mills*

Langton Long,
Blandford, Dorset.
Stables, c.1824; C.
R. Cockerell. A
bold design with
broadly-projecting
eaves

(114), Marshall Street, by J. Bonomi junior 1842–51, one of the most impressive monuments of the Egyptian Revival. *Armley Mills*, Armley, for B. Gott, c. 1800. *Armley House*, Gotts Park, c. 1781, remodelled by Smirke, with Ionic portico and (now demolished) flanking wings, c. 1818, for B. Gott, as the first Greek Revival mansion in West Yorkshire. Admired by Schinkel on his visit to Armley Mills in 1826 for turning the hill on which it stands into an Acropolis. *Burley Mills*, Kirkstall Road, c. 1800, for B. Gott. *Roundhay Park*, by J. Clark, 1826, for T. Nicholson, with giant Ionic portico and handsome top-lit staircase; park with lakes and sham ruins. *Wellington Bridge*, by J. Rennie, 1817–19.

Leicester. *County Rooms*, Hotel Street, by J. Johnson, 1792–1800, refined Classical composition with tripartite windows and good interiors. *New Hall* (now City Library), Wellington Street, by W. Flint, 1831, stuccoed Grecian. *United Baptist Chapel*, Charles Street, 1830, Grecian. Some Regency terraces survive, e.g. *The Crescent, King Street* and *Hastings Street. Gaol*, Welford Road, castellated pile by W. Parsons, 1825–8 and 1844–6.

Leigh Court, *Abbots Leigh, Avon*. By T. Hopper, 1814, for P. J. Miles, a banker. Greek Revival mansion with characteristically reticent Neo-Classical skyline and outstandingly impressive interiors. Dull entrance front of 9 bays with tetrastyle portico of giant unfluted Ionic columns; on 7-bay side façade the 5-bay centre is recessed behind screen of 4 Ionic columns. Entrance hall with shallow dome and ring of Ionic columns leads to palatial stair hall, 50ft long, 30ft wide and 40ft high. Double-flight staircase with sumptuous bronze balustrade, Ionic colonnades, and glazed coffering in the ceiling. Rich neo-Grecian plasterwork throughout, e.g. Morning Room ceiling. Entrance lodge in the form of Ionic triumphal arch.

Leighton Hall, *Yealand Conyers, Lancashire*. Palladian house of c. 1765 prettily Gothicised c. 1810 for R. Gillow, the celebrated Lancaster cabinet maker. Good interiors, e.g. Gothic entrance hall leading to elegant curved staircase (Extended 1870.)

Leith, *Edinburgh. North Leith Church*, by W. Burn, 1814–16, almost his first work, a Grecian version of St Martin-in-the-Fields. *Exchange Buildings*, Constitution Street, by T. Brown, 1809–10. *Custom House*, by R. Reid, 1811–12. *Trinity House*, by T. Brown, 1816–17. *Town Hall*, by R. & R. Dickson, 1827–8, heavy Palladian composition with engaged Ionic order.

Lennox Castle, *Lennoxtown, Central Region*. (12.) By D. Hamilton, 1837–41, for J. L. Kincaid Lennox. Large neo-Norman pile but lighter and more Regency in feel than Hopper's Penrhyn Castle (q.v.). of c. 1825–44.

Letham Grange, *near Arbroath, Tayside Region*. By A. Simpson, 1825–30, for J. Hay.

Letheringsett Hall, *Holt, Norfolk*. Remodelled by its brewer owner, W. Hardy, in 1808–9, with massive unpedimented Greek Doric portico, and in 1832–3 with elegant stair hall containing unusually curved staircase. On each occasion Hardy was his own architect. Drawing room with high coffered cove and bold anthemion frieze.

Lewes, *East Sussex. County Hall*, High Street, by J. Johnson, 1808–12. (Ground floor originally open.) *Nos. 1–4 Castle Place*, by A. Wilds, c. 1810, with characteristic ammonite capitals. *Priory Crescent*, c. 1834–5.

Leys Castle, *Highland Region*. By S. Beazley, 1833, for Col. J. Baillie, MP. Neo-Norman.

Lichfield, *Staffordshire*. (105.) *George Hotel*, Bird Street, late C18 9-bay Classical front with segmentally vaulted ballroom inside. *Newton's College*, The Close, by J. Potter, 1800–2, 11-bay Classical front.

Lilburn Tower, *Northumberland*. By Dobson, 1829–37, for H. J. W. Collingwood. Picturesque neo-Jacobean composition with shaped gables. (Interior mutilated.)

Lilleshall Hall, *Salop*. By Wyatville, 1826–33, for 2nd Duke of Sutherland. With Wyatville's favourite canted plan in a neo-Tudor style which is beginning to look Early Victorian.

Limpley Stoke, *Wiltshire*. (109.) *Dundas Aqueduct*, by J. Rennie, c. 1795–7.

Lincoln. *Assize Courts* (81), Castle, by R. Smirke, 1823–30, Gothic. *Lawn Asylum*, Union Road, by R. Ingleman, 1819–20, imposing Grecian design.

Linden House, *near Long Horsley, Northumberland*. By C. Monck, 1812–13, for his friend C.W. Bigge. Porch of unfluted Greek Doric columns.

Linton Park, *Kent*. 7-bay house of 1730s remodelled c. 1825 by T. Cubitt for 5th Earl Cornwallis. Cubitt stuccoed the house, added 2 4-bay wings, top storey, giant Corinthian portico and arcaded basement: a dramatic aggrandisement of the kind Nash excelled in. Fine top-lit staircase.

Little Dean, *Gloucestershire*. *Gaol* (now police station and County Record Office), by W. Blackburn, 1787–91.

Little Ouseburn, *North Yorkshire*. *Thompson Mausoleum*, in churchyard, c. 1790, grave Neo-Classical rotunda with attached unfluted Greek Doric columns.

Littleborough, *Greater Manchester*. *Holy Trinity*, by T. Taylor, 1818–20, Gothic with W tower and spire. (Chancel 1889.)

Liverpool, *Merseyside*. *St Andrew*, Rodney Street, by J. Foster, 1823–4, with twin-towered Grecian front influenced by Cockerell's Hanover Chapel. *St Bride*, Percy Street, by S. Rowland, 1830–1, giant portico of 6 unfluted Ionic columns. *St Luke*, St Luke's Place, by J. Foster, 1802, 1811 and 1826–31, neo-Perp with elaborate W tower. (Gutted.) *St George's Hall* (24, 25, 26, 84), designed 1840–1 by H. L. Elmes and completed 1856 as the finest Neo-Classical public building in Britain. Giant Corinthian portico at S end, massive apse at N end. Great Hall inspired by Baths of Caracalla, Rome. Richly ornamented interior of Concert Hall, by C. R. Cockerell, 1851–3, *Town Hall*, Castle Street, begun 1749 by J. Wood, extended 1789–92 by J. Wyatt and J. Foster, gutted 1795 and reconstructed by c. 1820. Tall dome, rich Empire Style interiors. *Lyceum Club* (92, 93), Bold Street, by T. Harrison, 1800–3, bold ashlar-faced exteriors with tripartite windows in segmental arches and recessed Ionic centrepiece. Domed (former) library inside. *Wellington Rooms* (84), Mount Pleasant, by E. Aikin, 1815–16, impressive largely blank Neo-Classical façade enlivened with carved wreaths, swags in panels, Corinthian pilasters and, in centre, semi-circular bow ringed with Corinthian columns and crowned by prominent row of continuous antefixae. *Medical Institution*, Hope Street, by C. Rampling, 1836–7, with hexastyle Ionic portico and good

interiors. *Royal Bank*, Dale Street, by S. Rowland, 1837–8. Numerous Regency terraces survive, e.g. *Abercromby Square*, *Gambier Terrace, Huskisson Street, Percy Street, Rodney Street* and *Montpelier Terrace. Albert Dock* (32, 111), by J. Hartley and P. Hardwick, 1841–5, justly famous functional buildings in style reminiscent of Ledoux. *St James's Cemetery*, by J. Foster, 1827–9, with good Grecian monuments of 1820s and 30s. *Allerton*: Some Grecian villas for merchants survive, e.g. *Allerton Hall, Springwood, Calderstones* and *Allerton* (or *Grove House*), by T. Harrison, c. 1815, for J. Fletcher (gutted). *Everton St George* (73), Heyworth Street, by T. Rickman and Cragg, 1813–14, big neo-Perp church with tower and amazing iron interior, iron tracery, galleries, ceiling, etc. *Liverpool Collegiate High School* (96), Shaw Street, by H. L. Elmes, 1840–3, neo-Perp. *Toxteth: St Patrick* (RC), Park Place, by J. Slater, 1821–3, Latin-cross plan with Greek Doric colonnades.

Liversedge, *West Yorkshire. Christ Church*, by T. Taylor, 1812–16, large, neo-Perp, with W tower.

Llanaeron, *Dyfed*. By Nash, c. 1794, for Major Lewis. Stuccoed villa in park.

Llanarthney, *Dyfed. Paxton's Tower*, large triangular castellated folly, perhaps by S. P. Cockerell, c. 1805, for Sir W. Paxton in memory of Lord Nelson. (National Trust.)

Llanerchydol, *Welshpool, Powys*. Remodelled in Picturesque Regency Gothic (perhaps by the Reptons), 1820, for D. Pugh. Neo-Perp interiors, e.g. impressive stair hall and drawing room.

Llangattock Park House, *Llangattock, Powys*. By T. H. Wyatt, c. 1838, for Duke of Beaufort. Stone neo-Tudor villa.

Llantarnam Abbey, *Gwent*. Remodelled in Elizabethan style by T. H. Wyatt, 1834, for R. S. Blewitt.

Lochwinnoch Church, *Strathclyde Region*. 1792, simple Gothic octagon.

LONDON

City of London

Bank of England (99), Threadneedle Street; all that survives of Soane's work are sections of rusticated outer screen walls (1795 and 1823–6) and mutilated Tivoli Corner (1805) with its Corinthian order inspired by the Temple of Vesta at Tivoli. *City Club*, Old Broad Street, by P.

Hardwick, 1833–4, stuccoed 7-bay Classical front; plain interiors though coffee room is enlivened with 3 large round-arched tripartite windows. *Custom House*, Lower Thames Street, by D. Laing, 1812–17; rebuilt to modified design by R. Smirke, 1825–7, after collapse of central portion. Austerely Classical with 13-bay Long Room on 1st floor. *Fishmongers' Hall* (104), London Bridge Approach, by H. Roberts, 1821–5. Roberts was a pupil of Smirke whose Grecian manner is echoed in this exceptionally refined building. Excellent Empire Style interiors (restored 1929 and 1951). *Goldsmiths' Hall* (104), Foster Lane, by P. Hardwick, 1829–35, remarkable neo-baroque composition in Portland stone with engaged Corinthian order; rich ceremonial interiors, especially staircase, hall and courtroom. *Stationers' Hall*, Stationers' Hall Court, Ludgate Hill, E front by R. Mylne, 1800–1, exceptionally elegant composition with tall round-headed windows and subtle doorway with segmental lunettes over. *Trinity House*, Tower Hill, by S. Wyatt, 1792–4, exquisite 5-bay façade with tripartite windows and characteristically reticent silhouette. Bombed in the war, but the façade, elegant semi-circular staircase and courtroom have been rebuilt.

City of Westminster
1. **Belgravia**. Vast development of stuccoed terraces à la Nash undertaken for Earl of Grosvenor by T. Cubitt, c. 1825 onwards. *Belgrave Square*, by G. Basevi, 1825–40, with free-standing corner mansions by other architects, e.g. No. 12, by Smirke, c. 1833, and Sefton House, by P. Hardwick, 1842. Nearby are *Halkin Place* and *Motcomb Street* with Greek Doric *Pantechnicon*. *Lowndes Square*, 1836–49. *Upper Belgrave Street*, *Belgrave Place*, *Eaton Place* and *Chester Square*. Cubitt's *Eaton Square*, 1825–53, has as an important accent H. Hakewill's *St Peter's Church*, 1824–7, with its hexastyle Ionic portico. *Ebury Street*, long Late Georgian terraces with *Pimlico Literary Institution*, by J. P. Gandy, 1830: striking Greek Doric portico in antis. *Victoria Square*, Pimlico, by Sir M. Wyatt, 1837.
2. **Buckingham Palace Area**. *Buckingham Palace* (77, 78, 79, 80), remodelling of C18 house by Nash for George IV, 1825–30. Entrance front is now of 1913 but W garden front is largely Nash: long episodic composition of 21 bays broken by 4 1-bay features of pairs of coupled Corinthian columns and, in centre, a far-projecting semi-circular 5-bay bow ringed with Corinthian columns and (originally) domed. Inside this bow on 1st-floor is the best of Nash's surviving interiors, the Music Room, with dark blue scagliola columns. Adjacent is his Blue Drawing Room. Other interiors are richer and heavier, being completed by Blore in 1830s. *Wellington Barracks*, Birdcage Walk, by F. Smith and P. Hardwick, 1833 onwards, long stuccoed ranges with Greek Doric porches. (Rebuilt behind replica façades.)
3. **Hyde Park Corner Area**. *Hyde Park Screen* and *Arch*, elegant Ionic composition by D. Burton, 1824–5. *Constitution Arch*, 1827–8, by D. Burton (resited 1883), with giant Corinthian coupled columns. *Apsley House*, Adam mansion of 1770s richly remodelled by B. D. Wyatt, 1828–9, for 1st Duke of Wellington; Bath stone Corinthian portico with Francophile interiors, e.g. *Waterloo Gallery*. *St George's Hospital* (87), by Wilkins, 1828–9, stuccoed neo-Grecian with details borrowed from the Thrasyllus Monument in Athens.
4. **Mayfair Area**. *St Mark*, North Audley Street, by J. P. Gandy, 1825–8, with memorable façade of giant Erectheion Ionic columns in antis crowned by imaginative neo-Grecian lantern. (Later interior.) *Dudley House*, 100 Park Lane, smart stuccoed mansion by W. Atkinson, 1824, for 4th Viscount Dudley and Ward. *39 Lower Brook Street*, additions and alterations by Wyatville for himself, 1821–3. *Marble Arch* (77), Cumberland Gate, designed by Nash, 1828, as entrance to Buckingham Palace but moved to present site 1851; modelled on Arch of Constantine, Rome. *Royal Institution*, Albemarle Street, C18 houses remodelled c. 1800 and provided with imposing columnar façade by Vulliamy, 1838.
5. **Paddington Area**. *St Mary* (66), Paddington Green, by J. Plaw, 1788–91, small but elegant Classical church with unusual octagonal gallery below dome. *Nos 3 & 5 Porchester Terrace*, by the great gardener J. C. Loudon, 1823–4, for himself; 'double detached villa' with

circular domed conservatory and verandah. *Connaught Square*, c. 1828–30. *Kensal Green Cemetery* with impressive Grecian chapels by J. D. Paul, c. 1835, and many elaborately architectural mausolea and monuments.

6. **Pall Mall Area**. *Athenaeum Club* (91, *92*), Waterloo Place, by D. Burton, 1827–30, stuccoed façades with modest Doric portico but full-scale cast of the Parthenon frieze; magnificent staircase and 1st-floor drawing room. *Carlton House Terrace* (*35*), by Nash, 1827–33, imposing stuccoed palaces raised above the Mall on colonnades of (cast-iron) Greek Doric columns. *Duke of York's Column*, Carlton Gardens, by B. D. Wyatt, 1831–4, Tuscan. *Oxford and Cambridge Club*, Pall Mall, by R. & S. Smirke, 1835–8, elegantly rusticated Classical façade in stucco; plain Greek Revival interiors (staircase altered). *Reform Club* (*26*, *27*, *91*), Pall Mall, by, Barry, 1837–41, monumental Portland stone façade inspired by the Palazzo Farnese; interior planned round great top-lit galleried saloon from which leads off the tunnel-vaulted staircase. Perhaps Barry's finest building. *Royal Opera Arcade* (*102*, *103*), Pall Mall, by Nash, 1816–18. *Travellers' Club*, Pall Mall (*28*, *91*) by Barry, 1829–32, original plan round open cortile; charming 1st-floor library with 2 screens of Corinthian columns; prettily ornamented Italianate garden front. *United Service Club* (*91*), Pall Mall, by Nash, 1826–8, enormous interiors planned, like the Athenaeum, round giant staircase.

7. **Piccadilly Area**. *The Albany*, addition of gentlemen's chambers known as the Rope Walk running N to Savile Row, by H. Holland, 1803–4. *Burlington Arcade* (*102*), Piccadilly, by S. Ware, 1815–18. (Partially rebuilt.)

8. **St James's Area**. *Carlton (formerly Arthur's) Club* (*91*), St James's Street, by T. Hopper, 1826–7, stone-faced front of old-fashioned but satisfying Palladian design with engaged Corinthian order on 1st floor, impressive staircase. *Clarence House* (*77*), St James's Palace, rebuilt by Nash, 1825–8, for Duke of Clarence. (Altered 1870s and later.) *Crockford's Club*, St James's Street, by B. D. Wyatt, 1827, with Louis XIV Revival interiors. (Much altered inside and out.) *Lancaster House* (*38*), Stable Yard, by R. Smirke, B. D. Wyatt and Barry, 1820–38, begun for Duke of York and completed for Duke of Sutherland. One of the most sumptuous Late Neo-Classical houses in the country. Bath stone with giant Corinthian porticos; interior organised round immense marble-lined staircase crowned by high lantern adorned with caryatids. Interiors such as the tripartite Gallery have neo-Rococo touches. *32 St James's Square*, by S. P. & C. R. Cockerell, 1819–21, for their cousin the Bishop of London. White brick with 3 prominent Venetian windows. (Interiors altered.)

9. **St Martin's Area**. *Canada House* (formerly Royal College of Physicians and Union Club) (*91*, *93*), Trafalgar Square, by R. Smirke, 1822–7, Greek Revival (remodelled 1925). *Fribourg and Treyer* (*104*), Haymarket, late C18 shop-front. *Haymarket Theatre* (*104*), by Nash, 1820–1, with pedimented hexastyle Corinthian portico. (Interiors modern.) *National Gallery* (*77*), Trafalgar Square, by Wilkins, 1833–8, episodic Picturesque façade with Corinthian portico and dome too small in scale for whole composition. *St Martin's Schools*, St Martin's Place, by Nash, c. 1830, stuccoed with giant Ionic pilasters and round-headed windows.

10. **St Marylebone Area**. *St Mary*, Marylebone Road, by T. Hardwick, 1813–17, with Corinthian portico aligned on to Nash's York Gate entrance to Regent's Park. *All Souls'*, Langham Place, by Nash, 1822–5, with amusing circular portico and spire. *Christ Church*, Cosway Street, by P. Hardwick, 1822–4, Commissioners' church with Ionic portico at E end below massive square tower with free-standing Corinthian columns surrounding the main storey. Further giant Corinthian columns within. *Holy Trinity* (*70*), Marylebone Road, by Soane, 1826–7, with unpedimented Ionic portico and complicated tower; similar to his St John, Walworth, but not especially characteristic of his personal style. *St Mary*, Wyndham Place, by R. Smirke, 1821–3, related to Bryanston Square; circular tower ringed at its base with bold Ionic colonnade. Galleries inside support Doric columns; segmental coffered ceiling. Church is virtually identical to Smirke's St Ann, Wandsworth, and St Philip, Salford. *Our Lady* (RC), Lisson Grove, by J. J. Scoles, 1833–6, Commissioners' Gothic style with mock transepts containing (originally) houses

for the donors and priest. *St John's Wood Chapel*, St John's Wood, by T. Hardwick, 1813–14, with Ionic porch and turret; attractive interior with galleries containing Tuscan and Ionic columns. Several villas and terraces of c. 1820–40, survive in *St John's Wood*. *Bryanston Square*, with Ionic features, *Montagu Square*, and adjacent streets by J. Parkinson, 1811. *Gloucester Place* and *Dorset Square*, both c. 1800. *Regent's Park* (7, 37, 40, 77) lined with Nash's elegant stuccoed terraces on E and W sides, 1821–30: *Gloucester Gate, St Katharine's Royal Hospital* (by A. Poynter, 1826–8, Gothic), *Cumberland Terrace, Chester Terrace* (19), *Cambridge Terrace, Park Square, Park Crescent, York Terrace, Cornwall Terrace* (D. Burton), *Clarence Terrace* (D. Burton), *Sussex Place, Hanover Terrace* and *Kent Terrace*. Some of the villas (much altered) in park survive, e.g. *The Holme* (by J. Burton, c. 1818), *Nuffield Lodge* (by D. Burton, 1822–4) and *St John's Lodge* (by J. Raffield, 1816–18). Important fragments also survive of Nash's *Park Villages East* and *West*, an influential layout of Italianate and neo-Tudor villas.
11. **Soho Area**. St Anne, Wardour Street, strange Soanean tower by S. P. Cockerell, 1802–3.
12. **Strand Area**. St Dunstan in the West, Fleet Street, by J. Shaw, 1829–33, octagonal Gothic church with S tower crowned by octagonal lantern with tall unglazed Perp openings: a feature inspired by the medieval All Saints Pavement, York. (Former) *Charing Cross Hospital*, Agar Street, by D. Burton, 1831–4, with rounded Corinthian corner. *Covent Garden Market* (100, 101), by C. Fowler, 1828–30, for 6th Duke of Bedford. (Altered by Cubitt, 1870s.) With its granite Tuscan columns and glass-roofed arcades this has recently been beautifully restored. *Hoare's Bank* (99), Fleet Street, by C. Parker, 1829–32, remarkable survival of Georgian family bank. *Law Society*, Chancery Lane, by Vulliamy, 1831, with Grecian portico à la Smirke. *Somerset House*, Strand, E wing forming King's College, by R. Smirke, 1830–5, tactful addition in style of Chambers. *Nos. 430–49 Strand*, triangular block of shops with fronts in Adelaide Street and William IV Street, by Nash, c. 1830. (Gutted internally and mutilated externally.) *Theatre Royal* (104, 104) Drury Lane, by B. D. Wyatt, 1811–12, with elegant rotunda and staircases; portico and colonnade by S. Beazley, 1831.
13. **Whitehall Area**. *Board of Trade* (77), Whitehall, by Soane, 1824–7, remodelled by Barry, 1844, though preserving Soane's Corinthian order. *Richmond Terrace*, Whitehall, by H. Harrison, 1822.

Borough of Barnet
Mill Hill School (94, 95, 95, 97), by Sir W. Tite, 1825–7, extensive institutional pile with giant Greek Ionic portico.

Borough of Bromley
Sundridge Park, by J. Nash, H. Repton and S. Wyatt, 1799, for Sir C. Scott, Bt. Extensive and flashy stuccoed mansion with extremely original plan, the essence of which is a domed Corinthian tempietto flanked by receding wings. In tempietto is a spectacular circular staircase with screens of Ionic and Corinthian columns. Park by Repton.

Borough of Camden
1. **Hampstead**. Enchanting complex of C18 and early C19 houses often linked by narrow lanes and stepped passages, e.g. *Holly Walk, Holly Place* (with simple Catholic church, 1817), *Hollyberry Lane, Benham's Place, Prospect Place*, and *Downshire Hill* with *Keats's house* and *St John's Church* (extended 1843).
2. **Holborn**. *British Museum* (10, 77, 89, 93), Great Russell Street, by R. Smirke, 1823–46, grandest of all Neo-Classical temples of the arts, with its Greek Ionic colonnade, grandly austere staircase and superb King's Library with brass gallery and crisp plasterwork ceiling. *Gray's Inn*, mainly C17 except for *Verulam Buildings* (1805–11) and *Raymond Buildings* (1825). (Former) *Royal College of Surgeons* (93), Lincoln's Inn Fields, by G. Dance, 1806–13 (22), with Greek Ionic portico; remodelled by Barry, 1835–7; interior gutted and remodelled after World War II. *Sir John Soane's Museum*, Lincoln's Inn Fields (20, 21), Soane's own eccentric and eminently Picturesque house-cum-museum designed for himself, 1792–1824, by the most original architect at that time in the country. The complexity and variety of its planning are not easily described but

especially characteristic interiors are the Library with semi-Gothic hanging arches, and Breakfast Room with shallow dome supported only at the corners and studded with small convex mirrors.

3. **St Pancras.** *All Saints*, Camden Street (162), by W. & H. W. Inwood, 1822–4, lively Greek Ionic semi-circular portico crowned with anthemion antefixae; cylindrical tower with Ionic columns; interior with curved apse, galleries on Ionic columns, and flat ceiling. *St Mary*, Eversholt Street, Somers Town, by W. & H. W. Inwood, 1822–4, mean stock-brick Gothic church with thin tower and broad W front. Condemned by Pugin in *Contrasts* (1836), and by Summerson who describes it as 'one of the most pitiful performances in Gothic revivalism ever perpetrated'. *St Pancras* (67, 68, 71), Woburn Place, by W. & H. W. Inwood,

1819–22, the most elaborately Grecian church in the country with the celebrated copies of the Erectheion caryatids at E end and, at W end, a hexastyle Erectheion Ionic portico surmounted by impressive 2-tiered tower modelled on the Tower of the Winds in Athens. *University College*, Gower Street, by Wilkins, 1827–9, with impressive decastyle Corinthian portico approached by elaborate external staircase. *Fitzroy Square*, S and E sides by R. Adam, 1794, impressive Ionic composition in Portland stone; N and W sides, 1827–35, in stucco. Duke of Bedford's Bloomsbury estate developed by J. Burton, c. 1800–14, e.g. *Russell Square* and nearby streets, *Montague Street* and *Bedford Place*. *Bloomsbury Square* and *Russell Square* originally planted by Repton, c. 1800. From 1824 onwards date T. Cubitt's

All Saints, St Pancras, London, 1822–4; W. & H. W. Inwood. The semi-circular portico has a beautifully composed Greek Ionic order

Tavistock Square (W side), Woburn Place, Endsleigh Street, and parts of Gordon Square and Euston Square. Torrington Square. Mecklenburgh Square (E side), by J. Kay, 1810–21. Further early C19 houses in Guilford Street, Doughty Street, Brunswick Square, Woburn Walk, Duke's Road, Argyle Square and Regent Square. Highgate Cemetery, begun 1839 by S. Geary. Soane family tomb, St Pancras Gardens, St Pancras Road, by Soane, 1816.

Borough of Ealing

Pitzhanger Manor (59), by G. Dance, 1768, remodelled by Soane for himself, 1800–2, with stock-brick entrance front inspired by Arch of Constantine, i.e. with 4 free-standing Ionic columns of Portland stone carrying Coade stone caryatids. Top-lit tunnel-vaulted entrance vestibule; front parlour with saucer dome incised with characteristic Soanean ornament; back parlour with equally characteristic star-fish vault. Primitivist entrance arch on corner of Ealing Green.

Borough of Enfield

Southgate Grove (now Grovelands), by Nash, 1797, for W. Gray. Pretty and rather elaborate Classical composition with coupled Ionic columns and pilasters, oval windows (borrowed from Chambers) in attic, and ground-floor windows with tympana ornamented with radial fluting round a shell: a device unique to Nash. Attractive interior with rooms open to each other through folding doors creating vistas out to the Repton park (now public).

Borough of Greenwich

St Michael, Blackheath, by G. Smith, 1828–9, stock-brick neo-Perp church with bizarre W tower and spire; part of the layout of Blackheath Park, c. 1825. The Paragon (34), Blackheath, by M. Searles, c. 1793, enchanting crescent of semi-detached houses linked by Tuscan colonnades. Colonnade House, South Row, early C19 7-bay house, perhaps by M. Searles. Macartney House, Chesterfield Walk, early C18 house altered by Soane, 1802, e.g. Greek Doric vestibule. Rotunda (Military Museum) (79), Woolwich Common, originally a ballroom by Nash erected in St James's Park, 1814, re-erected here 1819. Royal

Artillery Barracks (78–9, 79), Artillery Place, immensely long, restrained Neo-Classical composition, E half 1775–82, W half finished 1808. Royal Military Academy (79), Academy Road, by J. Wyatt, c. 1800–6, vast castellated pile of yellow stock-brick.

Borough of Hackney

St John (66, 67), Mare Street, 1792–7, by J. Spiller, friend and sometime colleague of Soane whose style is reflected in this curious Greek-cross-plan church with its shallow segmentally vaulted nave. Striking contrast between the brown stock-brick church and the dazzlingly white Portland stone tower added by Spiller, 1812–13, in a Soanean baroque style. Clissold House, Clissold Park, Stoke Newington, Greek Revival villa by J. Woods, c. 1820, in park with lake.

Borough of Hammersmith

St Peter, by Lapidge, 1827–8, modest stock-brick church with engaged Ionic portico. Adjacent to the W is St Peter's Square, c. 1830, groups of stuccoed houses linked by low walls; gardens designed by Loudon. Hurlingham House, Fulham, mid C18 house altered by G. Byfield, 1797–8, for J. Ellis. Stuccoed river front with giant Corinthain pilasters.

Borough of Harrow

Harrow School (96), Speech Room wing, by C. R. Cockerell, 1819–20, neo-Tudor to blend with existing wing.

Borough of Hounslow

Syon House (101, 101), conservatory, by C. Fowler, 1827–30, for 3rd Duke of Northumberland, graceful composition like Georgian orangery with domed centre and quadrant wings.

Borough of Islington

1. Finsbury. St Barnabus, King Square, by T. Hardwick, 1822–6, Commissioners' church with modest unpedimented Ionic portico and needle spire. Attractive complex of early C19 streets and squares, e.g. on the New River Co.'s estate, Claremont Square and Myddelton Square; and on the Lloyd Baker estate, Lloyd Square and Lloyd Baker Street. Also Northampton Square and Wilmington Square.
2. Islington. St Mary Magdalene,

Holloway Road, by W. Wickings, 1812–14, interesting as a Late Georgian church untouched by Greek Revival. E tower with urns and pilasters; plain interior with Tuscan galleries and no chancel. Charming urban development of 1820s with modest terraced houses, e.g. *Canonbury Square, Compton Terrace, Tibberton Square, Liverpool Road, Gibson Square, Barnsbury Square, Mountford Crescent, Milner Square,* and *Cloudsley Square* with Barry's Gothic Revival *Holy Trinity Church* (1826–8) as its principal accent.

Royal Borough of Kensington and Chelsea

St Barnabus, Addison Road, by Vulliamy, 1827–9, stock-brick King's College chapel type, i.e. neo-Perp with 4 corner turrets. Interior with galleries on iron columns. (Chancel 1860.) *St Luke* (73), Sydney Street, by J. Savage, 1820–4, expensive and ambitious church which pioneered use in the Gothic Revival of stone for vaulting. *Royal Hospital,* Chelsea: *Stable Block,* 1814, and *Secretary's Offices,* 1818–19, both by Soane. E front of stables is a memorable Soanean composition of blank arches within blank arches. *Duke of York's Barracks* (formerly Royal Military Asylum), 1801–3, by J. Sanders, pupil of Soane. Stock-brick ranges with portico of giant unfluted Doric columns. *Paultons Square,* small houses of c. 1830. Countless attractive early C19 stuccoed terraces, many by Basevi, 1826–45, e.g. *Alexander Square, Egerton Crescent, Pelham Crescent, Pelham Place, Thurloe Square* and *Walton Place. Edwardes Square* especially pretty with Tuscan lodge. Later and more Italianate feel about the streets and villas of *Campden Hill. Brompton Cemetery,* octagonal chapel with colonnades, by B. Baud, 1838–41.

Borough of Lambeth

St Mark, Kennington, by A. B. Clayton & D. R. Roper, 1822, with Greek Doric portico in antis surmounted by circular Ionic tower with cupola. *St Matthew,* Brixton, by C. F. Porden, 1822–4, with tetrastyle Greek Doric portico in antis and elaborate E tower. *St John* (70), Waterloo Road, by F. Bedford, 1823–4, with Greek Doric portico and clever Grecian tower. (Interior gutted.) *St Luke,* West Norwood, by F. Bedford, 1823–5,

with hexastyle Corinthian portico and W tower. (Interior remodelled 1878.) *St Anne's House,* 363 Kennington Lane, 1824, probably by J. M. Gandy. Late C18 terraces in *Kennington Road. Lying-in-Hospital,* York Road, by H. Harrison, 1828, with Ionic façade. *Brockwell Hall,* Brockwell Park, by D. R. Roper, 1811–13, for J. Blades, glass manufacturer. Elegant villa in park with lake.

Borough of Lewisham

Merchant Taylors' Almshouses, Lee High Road, by W. Jupp, 1826, 3-sided quadrangle of simple Classical elevations in stock-brick.

Borough of Southwark

St George, Wells Way, by F. Bedford, 1822–4, with giant hexastyle Greek Doric portico and boldly rectilinear 2-tiered W tower. *Holy Trinity, Trinity Church Square,* by F. Bedford, 1823–4, with Corinthian portico, in a remarkably complete Regency square. *St Peter* (70), Liverpool Grove, Walworth, by Soane, 1823–5. Stock-brick with 4 giant Ionic columns of Portland stone recessed in screen at W end; slim circular tower ringed with Composite columns. Untouched interior with unfluted Doric columns supporting galleries surmounted by broad semi-circular arches. Soanean segmental arches separate nave from chancel and W bay. Original altar-piece. Flat ceiling. *St James* (69), Thurland Road, Bermondsey, by J. Savage, 1827–9, most expensive of the Commissioners' churches in London except for St Luke, Chelsea, and Holy Trinity, Marylebone. Stock-brick with Bath stone Ionic portico and mannered Grecian tower. Good interior with galleries on square piers supporting unfluted Ionic columns; flat coffered ceiling. *Dulwich Gallery* (89), by Soane, 1811–14, one of his most important and original works, 1st independent building erected as a picture-gallery in England. Especially memorable, the Greek Doric mausoleum to founder of the gallery, Noel Desenfans, surmounted by square lantern incised with Soane's characteristic grooved lines. *Imperial War Museum,* Lambeth Road, built as Bethlehem Hospital by J. Lewis, 1812–15; portico and dome by S. Smirke, 1838–46. *Nelson Square,*

Southwark, c. 1807–10, perhaps by S. P. Cockerell.

Borough of Tower Hamlets

All Saints, East India Dock Road, Poplar, by C. Hollis, 1821–3, with Greek Ionic stone portico surmounted by somewhat Gibbsian steeple. *St John* (70), Cambridge Heath Road, Bethnal Green, by Soane, 1826–8, Commissioners' church with 3-bay brick front divided by Soanean pilasters and crowned by odd tower with detached corner piers. Soane's elegant vestibule survives but nave has been remodelled. *St Paul*, The Highway, Shadwell, by J. Walters, 1820–1, stuccoed Greek Revival church with circular obelisk-crowned tower; interior with galleries on Tuscan columns and segmental vault. *Royal Mint*, Tower Hill, by Smirke and Johnson, 1809–11, undemonstrative Classical building with twin lodges. *Wapping Pierhead*, terraced houses, 1811, flanking former entry to Docks. *London Docks*, Wapping, by D. A. Alexander, 1796–1820, a few portions survive. *St Katharine Docks* (32, 111, 111), by Telford and Hardwick, 1825–8.

Borough of Wandsworth

St Ann, St Ann's Hill, by Smirke, 1820–2, Commissioners' church with Ionic portico and tall circular tower; gallery on square piers supporting Doric columns. *Crescent Grove*, early terrace by T. Cubitt, 1822.

London Colney, *Hertfordshire. St Peter*, by G. Smith, 1825–6, early example of the Norman Revival.
Longford Hall, *Salop*. By J. Bonomi, 1789–94, for R. Leeke. Massive stone house with Tuscan portico in the form of a porte-cochère; entrance hall and stair hall are similarly in Bonomi's heavy, almost crude, Neo-Classical style.
Longhirst House (49), *near Morpeth, Northumberland*. By Dobson, 1824–8, for W. Lawson. Impressive portico with Corinthian columns in antis leading to central apsed and domed hall connected to staircase with segmental coffered vault.
Longleat, *Wiltshire*. Elizabethan prodigy house remodelled by Wyatville for 2nd Marquess of Bath, 1806–11. Neo-Elizabethan interiors and great staircase with Soanean star-fish vault.
Longner Hall, *Salop*. By Nash, c. 1805,

for R. Burton. Asymmetrical Tudor Gothic with traceried verandah and spectacular staircase, fan-vaulted in plaster. Park by Repton.
Lovat Bridge, *Highland Region*. By T. Telford, 1811–14.
Lower Hardres, *Kent. St Mary*, by T. Rickman, 1831–2, Early English in flint.
Lude, *near Blair Atholl, Tayside Region*. By W. Burn, 1837–40, for J. P. McInroy. Dull Jacobethan house.
Luscombe Castle (14, 15), *near Totnes, Devon*. By Nash, 1799–1804, for C. Hoare. Revolutionary asymmetrical composition in Picturesque castellated style set in fine Repton park.
Luton Hoo, *Bedfordshire*. Adam's house of 1766–74 was remodelled by R. Smirke, c. 1815, for 2nd Marquess of Bute; by S. Smirke in 1843; and by Mewès and Davis in 1903. Result is a bland and bulky ashlar-faced Neo-Classical mansion dominated by the Edwardian additions. Superb Capability Brown park. (National Trust.)
Lutterworth, *Leicestershire. Town Hall*, by J. A. Hansom, 1836. On upper floor 4 Greek Ionic columns are set against large area of blank wall; curved side wings.
Lyme Park, *Cheshire*. Palladian mansion of c. 1725–35 by Leoni. L. W. Wyatt added the powerful Roman attic behind the pediment on S front, 1814–17, for T. Legh, and remodelled E front interiors, providing new dining room which is an early example of a neo-Wren style.
Lympsham, *Somerset. Manor House* (former Rectory), charming Gothick fantasy of c. 1820.
Lypiatt Park, *Gloucestershire*. By Wyatville, 1809, for P. Wathen (later Bagot). Domestic Tudor Gothic style. Best interior is the long Gothic corridor. (Alterations 1876.)
Mabledon Park, *Quarry Hill, Tonbridge, Kent*. Castellated mansion by J. T. Parkinson, c. 1805, for the builder, J. Burton, whose son Decimus remodelled it with additional towers in 1829.
Macclesfield, *Cheshire. St Alban* (RC), Chester Road, by Pugin, 1838–41, in graceful Perp style before he turned to the C14. *Town Hall and Assembly Rooms* (73, 84), by F. Goodwin, 1823–4, stylish Grecian façade with tetrastyle Ionic portico and tripartite windows. *Sunday School*, Roe Street, 1813–14, large functional block 10 bays long and 2 storeys high. *St George's Sunday Schools*,

High Street, by W. Grellier, 1835. *Card Factory* (112), Chester Road, late C18 mill.

Madeley, *Salop. St Michael,* by T. Telford 1794–6, octagonal Classical church with W tower. (Chancel 1910.)

Maesderwen, *near Llanfrynach, Powys.* Elegant Regency villa with bowed wings, seat of the de Winton family.

Maidstone, *Kent. Sessions House* (formerly Shire Hall), by R. Smirke, 1826–7, elegant Classical composition. (Subsequently enlarged.) *Gaol,* Lower Boxley Road, by R. Smirke and D. A. Alexander, 1811–19. *Royal Insurance (formerly Kent Fire) Office,* High Street, by J. Whichcord, 7 bays with engaged Ionic columns. *Oakwood Hospital* (87), St Andrew's Road, by J. Whichcord, 1830, magnificent late Classical pile. *The Mote,* near Maidstone, by D. A. Alexander, 1793–1801, for 1st Earl of Romney, austere and daunting Greek Revival mansion. In park, small circular temple or tholos by S. Nelson, 1801, early example of revived Greek Doric.

Malpas Court, *near Newport, Gwent.* By T. H. Wyatt, 1836–8, for T. Prothero. Gothic.

Mamhead, *Devon.* (30, 31, 57.) By Salvin, 1828–38, for R. W. Newman. Neo-Tudor with attractive conservatory and stableyard built to resemble an earlier castle. Rich and eclectic interiors including fan-vaulted staircase and Lower Gallery.

Manchester. *Portico Library* (now Lloyd's Bank) (92), Mosley Street, by T. Harrison, 1802–6, Greek Ionic portico in antis. *Art Gallery* (24, 26, 90) (built as Royal Institution of Fine Arts), Mosley Street, by Barry, 1824–35, fine Grecian work with Ionic portico and raised attic inspired by Schinkel's Schauspielhaus in Berlin. Good staircase. *Athenaeum* (92) (now part of Art Gallery), Princess Street, by Barry, 1837–9, in his palazzo style. *Regional College of Art,* Grosvenor Square, Chorlton-on-Medlock, incorporates the former Chorlton Town Hall, by R. Lane, 1830, with Greek Doric portico. *St George,* Chester Road, Hulme, by F. Goodwin, 1826–8, Commissioners' Gothic.

Mansfield, *Nottinghamshire. Town Hall,* Market Place, by W. A. Nicholson, 1836, Late Greek Revival.

Marden Hill, *near Tewin, Hertfordshire.* Chaste yellow-brick villa by F. Carter, 1790–4, for R. Mackay. This was rendered remarkable by the remodelling of 1818–19 for C. G. Thornton by Soane who provided the Ionic porch and, especially idiosyncratic, the staircase and adjacent 1st-floor vestibule with its vaulted bays.

Marford, *Clwyd.* Estate village with charming Gothick cottages, 1805, for G. Boscawen.

Margam Abbey, *West Glamorgan.* By T. Hopper, 1830–5, for C. R. Mansel Talbot. Elaborate Tudor Gothic with great octagonal tower. (Gutted.)

Margate, *Kent. Cobb's Brewery,* by W. Teanby, 1807–8, pedimented centre with wings and circular brewhouse behind.

Markham Clinton, *Nottinghamshire.* Boldly Greek *church* and mausoleum built for 4th Duke of Newcastle, 1831–2, by R. Smirke, with Doric portico and 2-tier octagonal lantern with free-standing Greek Doric angle columns. Also by Smirke the *Rectory* in 'Swiss Jacobean' style.

Marlow, *Buckinghamshire. Suspension Bridge,* by W. T. Clark, 1831–6.

Matfen Hall, *Northumberland.* By Rickman, 1832–5, for Sir E. Blackett, Bt. Jacobethan mansion with vast Gothic stair hall inspired by Fonthill. Chimney-piece by Chantrey made for Buckingham Palace.

Meldon Park, *Northumberland.* By Dobson, 1832, for I. Cookson. Fine Classical composition in ashlar; good interiors, especially the imperial staircase.

Melford Hall, *Long Melford, Suffolk.* Elizabethan mansion with Neo-Classical library and handsome colonnaded staircase added in 1813 by T. Hopper for Sir W. Parker, Bt. (National Trust.)

Mellor, *Lancashire. St Mary,* by Rickman & Hutchinson, 1827–9, Gothic Commissioners' church with tower and spire. *Woodford Hall,* 1798, 9-bay ashlar front with Ionic portico, attributed to J. Wyatt. (Gutted.)

Menai Straits, *Gwynedd.* (32, 108, 109.) *Suspension Bridge,* by Telford, 1819–26.

Merevale Hall, *Warwickshire.* By Blore, 1838–44, for W. S. Dugdale. One of the finest products of the Jacobean Revival, superbly placed on wooded hill above Atherstone. Generally symmetrical but with crowded Picturesque skyline and asymmetrically placed tower. Good interiors.

Merthyr Mawr, *near Bridgend, Mid Glamorgan*. By H. Wood, 1806–8, for Sir J. Nicoll. Regency villa in park.

Methven, *Tayside Region. Mausoleum*, by J. Playfair, 1793, for 1st Lord Lynedoch. Greek Revival Ledoux-inspired style.

Micheldever, *Hampshire. St Mary*, curious octagonal brick nave added to medieval church by G. Dance, 1808–10. (Chancel 1880.)

Milbourne Hall, *Penteland, Northumberland*. By J. Paterson, 1807–19, for R. Bates. Elegant Classical villa with canted bays and angles and an ingenious plan employing Paterson's characteristic oval rooms. S entrance front prolonged to the W with lower side wing which contains Tuscan porch and terminates in tower and cupola. Impressive octagonal stable block.

Mildenhall, *Wiltshire.* (Former) *School*, by R. Abraham, 1823–4, Gothic, cruciform, with top-lit octagonal centre.

Millichope Park, *Salop.* (50.) By E. Haycock, 1835–40, for the Rev. R. N. Pemberton. Uncompromising Greek Revival mansion with giant hexastyle Ionic portico and noble top-lit hall with 2 tiers of Ionic columns. Building was modified in 1970 when original entrance was removed: this was a curious affair in a semi-basement flanked by stunted Doric columns. Fine park with lake and temple on a rock, by G. Steuart, 1770.

Milne Graden, *near Coldstream, Borders Region*. Classical house by J. G. Graham, 1822, for Admiral Sir D. Milne.

Milton Hall, *Cambridgeshire*. Built c. 1790 for the Rev. S. Knight. 5-bay white-brick Neo-Classical house in style derived from Soane's East Anglian houses. Garden front has tripartite windows and 3-bay semi-circular bow. Façade is raised half a storey over the bow and is lit by a Diocletian window. Oval staircase. Remains of a Repton park.

Mitford Hall, *Northumberland*. By Dobson, c. 1828, for B. O. Mitford. Ashlar-faced Grecian villa with Tuscan conservatory.

Moggerhanger House, *Bedfordshire*. (59.) By Soane, 1809–11, for S. Thornton. Lively entrance front of stucco with semi-circular Greek Doric portico. Interiors mutilated for present use as Bedfordshire County Sanatorium (Park Hospital).

Monmouth, *Gwent. Shire Hall*, by E.

Haycock, 1829–30, Greek Revival, staircase with elegant glazed dome and screen of Greek Doric columns. The following buildings all by G. V. Maddox: *Market Hall* (now post office and museum), Priory Street, 1839, Grecian; *Priory Street*, 1837–9; *Methodist Chapel*, 1837, Ionic; *Masonic Hall*, 1837.

Montrose, *Tayside Region. Parish church*, by D. Logan, 1791, Gothic, with tower and spire by J. G. Graham, 1832–4. *St John's Free Church* (76), by W. Smith, with Greek Ionic portico and cupola. *Academy*, by D. Logan, 1815, Greek Ionic. *Museum*, Panmure Place, by J. Henderson, 1837. *Royal Infirmary*, by J. Collie, 1837–9, Greek Revival. *Bank of Scotland*, High Street, by W. Burn, 1839.

Monzie Castle, *Tayside Region*. By J. Paterson, c. 1795–1800, for Gen. A. Campbell. In Adam's castle-style. (Restored after a fire in 1908.)

Moreby Hall, *North Yorkshire*. By Salvin, 1828–33, for H. Preston. Impressive neo-Tudor mansion with battlemented staircase tower.

Morpeth, *Northumberland. Bridge*, by T. Telford, 1831.

Much Birch, *Hereford and Worcester. St Mary and St Thomas of Canterbury*, by J. Foster and W. Okely, 1837, characteristic Commissioners' Gothic.

Mulgrave Castle, *North Yorkshire*. (29.). By W. Atkinson, c. 1804–11, for 1st Earl of Mulgrave. Romantic castellated style but preserving an early Georgian core and some work by Soane of 1786–7. Fine park by Repton of 1793.

Musselburgh, *Lothian Region. Bridge*, by J. Rennie, 1803. (Widened 1924.)

Nanteos, *Dyfed*. (62.) Mid C18 mansion with centrepiece and massively Doric stables added by E. Haycock, c. 1839–49, for W. E. Powel.

Netherby Hall, *Cumbria*. C18 house incorporating peel tower remodelled in Baronial style by W. Burn, 1833, for Sir G. Graham, Bt.

New Galloway, *Dumfries and Galloway Region. Ken Bridge*, by J. Rennie, 1820–1.

New Lanark, *Strathclyde Region*. (112, 113.) Early C19 industrial town planned by Robert Owen.

Newark Park, *near Ozleworth, Gloucestershire*. C16 mansion remodelled by J. Wyatt, c. 1810, for L. Clutterbuck. Gothic S front and elegantly Neo-Classical hall and staircase.

Newbyth, *Lothian Region*. By A. Elliot,

1817–18, for D. Baird. 2-storeyed castellated house of 5 by 6 bays with symmetrical façades and horizontal crenellated skyline broken by tall turrets. (Interior remodelled during conversion into flats, 1972–5.)

Newcastle-upon-Tyne, *Tyne and Wear*. (39.) *All Saints* (65), by D. Stephenson, 1786–96, one of the most original Neo-Classical churches in the country; elaborate tower projecting in front of the church; Greek Doric entrance portico; oval nave. *St Thomas*, Barras Bridge, by Dobson, 1828–9, Early English with openwork belfry and vaulted interior. *Moot Hall* (84), Castle Garth, by J. Stokoe, 1810–12, impressive early Greek Revival building, 11 bays with Doric portico. In 1825–40 Grainger and Dobson rebuilt Newcastle town centre to make it one of the best examples of Neo-Classical town planning in Britain. Inspired by Nash's London, but carried out in local stone, scheme begins with *Eldon Square* (now mutilated) (40), 1825, *Leazes Crescent* and *Terrace* (40), 1829–34. Then came the *Triangle* (40), a block formed by *Market Street*, *Grey Street* (41) and *Grainger Street*. Nearby is the *Grey Column*, by B. Green, 1837–8, with statue by Baily. *Grey Street* is the finest street with Corinthian portico of the *Theatre Royal* by B. Green, 1836–7. The *New Markets* (102), by Dobson, 1835–6, large glazed area with impressive façades, e.g. to *Clayton Street*. *Literary and Philospphical Society* (90), Westgate Street, by J. Green, 1822–5, Grecian. *Newcastle General Cemetery* (81), Jesmond Road, chapels and Grecian entrance gates in Schinkelesque style, by Dobson, 1836. *Sandyford Park* (formerly Villa Reale), Sandyford Road, Jesmond, Grecian mansion by Dobson, 1817, for J. Dutton.

Newlaithes Hall, *Horsforth, West Yorkshire*. By R. Lugar, c. 1825, for C. Greenwood. Asymmetrical Tudor villa.

Newlands Church, *Borders Region*. 1838, Gothic, with T-plan.

Newport, *Gwent*. St Mary (RC), by J. J. Scoles, 1839–40, ambitious Gothic church.

Newport, *Isle of Wight*. *St Thomas of Canterbury* (RC), Pyle Street, 1791, modest Classical church. *Isle of Wight Institution*, by Nash, 1811, Classical. *Market House and Guildhall*, 1814–16, Classical.

Newton Don, *Near Kelso, Borders Region* (50.) By R. Smirke, c. 1815, for Sir A.

Don, Bt. Astylar Classical composition with 3-bay 3-storeyed centre with tripartite windows, flanked by 2 lower wings with shallow segmental 3-bay bows.

Newton Stewart Bridge, *Dumfries and Galloway Region*. By J. Rennie, 1812–13.

Nidd Hall, *Nidd, North Yorkshire*. Large, ashlared 3-storey Classical mansion. 8-bay S front; 14-bay E front, 3 canted bows. Core early C19, enlarged 1894.

Nigg, *Grampian Region*. Church, by J. Smith, 1828–9, Gothic with tower.

Nonsuch Park, *Surrey*. By Wyatville, 1802–6, for S. Farmer. Dull cemented neo-Tudor elevations but an early example of asymmetry.

Normanby Park, *Humberside*. (50.) By R. Smirke, 1825–30, for Sir R. Sheffield, Bt. Finest example of Smirke's uncompromisingly rectilinear Grecian style with subtle recessions and advances of both wall plane and skyline. Largely astylar though the tripartite windows are divided with slender Doric piers. Fine marble chimney-pieces by Westmacott. (Additions and alterations 1906.)

Normanton, *Leicestershire*. St Matthew, tower, by T. Cundy, 1826–9, inspired by baroque towers of Archer's St John, Smith Square, London. (Nave 1911.) Stables and farm buildings also by Cundy for the (now demolished) Normanton Park.

Norris Castle, *East Cowes, Isle of Wight*. By J. Wyatt, 1799, for Lord H. Seymour. Picturesque neo-Norman pile, castellated and asymmetrical. Kitchen garden with impressive embattled wall, farm buildings and 2 lodges also by Wyatt.

North Leach, *Gloucestershire*. (88.) *House of Correction* (now police station), by W. Blackburn, 1787–91. (Partly demolished.)

North Shields, *Tyne and Wear*. (106.) St Curthbert (RC), Albion Road, by R. Giles, 1821, inaccurate Gothic, but pretty interior with canted chancel framed by hanging arches. *New Quay and Market Place*, by D. Stephenson, 1806–17. Handsome Classical ranges including *Northumberland Arms Inn*.

Norwich, *Norfolk*. Gaol, Castle, by Wilkins junior, 1824–8, castellated. St Andrew's Hospital (86), Thorpe, by F. Stone, 1811–14, pedimented 7-bay centre with wings. *Jarrold's Works* (115), Cowgate, begun 1834 by J. Brown. *Albion Mills* (115), King Street, 1836–7. *Bracondale Lodge*, Martineau Lane, by

Wilkins senior, c. 1795, villa with dome of slightly Oriental outline, originally also a park by Repton.

Nottingham. *Judges' Lodgings* (now Record Office), High Street, by H. M. Wood, 1833, arresting Greek Revival façade; good interiors.

Nunnykirk, *Northumberland*. By Dobson, 1825, for W. Orde. Finest of Dobson's Classical houses; tripartite garden front with French-inspired horizontally-channelled rustication and Ionic colonnade. Impressive galleried and domed hall in centre of house.

Nutwell Court, *Lympstone, Devon*. By S. P. Cockerell, 1802, for 2nd Lord Heathfield. 5-bay stuccoed villa with tripartite windows in end bays. Gothic chapel at rear.

Oaklands, *near Okehampton, Devon*. Begun by C. Bacon, c. 1816, and completed by C. Vokins for A. Savile, MP. Elegant Greek Revival of pink sandstone with Ionic porticos.

Oaklands Park, *near Newnham on Severn, Gloucestershire*. Built c. 1830 for the Crawshay family, colliers in the Dean. Massive 7-bay entrance front of grey stone with unusually heavy overall rustication. Solid porch with rusticated arch and tripartite window over. Side elevation with semi-circular bow window commanding fine views.

Oakly Park, *Salop*. C18 house remodelled by C. R. Cockerell, 1819–36, for the Hon. R. Clive. 9-bay entrance front of 3 storeys flanked by 2 2-storeyed wings. Cockerell added twin Doric loggias, one of which leads into circular saucer-domed entrance vestibule and thence to noble staircase hall with a 1st-floor screen of Tower of the Winds columns supporting a cast of the Bassae frieze (which Cockerell had helped discover). Cockerell's library has contemporary shelving and fine chimney-piece. The Bromfield lodge also by Cockerell.

Ochtertyre, *Tayside Region*. *Mausoleum*, by C. H. Tatham, 1809, for Sir P. Murray, Bt., massive neo-Perp chapel of local granite.

Oddington House, *Gloucestershire*. Remodelled c. 1810 for Lady Reade. Classical with Doric porch and elegant curved staircase.

Old Hall Green, *Hertfordshire*. *St Edmund's College* (RC), by J. Taylor, 1795–9, 'Priest factory', simple Classical 15-bay block of 3 storeys. (Chapel by

Pugin, 1845–53.)

Oldham *Greater Manchester*. (97.) *St Mary*, Church Street, by R. Lane, 1827–30, Commissioners' Gothic style with tower. *Blue Coat School*, Horsedge Street, by R. Lane, 1829–34, 17-bay Gothic front. *Town Hall*, by J. Butterworth, 1840–1, with pedimented Ionic portico. (Enlarged 1879.)

Ombersley, *Hereford and Worcester*. (73.) Estate *church*, near Ombersley Court, by Rickman & Hutchinson, 1825–9, for Marchioness of Downshire. Decorated with W tower and spire. *Ombersley Court*, by Smith of Warwick, 1720s, but remodelled 1812–14 by J. Webb, for Marchioness of Downshire, with reticent 7-bay entrance front of 3 storeys with porch of 4 pairs of coupled Ionic columns. Some interiors by Webb including Chinese room and Dufour wallpaper room.

Osberton House, *Nottinghamshire*. (50.) By Wilkins, c. 1805, for F. F. Foljambe. Greek Doric portico, one of the first on an English country house. (Altered in the 1840s and 70s.)

Ospringe House, *Kent*. By C. Beazley, c. 1799, for I. Rutten. Greek Doric porch and circular staircase, top-lit with elegant balustrade.

Otterden Place, *Kent*. By W. Pilkington, 1802, for G. H. Wheler. Red-brick neo-Tudor alteration and extension of Elizabethan house. Solid decent work with Classical interiors.

Oulton, *West Yorkshire*. *St John*, by Rickman & Hutchinson, 1827–9, excellent Gothic church with spire, brick vaults and polygonal apse. Stands in the grounds of *Oulton Hall*, by R. Smirke, c. 1822, for J. Blayds. (Reconstructed after a fire in 1850 by S. Smirke.) Classical with tripartite windows. Stables, by J. Clark, 1837.

Owston Hall, *South Yorkshire*. By W. Lindley, 1794–5, for B. Cooke. 7-bay Classical house of simple design.

Oxburgh Hall, *Norfolk*. *Catholic chapel*, 1835, by A. W. Pugin or J. C. Buckler, Gothic.

Oxford. (94.) *St Clement*, Marston Road, by D. Robertson, 1827–8, neo-Norman with tower. *St Paul*, Walton Street, by H. J. Underwood, 1836, with Ionic portico. (Apse 1853.) *Balliol College*, alterations to (former) Hall and Library, by J. Wyatt, 1792–4, Gothic; W side of Garden Quad, by Basevi, 1826–7, Classical. *Oriel College*, W side of St

Mary's Quad, by D. Robertson, c. 1826, Gothic. *St Peter's College*, Master's Lodgings (formerly Canal House), by R. Tawney, 1827–9, with Greek Doric portico. *Ashmolean Museum and Taylorian Institution* (26, 89), by C. R. Cockerell, 1839–45, blending Greek, Roman and Mannerist elements in powerful and original way. *Botanical Gardens Library and Lecture Room* (now Magdalen College bursary), by H. J. Underwood, 1835, Greek Ionic. *Clarendon Press*, Walton Street, by D. Robertson, 1826–7, and E. Blore, 1829–30, with central triumphal arch. *Beaumont Street*, 1828, elegant terraces of ashlar-faced houses.

Oxton House, *Kenton, Devon*. Built 1781; E entrance front of 5 bays and 2 storeys with canted bows at each end; 6-bay S front. Bows connected by colonnade of 4 Greek Doric columns c. 1820. Attractive landscaped park with Swiss cottage and Gothic hermitage, c. 1800, and iron bridge with low end piers in the form of truncated Doric columns surmounted by urns.

Ozleworth Park, *Gloucestershire*. C18 house with elegant bowed Regency addition of 3 bays with Greek Doric porte-cochère.

Packington Hall, *West Midlands*. Interiors by J. Bonomi for 4th Earl of Aylesford from 1784 onwards, including remarkable Pompeiian Gallery. H. Hakewill added external terraces, 1812, and some interiors, 1828. Massive and unusual Greek Revival church of *St James* (22, 23) nearby, 1789–90, also by Bonomi.

Painswick House, *Gloucestershire*. Stone house of 1730s with wings added by Basevi, 1827–32, for his brother-in-law, W. H. Hyett, MP. Though Basevi's façades are in a Cotswold baroque style, i.e. sympathetic to the existing house, he added a Neo-Classical Corinthian entrance porch on E front leading into a chaste entrance hall with Ionic columns, flanked by groin-vaulted vestibules with Classical reliefs in rectangular panels. Basevi's new W wing contains a massively antique dining room with Corinthian columns, coffered ceiling and cleverly top-lit cast of a section of the Parthenon frieze.

Papworth Hall, *Cambridgeshire*. By G. Byfield, 1809, for C. M. Cheere. Flashy and rather coarse stuccoed Greek Revival mansion, with hexastyle Ionic portico on W front flanked by tripartite windows. 7-bay S front with semi-circular Greek Doric porch. E front with recessed portico of giant Ionic columns in antis. Impressive columnar hall with adjacent lobbies and staircase.

Parkend, *Forest of Dean, Gloucestershire*. St Paul, by the Rev. H. Poole, 1822, unusual Gothick octagon with 4 projecting arms and W tower. *Rectory*, Gothick, presumably c. 1820.

Paxton House, *Borders Region*. Mid C18 Palladian mansion with wing added by R. Reid, 1812–13, for G. Home. Contains picture gallery (now chapel) and superb Regency library with bowed end and fitted book-cases.

Pelwall House, *near Market Drayton, Salop*. (59.) By Soane, 1822–8, for his friend P. Sillitoe. Remarkable stone-built Classical house with Picturesque skyline, Soanean incised ornament and Ionic porch (somewhat altered). Interiors more altered, though vaulted Small Drawing Room survives. (House now decaying.) Even odder, the triangular lodge on N drive, with canted corners in a style half-way between Classic and Gothic.

Pennsylvania Castle, *Portland, Dorset*. By J. Wyatt, 1800, for J. Penn. Picturesque castellated pile in Portland stone.

Penpont, *Powys*. C17 house refronted 1813 with Doric loggia.

Penrhyn Castle, *Bangor, Gwynedd*. (54, 56, 56.) By T. Hopper, c. 1825–44, for G. H. Dawkins-Pennant. Mightiest of all neo-Norman castles, with keep inspired by Rochester, Great Hall by Durham, sumptuous library and exotically carved staircase. (National Trust.)

Penryn, *Cornwall*. Numerous simple early C19 buildings, including *Town Hall*, 1825, with neo-baroque tower of 1839.

Penshaw Hill, *Co. Durham*. Monument to 1st Earl of Durham, by J. & B. Green, 1844. Impressive Greek Doric temple on a hill, roof-less and wall-less.

Penylan, *Meifod, Powys*. 7-bay Regency house with Tuscan porch.

Penzance, *Cornwall*. (101.) St Mary, by C. Hutchens, 1832–6, Gothic. *Baptist Chapel*, Clarence Street, by P. Sambell, 1835–6, neo-Norman. *Market House*, by H. J. Whitling, 1835–6, long narrow building with, unusually, a dome; tall

Ionic portico at one end. *Egyptian House,*
6 Chapel Street (*171*), c. 1830, amazing
extravaganza closely modelled on P. F.
Robinson's (now demolished) Egyptian
Hall, Piccadilly, with winged disc, cavetto
cornices and corbel-arched windows with
aggressively canted sides. Attractive
Regency houses in *Clarence Place,*
Clarence Street and *Regent Square.*
Regency terraces, e.g. *Regent Square.*
Perridge House, *Devon.* By G. Byfield,
c. 1827, for H. L. Toll.
Perth, *Tayside Region. St Paul*, by J.
Paterson, c. 1800–7, large octagonal
Gothic nave with tower and spire. *St
Leonard* (76), King Street, by W. D.
Mackenzie, 1834, Classical with

Lysicrates Monument turret. *Kinnoull
parish church*, by W. Burn, 1826, neo-
Perp with Greek-cross plan. *Old Academy*
(*82*), Rose Terrace, by R. Reid, 1803–7,
ambitious Classical building in Adam
style, with broad 5-bay façade on
rusticated ground floor, tripartite
windows under segmental heads with
fan-glazing, engaged coupled Doric
columns and paterae. Domed octagonal
schoolroom on 1st floor. *County
Buildings* (7, 81, 82), Tay Street, by R.
Smirke, 1815–19, Greek Revival (in
striking contrast to Old Academy), with
octostyle Doric portico flanked by 2 3-
bay 1-storey wings; side elevation has
tripartite windows with Diocletian heads.

Egyptian House,
Penzance, c.1830.
Inspired by the
Egyptian Hall,
Piccadilly

Marshall Monument, by D. Morison, 1822–4, built for Perth Literary and Antiquarian Society and Public Library (remodelled 1854 as Perth Art Gallery), domed Pantheon with Ionic portico on podium. *Murray Royal Asylum for the Insane* (now Hospital) (87), Kinnoull, by W. Burn, 1827, with Roman Doric portico and central octagon; the earliest surviving asylum in Scotland. (Enlarged 1834 and 1865.) *Infirmary*, York Place, by W. D. Mackenzie, 1836, astylar with arched porte-cochère. (Former) *Exchange Coffee Rooms*, George Street, by W. D. Mackenzie, 1836, with incised Soanean ornament. *Prison*, Edinburgh Road, by R. Reid, 1810–12, with 4 radial blocks. (Partly rebuilt 1842.) (Former) *Waterworks*, Tay Street, by A. Anderson, 1832, with impressive cast-iron domed reservoir adorned with Ionic pilasters and swagged frieze; chimney in the form of a tall Doric column. *Salutation Hotel*, South Street, front of c. 1800, perhaps by Reid, with eye-catching tripartite window under giant lunette with fan-glazing. *St John Street*, laid out 1796–1801. *Blackfriars House*, Atholl Place, c. 1790. *Atholl Crescent* and *Place*, 1797–1805. *Marshall Place*, 2 terraces by Reid, 1801. *St Leonards Bank*, villas, perhaps by Reid. *Barossa Place. Boatland House*, Isla Road, c. 1820, villa with semi-circular bow and oval stairs.

Phillips House, *Dinton, Wiltshire*. (50.) By Wyatville, 1812–17, for W. Wyndham. Neo-Classical mansion of great austerity and refinement; 9-bay ashlar-faced front with hexastyle Ionic portico. Domed imperial staircase with brass balustrade. (National Trust.)

Pitcairns, *Dunning, Tayside Region*. By W. Burn, 1827, for J. Pitcairn. Tudor Gothic mansion.

Pitcaple Castle, *Grampian Region*. Baronial-style additions to old tower by W. Burn, c. 1830, for H. Lumsden.

Pitshill, *near Tillington, West Sussex*. Main E front is mid C18 but plain N and W sides were modified in 1790s from designs by Soane for W. Mitford. Fine landscaped park.

Plas Newydd, *Anglesey, Gwynedd*. Gothicisation begun by J. Wyatt, 1795, for 1st Earl of Uxbridge, and completed by J. Potter, 1823. Architecturally unrewarding but superbly sited overlooking Menai Straits. Nearby at Llanfairpwll the *Anglesey Column*, by T. Harrison, 1816, to commemorate 1st Marquess of Anglesey. (National Trust.)

Pleasington, *Lancashire*. *St Mary and St John Baptist* (RC), by J. Palmer, 1816–19, large and rather fantastical Gothic church.

Plymouth, *Devon*. (43, 92, 106.) *Custom House*, by D. Laing, 1810, refined composition with 5 round-arched windows on 1st floor. *Town Hall*, Devonport, by J. Foulston, 1821–3, Greek Doric. Nearby in Ker Street is the *Library* (now Oddfellows' Hall), by Foulston, 1823, neo-Egyptian, and *Column*, by Foulston, 1824, Greek Doric. *Royal William Victualling Yard*, Stonehouse, by J. Rennie, 1826–32, vast and impressive complex in an unexpectedly Hawksmoorian style. *Athenaeum Terrace, The Crescent* and *Sussex Place*, by G. Wightwick, 1832–6. *Albemarle Villas, St Michael's Terrace* and other villas in Stoke Damerel, by J. Foulston, 1825–36.

Polesden Lacey, *Surrey*. By T. Cubitt, 1821–3, for J. Bonsor. Simple Regency villa with long Ionic colonnade on SE front. Now more interesting for the Edwardian additions and remodelling. (National Trust.)

Pont Cysyllte Aqueduct, *near Llangollen, Clwyd*. (110, 111.) By Telford, 1794–1805. The supreme achievement of canal engineering: 19 cast-iron arches on immense stone piers carry the Shropshire Union Canal in a cast-iron trough 127ft above the Dee. Admired by Sir Walter Scott.

Pontefract, *West Yorkshire*. (84.) *Court House*, by C. Watson, 1807–8, with Greek Ionic portico.

Poole, *Dorset*. *Custom House*, 1813, jaunty 3-bay façade with twin curved staircase leading up to entrance. Beside this is the *Harbour Office*, 1822, with Tuscan colonnade. *Beech Hurst*, High Street, 1798, for S. Rolles, 5-bay, 3-storey red-brick house with semi-circular Tuscan porch. *Mansion House*, Thames Street, c. 1800, imposing 5-bay red-brick front of 3 storeys with tall blank arcading linking the windows on ground and 1st floors.

Port Eliot, *St German's, Cornwall*. (59, 60.) Medieval and mid C18 house remodelled by Soane, 1804–6, for 2nd Lord Eliot. S and E fronts in subdued castellated style; good interiors, e.g.

circular drawing room with Soanean incised lines on ceiling. Gothic porch and entrance hall by H. Harrison, 1829. Park by Repton, 1792.

Potarch Bridge, *Grampian Region*. By T. Telford, 1811–15.

Powderham Castle, *Devon*. Medieval and Georgian castle with castellated additions by J. Wyatt, 1794–6, for 3rd Viscount Courtenay. Includes superb Music Room with coffered dome and furniture by Marsh & Tatham. Further castellated alterations by C. Fowler, 1837–48.

Powfoulis, *Central Region*. Ornamental Gothic mansion, c. 1830, with symmetrical façade and pinnacled skyline.

Preston, *Lancashire*. *Christ Church*, Bow Lane, by J. Latham, 1836, neo-Norman. *St Ignatius* (RC), Meadow Street, by J. J. Scoles, 1833–6, Gothic. (Additions 1858.) *St Mary*, St Mary's Street, by J. Latham, 1836–8, large neo-Norman church with strange W tower. *St Peter*, St Peter's Square, by Rickman & Hutchinson, 1822–5, Gothic Commissioners' church. (Steeple 1851.) *St Thomas*, Lancaster Road, by J. Latham, 1837, neo-Norman with tower, spire and polygonal apse.

Preston Grange, *Prestonpans, Lothian Region*. Remodelled in Baronial style by W. H. Playfair in 1830 and 1850 for the Suttie family. Large but not specially interesting.

Preston Hall, *Lothian Region*. By R. Mitchell, 1791–4, for A. & Sir J. Callander, Bt. 7-bay Palladian front on rusticated basement, the central 3 bays pedimented and adorned with Ionic pilasters; flanked by link ranges leading to 5-bay wings. Rich Adam-style interiors, especially the elaborate domed staircase with screens of Corinthian columns. Fine stable block, lodges and park.

Prestwick Lodge, *near Ponteland, Northumberland*. By Dobson, 1815, for P. Fenwick. 3-bay Greek Doric villa.

Prestwold Hall, *Leicestershire*. Mid C18 house altered by Wilkins senior, 1805, for C. J. Packe, and completely remodelled by W. Burn, 1842–4, for C. W. Packe. Magnificent marbled interiors in rich Classical taste.

Prior Park, *Bath, Avon*. John Wood's Palladian mansion, begun 1735, has elaborate external staircase, wings and

interiors by H. E. Goodridge, 1829–34 and 1836, for Bishop Baines. Magnificent Classical chapel by J. J. Scoles, 1844, with colonnaded interior inspired by Versailles chapel.

Pudsey, *West Yorkshire*. *St Laurence*, by T. Taylor, 1821–4, large simple Gothic church with W tower.

Purley House, *Berkshire*. By J. Wyatt, c. 1800. Elegant stone house with Tuscan porte-cochère, curved bow and good interiors.

Quatford Castle, *Salop*. Castellated mansion built for himself in 1829–30 by J. Smalman, builder and architect.

Quernmore Park Hall, *Lancashire*. 5-bay Classical house flanked by pavilions with tripartite windows, built 1795–8 for C. Gibson, and sometimes attributed to T. Harrison on stylistic grounds. Best interior is the 2-storeyed colonnaded hall by Alexander Mills, 1842, with coved ceiling and heavy Greek Revival plaster-work. Fine park by Staffordshire landscape-gardener and architect John Webb.

Raehills, *near Moffat, Dumfries and Galloway Region*. By A. Stevens, 1786, for 3rd Earl of Hopetoun. In Adam's castle-style, and enlarged by W. Burn, 1829–34, for J. J. Hope Johnstone.

Rainhill, *Merseyside*. (73.) *St Bartholomew* (RC), Rainhill Stoops, by J. Dawson, 1838–40, unusual temple church with Ionic portico and Italianate interior, richly polychromatic, with coffered tunnel vault and apse.

Rainscombe House, *near Oare, Wiltshire*. By T. Baldwin of Bath, c. 1816, for the Rev. J. Rogers. Refined ashlar-faced 5-bay Classical block ornamented with blank round-headed niches and Ionic porches.

Ramsey Abbey, *Cambridgeshire*. Limp Gothic mansion by Soane, 1804–7, and more especially by Blore, 1838–9, for E. Fellowes. Incorporates portions of medieval and C16 work.

Ratho, *Lothian Region*. *Ratho Hall*, c. 1800, plain 5-bay Classical front with elegant interiors. *Ratho Park*, by W. Burn, 1824, for J. Bonar with symmetrical Jacobethan S front but more interestingly grouped entrance front. Dignified Greek Revival interiors.

Read Hall, *Lancashire*. By G. Webster of Kendal, 1818–25, for J. Fort. Classical house of great dignity in warm brown stone, 9-bay front with 3-bay domed bow ringed with Ionic colonnade. Rich interiors, especially the extensive entrance hall.

Reading, *Berkshire. St James* (RC), Forbury Road, by Pugin, 1837–40, in a neo-Norman style he would have rejected later. (Much altered.) (Former) *Congregational Chapel*, Castle Street, by J. J. Cooper, 1837, with Soanean detail. *St Mary*, Castle Street, imposing hexastyle Corinthian portico and (now destroyed) cupola added 1840, by H. & N. Briant, to late C18 church. *Simeon Monument*, Market Place, obelisk by Soane, 1804. *Royal Berkshire Hospital* (87), London Road, by H. Briant, 1837–9, impressive pile with giant Ionic portico. *Barclay's Bank*, King Street, 1838–9, palazzo by H. & N. Briant. Several Late Georgian terraces, e.g. *Southampton Street, Queen's Crescent, Eldon Square* and *London Road*.

Redcar, *Cleveland. St Peter*, Redcar Lane, 1828–9, by I. Bonomi, Gothic with W tower.

Rendlesham, *Suffolk.* 2 remarkable lodges to the former hall, Gothick follies.

Renishaw Hall, *Derbyshire.* Enlarged in a Gothic style, by J. Badger, 1793–1808, for Sir S. Sitwell, Bt.

Rheola, *West Glamorgan.* Small house modestly enlarged by Nash, c. 1812, for his friend J. Edwards. Classical. (Later additions.)

Ringwould House, *Kent.* By Soane, 1813, for the Rev. J. Monins. Small plain house of yellow brick on cliffs near Dover. Characteristic pilaster strips on entrance front, but interiors have little of interest.

Ripon, *North Yorkshire. Holy Trinity*, Kirkby Road, by T. Taylor, 1826–7, large Gothic ashlar-faced church with broach spire. (Later alteration.)

Rise Hall, *Humberside.* 1815–20, for R. Bethell, probably by Watson and Pritchett. Ambitious ashlar-faced Greek Revival mansion with Ionic portico, impressive entrance hall and top-lit staircase hall.

Roche Court, *near Winterslow, Wiltshire.* By C. H. Tatham, c. 1805, for F. T. Egerton. 4-bay 2-storey entrance front with 4-columned Tuscan portico. Dull design for this interesting architect.

Rode Hall, *Cheshire.* Large, irregular and rather featureless C18 house altered 1810–12 for R. Wilbraham by L. W. Wyatt who provided the Empire Style dining room with green scagliola Ionic columns.

Rood Ashton House, *West Ashton, Wiltshire.* By Wyatville, 1808, for R. G. Long. Large castellated house, altered by T. Hopper, 1836. (Now a ruin.)

Rookesbury, *near Wickham, Hampshire.* By C. H. Tatham, 1820–5, for the Rev. W. Garnier. Stuccoed Greek Revival mansion with Ionic portico and good interiors. Octagonal castellated tower in grounds, 1826, also by Tatham.

Ross Priory, *Strathclyde Region.* Remodelled in Gothic style by J. G. Graham, 1812, for H. Macdonald Buchanan.

Rowton Castle, *Salop.* Early C18 house transformed into eminently Picturesque castellated composition with large round tower by G. Wyatt, 1810–12, for Col. R. Lyster. (Further additions c. 1824–8.)

Rudding Park, *North Yorkshire.* Begun 1805 for the Hon. W. Gordon and completed c. 1825 by R. D. Chantrell for Sir J. Radcliffe, Bt. Perfect expression of the Classical style associated with S. and L. W. Wyatt, relying for its effect on smooth, chaste forms, perfectly cut ashlar, unmoulded window surrounds and shallow segmental bays of which there are as many as 5 at Rudding. Elegant but understated interiors and noble stair hall with stairs rising in 1 arm, returning in 2.

Rug Hall, *Clwyd.* (*175.*) Severe Classical mansion with Ionic portico, c. 1800; recently reduced in size. Park laid out by Repton, 1793, for Col. E. V. W. Salusbury.

Rugby School, *Warwickshire.* (96, 96.) Irregular Tudor Gothic quadrangle by H. Hakewill, 1809–16. Influential design.

Ryde, *Isle of Wight. Town Hall*, Lind Street, by J. Sanderson, 1830, with colonnaded front. Several Regency houses including *Brigstocke Terrace*, c. 1832.

Ryes, The, *Little Henny, Essex.* Built by R. Lugar, 1810, as shooting box for N. Barnardiston. Irregular villa stylistically close to Lugar's Yaxham Rectory, Norfolk. Greek Doric porch, Italianate eaves, 2-storeyed bow.

Sacombe Park, *Hertfordshire.* Extensive Greek Revival house of yellow brick, built c. 1802–8. W entrance front of 9 bays and 2 storeys with tetrastyle Greek Doric porch, 9-bay E front with semi-circular bow in centre. Show-piece is the 11-bay S front with segmental bows at each end linked by colonnade of 6 giant but oddly attenuated Greek Doric columns. Fine staircase under oval dome.

St Asaph, *Clwyd*. (Former) *Bishop's Palace*, 1791, with domed bow, W wing by Blore, 1830–1, neo-Tudor.

Salford, *Greater Manchester*. (84.) *St Philip*, St Philip's Place, by R. Smirke, 1822–4, with semi-circular Ionic portico and circular domed tower, virtually identical to his St Ann, Wandsworth. *St Thomas*, Broad Street, Pendleton, by R. Lane and F. Goodwin, 1829–31, in Commissioners' Gothic style. *Town Hall and Assembly Rooms*, Bexley Square, by R. Lane, 1825–7, ashlar-faced with Greek Doric portico. *Buile Hill*, Eccles Old Road, by Barry, 1825–7, for Sir T. Potter, Grecian villa in style of Smirke with tripartite windows. (Later additions; now museum.)

Salisbury, *Wiltshire*. (105.) *Guildhall*, Market Place, by R. Taylor and W. Pilkington, 1788–95, enlarged 1829 by T. Hopper who formed the Tuscan portico. *White Hart Hotel*, St John Street, late C18 front of 9 bays and 3 storeys with pedimented Ionic portico (perhaps early C19) standing on 3-bay porte-cochère.

Salperton Park, *Gloucestershire*. Gabled C17 house modernised for J. Brown in 1817 with large 5-bay wing ornamented with horizontally-channelled rustication on ground floor and a pediment; flanked on either side by 2-bay 2-storey wings. Architect was R. Pace who specialised in making restrained Classical additions to houses in this part of the country.

Salthrop House, *Wroughton, Wiltshire*. c. 1795, 3-bay ashlared entrance front with curved bow, curved central staircase below oval skylight.

Saltmarshe Hall, *Laxton, Humberside*. By C. Watson, 1818–28, for P. Saltmarshe. Ashlared 2-storeyed block of 5 by 5 widely spaced bays in refined but understated Classical style close to Dobson's. Unmoulded window surrounds, severely plain skyline, only external adornment being the semi-circular Tuscan porch on N entrance front.

Saltoun Hall, *Lothian Region*. By W. Burn, 1818–26, for A. Fletcher. Impressive castellated Gothic pile with central tower inspired by Taymouth Castle. Spectacular sequence of rib-vaulted Gothic interiors.

Sandhurst, *Berkshire*. *Royal Military Academy*, 1807–12, by J. Sanders, Soane's first pupil. Long dignified façade with giant portico, an early use of the Greek Doric order. (Later additions.)

Sandridge Park, *Stoke Gabriel, Devon*.

Rug Hall, Clwyd, c. 1800. A dauntingly severe Neo-Classical mansion of which the left-hand block has now been removed

(*13.*) By Nash, c. 1805, for Lady Ashburton. Stuccoed Italianate villa with round and square towers. Similar to Cronkhill (q.v.) but less successfully grouped. Superbly placed above R. Dart. Extensive stables with Picturesque spirelet.

Sarsden, *Oxfordshire*. *Sarsgrove House*, substantial cottage orné by G. S. Repton, c. 1825, with ornamental barge boards and Tudor chimney stacks, but with more of an Early Victorian than Regency feel. Interesting Soanean drawing room with elliptical arches and groined ceiling, though the lines are smooth and not sharp as Soane would have had them. House was built for the 2 unmarried daughters of J. H. Langston, MP, of nearby *Sarsden House*, built c. 1690, altered c. 1825 by G. S. Repton who added Ionic porticos and octagonal domed hall. Park and lake by H. Repton, 1795.

Scampston House, *Humberside*. By T. Leverton, 1803, for W. T. St Quintin. 9-bay S front with domed bow adorned with Doric pilasters. Another bow on 5-bay W front ringed with detached Tuscan columns. Interiors equally chaste and elegant. Park and bridge of 1770s by Capability Brown.

Scarborough, *North Yorkshire*. (90.) *Museum*, by R. H. Sharp, 1828–9, tall domed rotunda, a most unusual shape for a museum at this date. (Later wings.) Stands in *The Valley*, landscaped in 1830s with villas of 1840s, approached via *The Crescent*, c. 1835, by R. H. & S. Sharp.

Scarisbrick Hall, *Lancashire*. (31.) By Pugin, 1837–45, for C. Scarisbrick. Amongst the earliest and most lavish of his Gothic Revival houses. Exuberant S front with richly carved neo-Perp oriel windows; inside, Great Hall, King's Room and staircase are similarly elaborate. (Later additions.)

Scone Palace, *Tayside Region*. (29, 57.) By W. Atkinson, 1803–12, for 3rd Earl of Mansfield. Undemonstrative castellated exteriors but first house in Scotland in which every interior was neo-Gothic, the best being the Long Gallery and the Octagon.

Scotney Castle, *Kent*. (30, 57, 60.) By Salvin, 1837–43, for E. Hussey. Neo-Elizabethan house, asymmetrical and castellated, with neo-Jacobean interiors. Picturesquely sited to catch view in the valley below of original medieval castle surrounded by moat. (National Trust.)

Seaham Harbour, *Co. Durham*. New town planned for 3rd Marquess of Londonderry, by J. Dobson, 1828. *St John*, by T. Prosser, 1835–7, neo-Perp church. Greek Revival *Londonderry Institute*, Tempest Place, is later than it looks: 1853–5, by T. Oliver.

Sedbury Park, *Tidenham, Gloucestershire*. Remodelled by R. Smirke, 1826, for G. Ormerod. Arresting 3-storeyed S entrance front of 3 widely spaced bays, the central bay breaking forwards and emphasised with porte-cochère of unfluted Greek Doric columns. These are continued round the corner to serve as a loggia along W front which has 5 bays and 3 storeys with crowning balustrade. Domed hall altered in 1890s. House has been wrecked by extensive recent additions to the N and E.

Sedgley, *near Dudley, West Midlands*. *All Saints*, Vicar Lane, by T. Lee, 1826–9, in Commissioners' Gothic with tower. *St Chad and All Saints* (RC), Catholic Lane, 1823, Gothic.

Seton Castle, *Lothian Region*. (177.) By R. Adam, 1790–1, for A. Mackenzie. Theatrically handled approach through forecourt to small but vigorously modelled castle-style house reminiscent of Vanbrugh Castle, Blackheath.

Settle, *North Yorkshire*. *Holy Ascension*, by T. Rickman, 1836–8, simple lancet Gothic with SW porch tower. *Town Hall*, Market Square, by G. Webster, 1832, Jacobean Revival.

Sezincote House, *Gloucestershire*. (59.) By S. P. Cockerell, c. 1805, for his brother, Sir C. Cockerell, Bt. Lovely neo-Moghul fantasy for retired nabob in golden local stone with Indian garden buildings by Thomas Daniell and exquisite Reptonian park. 2-storeyed main block, 9 bays by 5, crowned by emphatic *chujja* or Indian cornice above which rises the onion-shaped copper dome. This block is Picturesquely extended by a 15-bay quadrant conservatory terminating in an octagonal pavilion. Principal interiors, Classical not Indian, are on 1st floor, finest being the Saloon with a great canted bay and high cove painted and gilded in *trompe-l'oeil* trellis-work. Central flier of the graceful tripartite staircase is unusually carried on exposed cast-iron girders, pierced in guilloche pattern. *Beehive Lodge* on the

Seton Castle, Lothian Region, 1790–1; Adam. The happiest surviving example of Adam's personal castle-style

Worcester Road, by C. R. Cockerell, 1823.
Sheffield, *South Yorkshire. Carver Street Methodist Church* (74, 75), by the Rev. W. Jenkins, 1804, influential design with arched 1st-floor windows. *Nether Independent Chapel*, Norfolk Street, by Watson and Pritchett, 1827. *Cutlers' Hall* (Chamber of Commerce) (104), Church Street, by S. Worth and B. B. Taylor, 1832, richly Corinthian. (Enlarged 1860s and 80s.) (Former) *Savings Bank*, Surrey Street, by R. Potter, 1831, Italianate. *City Training College* (97), Ecclesall Road, by J. G. Weightman, 1835, Gothic. *King Edward VII Grammar School* (95), Glossop Road, by W. Flockton, 1837–40, immensely ambitious with Corinthian portico. *Botanical Gardens*, Clarkehouse Road,

Grecian gatehouse, by B. B. Taylor, 1836, and 3 contemporary glass-houses. *General Cemetery*, Cemetery Road, Greek Doric Chapel and Offices, by S. Worth, 1836, and Egyptian entrances. Terraces and villas in *Glossop Road*, e.g. *The Mount*, by W. Flockton, c. 1835, Grecian. *Banner Cross*, Eccleshall, by Wyatville, 1817–21, for Gen. W. Murray, freely grouped castellated house.
Sheringham Hall, *Norfolk*. (60.) By J. A. Repton, 1813–19, for A. Upcher. Simple white-brick villa in delicious park by his father, H. Repton, with tantalising views of the sea. 5-bay S front has colonnade of coupled Doric columns forming a loggia in the recessed 3-bay centre. Chaste interiors except for the comfortable bow-windowed library which survives as furnished in 1839 with

fitted concave book-cases of polished rosewood.

Shrewsbury, *Salop*. St Chad (65, 66, 66, 81), by G. Steuart, 1790–2, inventive Neo-Classical experiment with circular nave and massive 3-tiered tower preceded by pedimented Doric portico and crowned by a Corinthian rotunda. Inside, circular vestibule leads into an apsed ante-room with twin curved staircases and so into the nave with a gallery supporting attenuated Corinthian columns of cast iron. *St Alkmund*, nave and chancel by J. Carline, 1794–5, Gothic; E window with cast-iron tracery and painted glass by F. Eginton. (Later alterations.) *St George*, Drinkwater Street, Frankwell, by E. Haycock, 1829–32, Gothic, with hotly coloured contemporary glass by D. Evans in E window. *County Gaol*, Howard Street, by J. H. Haycock and executed by T. Telford, 1787–93, Classical with central octagonal chapel. *Lord Hill's Column*, by E. Haycock and T. Harrison, 1814–16, Greek Doric, enormous. *Royal Salop Infirmary* (87), St Mary's Place, by R. Smirke, 1826, impressive Greek Doric pile. *Music Hall*, The Square, by E. Haycock, 1839–40, Grecian. *Butter and Cheese Market*, Howard Street, by Fallows and Hart, 1835, Greek Doric. *Benyon, Bage and Marshall's Flax Spinning Mill* (Allied Breweries) (112), Spring Gardens, Ditherington, 1796–7, important early iron-frame building.

Shugborough, *Staffordshire*. (21, 50.) Late C17 and mid C18 house remodelled by S. Wyatt, 1790–8, for 1st Viscount Anson. Striking Ionic colonnade on E front boasting 8 giant columns of slate-encased timber, flanked by Wyatt's characteristic domed bows. Excellent Wyatt interiors, e.g. entrance hall, saloon, staircase and Red Drawing Room with elegant coved ceiling. In park, the celebrated Greek Revival garden buildings by Athenian Stuart of 1760s. (National Trust.)

Sibton Park, *Suffolk*. 1827, 2-storeyed and rendered, with a crowning balustrade and semi-circular entrance portico of 4 giant Ionic columns. Good interiors. Similar to Foxboro Hall (q.v.), of which the architect is also unknown.

Sidmouth, *Devon*. *Fortfield Terrace*, begun c. 1790 by M. Novosielski. Few other terraces but numerous villas and cottages ornés, e.g. *Woodlands Hotel*,

Knowle Hotel and *Royal Glen Hotel*.

Skellingthorpe Hall, *Lincolnshire*. Impressive Greek Revival house, c. 1830, with Doric portico in antis.

Skutterskelfe House (formerly Leven Grove), *Rudby-in-Cleveland, Cleveland*. By Salvin, 1831, for 10th Viscount Falkland. Plain Classical block, 7 bays by 5.

Sleaford, *Lincolnshire*. *Sessions House*, Market Place, by H. E. Kendall, 1830, neo-Tudor with open arcades. *Carr's Hospital*, Eastgate, by H. E. Kendall, 1830 and 1841–6, castellated.

Somerley, *Hampshire*. By S. Wyatt, 1792–5, for D. Hobson, a Salford manufacturer. 5-bay block with Ionic colonnade on S front and elegant entrance hall, staircase and libraries. All this survives embedded in a remodelling and extension (now partly demolished) of 1869–74.

Southborough Place, *Ashcombe Avenue, Surbiton, Surrey*. By Nash, 1808, for T. Langley. 7-bay villa with Tuscan eaves and octagonal porch.

Southill, *Bedfordshire*. Remodelled by H. Holland, 1796–1800, for S. Whitbread, the brewer. Understated Classical exteriors with Ionic colonnade and loggias along S front. Exquisite interiors important for their contemporary furniture and fittings. Painted Parlour has Louis XVI painted ornament in Pompeiian style, perhaps by T. Pernotin.

Spetchley Park, *Hereford and Worcester*. By J. Tasker, 1811–c. 18. Massive and heavy Greek Revival mansion of Bath stone with portico of 4 unfluted Ionic columns on W entrance front; S front has tripartite windows in the end bays and semi-circular bow with Ionic pilasters. Both architect and patron were Catholics and the impressive interiors include a handsome chapel.

Spilsby, *Lincolnshire*. *Sessions House and House of Correction*, by H. E. Kendall, 1824–6, with Greek Doric portico against plain side wings.

Spott House, *Lothian Region*. C17 or earlier house remodelled in Scots Baronial style by W. Burn, 1830, for J. Sprot.

Stafford. *Shire Hall*, Market Place, 1794, by J. Harvey, an assistant of S. Wyatt whose style is reflected in this elegant building. 9-bay ashlared front with engaged (almost Greek) Doric columns; good interiors. *Gaol*, Gaol Road, by T.

Cook, 1793–4. (Enlarged 1832.) *St George's Hospital*, Gaol Road, 1814–18, 31-bay front. *Fernleigh Hospital* (formerly Workhouse), Marston Road, by T. Trubshaw, 1837–8, extensive complex. *Lloyd's Bank*, Market Square, c. 1795. *Rowley Hall*, Rowley Avenue, perhaps by W. Keen, c. 1817, Grecian.

Staines, *Surrey. Bridge*, by J. Rennie, 1829–32.

Stamford, *Lincolnshire*. (104, 105, 106.) Generally thought of as a medieval, C17 & C18 town, although there is much stone-fronted Neo-Classical work of high quality carrying a Late Georgian style into 1840s. *Austin House*, Austin Street, c. 1800, elegant pile with 2 3-storeyed bows with Gothick glazing bars. *Library* (formerly market), High Street, by W. Legg, 1804, with Tuscan portico. *Stamford Hotel*, St Mary's Street, by J. L. Bond, c. 1810–20, spectacular 9-bay façade of metropolitan splendour with engaged Corinthian order; above handsome entablature a figure of Justice by J. Rossi; good interiors. *Congregational Chapel*, Star Lane, 1819, red brick with windows in elegant arched recesses. *Bath House*, Bath Lane, 1823, Gothic. *Stamford and Rutland Infirmary*, Deeping Road, by J. P. Gandy, 1826–8, Tudor Gothic. *Rutland Terrace*, 1829–31, 34 bays, 3 storeys, giant pilasters with anthemion capitals, overlooking undulating Welland meadows, the perfect example of Regency *rus in urbe*. *Truesdale's Hospital*, Scotgate, by Basevi, 1832, 12 Tudor Gothic almshouses round courtyard. *14 Barn Hill*, c. 1840, severe 3-storeyed Classical house with tripartite windows. *Stamford Institution* (now YMCA), St Peter's Hill, by B. Browning, 1842, with imposing Graeco-Egyptian tapered doorway. *Rock House*, 1842, elaborate villa in style verging on the Italianate; recessed centre flanked by pedimented bays with bay windows; giant Corinthian pilasters and miniature columns; rich plasterwork inside. *Barn Hill House*, N front of 1843 by B. Browning with portico of fluted Roman Doric columns. *13–14 St Mary's Street*, 1849, good shop-fronts with Erectheion Ionic columns. Several early C19 shop-fronts, e.g. *7 High Street* and *4 St Mary's Street*.

Stanage Park, *Powys*. Rebuilt by J. A. Repton, 1803–7, for C. Rogers (with additions by E. Haycock, 1845). Extensive, scattered, informal Gothic pile: quintessence of the Picturesque in superb Repton park.

Stand, *Greater Manchester. All Saints*, Church Lane, by Barry, 1822–5, Commissioners' church in fetching unarchaeological Gothic.

Stanfield Hall, *near Wymondham, Norfolk*. By Wilkins senior, 1792, for the Rev. G. Preston. Neo-Elizabethan. (Altered 1830–5.)

Stirling, *Central Region. Athenaeum*, King Street, by W. Stirling, 1814–16, plain Georgian 3-storeyed curved frontage on corner site, dominated by tall but lifeless tower of 5 stages capped with spire. *Court House and Gaol*, by R. Crichton, 1806–11. *Bank of Scotland*, King Street, by W. Burn, 1833, Italianate, 5 bays and 3 storeys. *Melville Terrace*, c. 1807 onwards, detached or semi-detached villas. *Allan Park*, c. 1810–27, L-shaped street of villas and terraced houses, partly by A. Bowie. *Queen Street*, c. 1820, terraced houses. *Craigs House*, by A. Bowie, c. 1820, for R. Gillies, elegant 3-bay villa with tripartite windows ornamented with radial fluting in the tympana.

Stobo Castle, *Borders Region*. By A. & J. Elliot, 1805–11, for Sir J. Montgomery, Bt. Symmetrical and fortress-like castellated mansion with round angle towers. Good Classical interiors.

Stobs Castle, *Borders Region*. By R. Adam, 1792–3, for Sir W. Elliott, Bt., in the castle-style.

Stockport, *Greater Manchester. St Thomas* (71, 73), Wellington Road South, by Basevi, 1822–5, expensive Commissioners' church in Grecian style with handsome Ionic portico containing open double staircase of stone leading to the galleries. *Tiviot Dale Wesleyan Methodist Chapel*, by R. Lane, 1825–6. *Sunday School*, Duke Street, 1805–6 and 1835–6, functional 14-bay block of 4 storeys. *Infirmary* (87), Wellington Road South, by R. Lane, 1832–3, with impressive Greek Doric portico. *Woodbank Park*, Woodbank, by T. Harrison, 1812, for P. Marsland, 3-bay Classical villa with tripartite windows.

Stockton-on-Tees, *Cleveland. Holy Trinity*, by J. & B. Green, 1834–5, Gothic with massive W tower and internal galleries. (Later alterations and additions.)

Stoke Poges, *Buckinghamshire. Monument* to Thomas Gray in churchyard, by J. Wyatt, 1799, handsome sarcophagus on 20ft-high pedestal. *Stoke Park*, begun by R. Nasmith for John Penn, and completed by J. Wyatt, c. 1793-7, with remarkable Greek Doric colonnades and dome (altered later). In the grounds, memorial *column* to Sir Edward Coke, by J. Wyatt, 1800, 60ft-high Roman Doric column with statue by Rossi.

Stoneleigh, *Warwickshire. Stoneleigh Abbey*, extensive castellated stables, 1813, by C. S. Smith who also remodelled parts of the Abbey, 1837-9. *Sowe Bridge*, by J. Rennie, 1814.

Stonyhurst, *Lancashire.* Great Elizabethan mansion with C19 additions for the Jesuits including impressive Catholic church of St Peter, by J. J. Scoles, 1834-5, neo-Perp with corner turrets.

Storrs Hall, *Bowness-on-Windermere, Cumbria.* (50, *180*.) By J. M. Gandy, 1808-11, for J. Bolton. Chunky Greek Revival house with 5-bay entrance front, the centre 3 bays recessed and provided with Doric colonnade sporting prominent antefixae. End bays with pilaster strips and tripartite windows with corbelled pediments. Top-lit entrance hall and staircase. Octagonal temple of 1804 on shore of lake.

Stourhead, *Wiltshire.* Palladian mansion of 1720s by Campbell with wings added 1793-5 and Corinthian portico in 1840 by C. Parker to Campbell's designs. In the wings spacious Picture Gallery and perfect Regency Library with segmental tunnel vault, lunette window with stained glass after Raphael, and contemporary Chippendale furniture. (National Trust.)

Stowe, *Buckinghamshire.* C18 palace containing library (now headmaster's room), by Soane, 1805-6, for 1st Marquess of Buckingham, in Strawberry Hill Gothick.

Stowell Park, *Wilcot, Wiltshire.* Stuccoed house, c. 1813, with 6-columned Doric verandah.

Stracathro House, *Tayside Region.* (10, 50.) By A. Simpson, 1828, for A. Cruickshanks. Magnificent Roman composition with Corinthian portico extending into side wings in the form of a screen, as at Basevi's Fitzwilliam Museum of 1830s. Top-lit hall with screens of columns and rich marble floor.

Strathallan Castle, *Tayside Region.* Enlarged and regularised in symmetrical Gothic style by R. Smirke, 1817-18, for Lord Strathallan.

Stratton Park, *Hampshire.* (50.) Massive portico of unfluted Greek Doric columns is all that survives of Dance's work for

Storrs Hall, Bowness-on-Windermere, Cumbria, 1808-11; J. M. Gandy. The Greek Revival at its heaviest and most self-conscious

Sir F. Baring, Bt., 1803–6. *London Lodge* also by George Dance, as well as 5 pairs of cottages in the estate village of *East Stratton.*

Stretton-on-Dunsmore, *Warwickshire*. *All Saints*, by T. Rickman, 1835–7, Gothic with accurate C14 & C15 details.

Stroud, *Gloucestershire*. *Holy Trinity*, Stroudshill, by J. Foster, 1838–9, in Commissioners' Gothic style with polygonal apse. *Congregational Church*, Bedford Street, by C. Baker of Painswick, 1835–7, characteristic non-conformist Classical front, pedimented with engaged columns and Venetian window, domed circular entrance hall. *Subscription Rooms*, by Basevi and C. Baker, 1833–4, 5-bay Classical composition with good interiors.

Stubton Hall, *Lincolnshire*. By Wyatville, 1813–14, for Sir R. Heron. Elegant Neo-Classical villa with Wyatt motifs, e.g. shallow bow and tripartite windows. Tuscan portico and porch later. Conservatory projecting at canted angle from S front now demolished. (Spoilt by modern additions for its present use as school.)

Studley Castle, *Warwickshire*. By S. Beazley, for Sir F. L. H. Goodricke, Bt. Symmetrical neo-Norman and Gothic composition building up to central keep crowned by grotesque octagonal top storey.

Sunderland, *Tyne and Wear*. *Exchange*, by J. Stokoe, 1812–14. Regency houses, e.g. in *John Street, Foyle Street* and *Athenaeum Street.*

Swansea, *West Glamorgan*. (93.) *Royal Institution of South Wales*, by F. Long, 1838–40, with Greek Ionic portico, one of the few Greek Revival monuments in Wales of a type familiar in England and Scotland.

Sweeney Hall, *Salop*. By J. H. Haycock, 1805, for T. N. Parker. Stone house with 5-bay front adorned with giant Tuscan pilasters.

Swerford House, *Hook Norton, Oxfordshire*. C18 house remodelled by J. M. Gandy, 1824, for Sir R. Bolton. N entrance front with screen of 2 Greek Doric columns flanked by gabled wings with Soanean pilaster strips and tripartite windows. E front of 5 bays and 2 storeys plus dormer windows. House is placed on steeply sloping site so that S front, with tall canted bows, is 3 storeys high.

Swinton Park, *North Yorkshire*. (60, 64.) 1690s house (extended by Carr of York, 1764–7), enlarged 3 times for W. Danby in 1791–6 and 1813–15 by J. Foss, and in 1821–4 by R. Lugar who castellated what had previously been a Classical house. Foss's S wing of 1790s contains a drawing room with curious high coving decorated by J. Wyatt. Lugar's large round tower was heightened 1890. Late Picturesque park with lake and Druid's Temple (64), c. 1800.

Swithland Hall, *Leicestershire*. By J. Pennethorne, 1834, for 4th Earl of Lanesborough. Elaborate and unusual neo-Grecian stuccoed mansion: end bays of the central block are pedimented and have curious tripartite oriel windows on ground floor. This block is linked by 1-bay wings to far-projecting 3-bay pavilions. (Somewhat decayed.) Neo-Tudor lodge, 1838.

Talacre Hall, *Clwyd*. By T. Jones, 1824–7, for Sir P. Mostyn. Tudor Gothic.

Tatton Park, *Cheshire*. (50, 60.) Begun by S. Wyatt for W. Egerton, 1785–91, and completed to modified scheme by L. W. Wyatt, 1807–25. Elegant Neo-Classical mansion, plain except for giant Corinthian portico. Best interiors are the screened tripartite entrance hall, staircase and library. Park by Repton with orangery, Lysicrates Monument (by W. Cole, c. 1820) and Rostherne Lodge (by J. Hakewill, 1833, Greek Doric). (National Trust.)

Taymouth Castle, *Tayside Region*. (57, 58.) By A. & J. Elliot, 1806–10, for 1st Marquess of Breadalbane. Fantastic towering Gothic stair hall. Enlarged by W. Atkinson, 1818–28, and by J. G. Graham, 1838–9.

Tenby, *Dyfed*. A town sometimes described, over-optimistically, as the Brighton of West Wales. Developed as a Regency seaside resort after 1800 by Sir William Paxton, for whom S. P. Cockerell built the *Public Baths* (now Laston House), St Julian's Street, 1811.

Terling Place, *Essex*. By J. Johnson, c. 1772–8. Altered by Hopper, 1818–21, for Col. J. Strutt, with 2 wings, new entrance front, library, staircase and superb 2-storeyed galleried saloon. With its cast of the Parthenon frieze, screens of yellow scagliola Ionic columns and shallow saucer dome, the saloon is one of the most accomplished if least-known monuments of the Greek Revival in domestic architecture.

Tewkesbury, *Gloucestershire. Mythe Bridge*, by T. Telford, 1823–6.
Theale, *Berkshire. Holy Trinity* (29), by E. W. Garbett, 1820–2, remarkable essay in Early English Revival inspired by Salisbury Cathedral. Tower by J. Buckler, 1827–8. (Apse 1892.)
Theale, *Somerset. Christ Church*, by R. Carver, 1828, Gothic with canted E window, no tower.
Thickthorn Hall, *Hethersett, Norfolk.* Stuccoed early C19 house of 3 widely spaced bays divided on S front by broad Doric pilasters. 1-storeyed extension forming kind of loggia round 3 sides.
Thornes, *near Wakefield, West Yorkshire. St James*, by S. Sharp, 1829–31, Classical.
Thorpe Perrow, *near Firby, North Yorkshire.* By J. Foss, c. 1802, for M. Milbanke. Late Palladian or Adamish house with 11-bay front with 3-bay pediment, Ionic porte-cochère and tripartite windows. Interiors altered though fine staircase survives.
Thrybergh Park, *South Yorkshire.* By J. Webb, c. 1820, for Col. J. Fullerton. Castellated Gothick; symmetrical front, rib-vaulted entrance hall and stair hall.
Toddington Manor, *Gloucestershire.* Vast accurately detailed neo-Perp mansion built 1820–35 from designs by its owner, C. Hanbury Tracy, 1st Lord Sudeley.
Tongland Bridge, *near Kirkcudbright, Dumfries and Galloway Region.* (108.) By T. Telford, 1805–6, castellated.
Torquay, *Devon.* (43.) Development of Regency Torquay began with *High Terrace*, c. 1811, *Park Place* and *Crescent*, *Vaughan Parade* and *Beacon Terrace*, 1830, all by J. Harvey.
Torrisdale Castle, *Kintyre, Strathclyde Region.* Probably by J. G. Graham, c. 1815, for Gen. K. MacAlister. Castellated and stylistically close to J. G. Graham's Edmonstone Castle (q.v.).
Townley Hall, *Lancashire.* Partly medieval house to which Wyatville made some external Gothic alterations, 1817–19, for P. Townley. Interiors Classical, e.g. dining and drawing room.
Tranent, *Lothian Region.* (87.) *St Joseph's School* (formerly George Stiell's Hospital), by W. Burn, 1821–2, Greek Ionic, ashlar-faced. (Later alterations and additions.)
Trebursey House, *near Launceston, Cornwall.* By Wyatville, c. 1820, for 2nd Earl of St Germans. Gothic with crow-stepped gables.

Tregothnan, *near Truro, Cornwall.* (9, 57, 60.) Elaborate Tudor Gothic mansion (incorporating C17 house) by Wilkins, 1816–18, for 4th Viscount Falmouth. Built of local brown porphyry with pinnacles, etc., of cement modelled on the details of Wilkins's favourite building, East Barsham Manor, Norfolk. Interiors Classical save for the grand staircase rising in 1 arm, returning in 2, with elaborate Gothic metal balustrade. (Sympathetic extensions to S by Vulliamy, 1842–6.) Superb park & setting.
Tregrehan House, *St Blazey, Cornwall.* By G. Wightwick, c. 1804–5, for Col. E. Carlyon. Granite with 7-bay entrance front and Ionic colonnade. Gothic lodge.
Trelissick House, *near Truro, Cornwall.* (48.) By P. F. Robinson, 1824, for T. Daniell. Grandest Neo-Classical mansion in Cornwall, with N entrance front of 9 bays and 2 storeys with tetrastyle unpedimented 1-storey portico of fluted Greek Doric columns; tall dormers suggest an earlier core. S garden front of 11 bays with hexastyle portico of giant Erectheion Ionic columns and conservatory adjoining.
Tremadoc, *Gwynedd.* Model coaching-town laid out 1805–12 for W. Madocks. *Square*, with hotel and arcaded market hall. *Church*, 1806, Gothic, and *Peniel Chapel*, opposite, 1811, with Tuscan portico. Near the town is *Tanyrallt*, verandahed Regency villa built for Madocks, c. 1800, and rented by the Shelleys 1812–13.
Trentham Hall, *Staffordshire.* (28, 64.) By Barry, 1834–9, for 2nd Duke of Sutherland. Demolished except for Italianate garden buildings. *Mausoleum*, for 2nd Marquess of Stafford, by C. H. Tatham, 1807–8, remarkable Primitivist block in manner of Ledoux with Greek-cross plan and emphatically canted walls.
Truro, *Cornwall. St John*, by P. Sambell, 1827–8, Grecian. (Altered.) *Methodist church*, Union Place, 1830, 3-bay pedimented front with Greek Doric porch. *Doric Column*, Lemon Street, by P. Sambell, 1835, to commemorate the explorer Richard Lander. Georgian houses in *Lemon Street*, begun 1794; *The Parade*, Malpas Road; and *Walsingham Place*.
Tulliallan Castle, *Fife Region.* (57.) Gothic pile, by W. Atkinson, 1817–20, for Viscount Keith.
Tunbridge Wells, *Kent. Holy Trinity*, Church Road, by D. Burton, 1827–9,

uninspired Gothic. *Christ Church*, High Street, by J. Palmer Brown, 1836–41, uninspired Norman. *Bath House*, Bath Square, by J. T. Groves, c. 1804, stuccoed with Tuscan pilasters. (Mutilated.) *Corn Exchange*, 1801–2, Greek Doric, built as theatre; next door is the (former) *Royal Sussex and Victoria Hotel*, stuccoed with giant pilasters. Numerous Late Regency houses and terraces, e.g. *Mount Sion*, 1830s, with shallow bows; but show-piece is the *Calverley Park estate* (40) laid out from 1828 by D. Burton for J. Ward: 19 Italianate villas disposed in a rough semi-circle approached through Victoria Lodge, a Greek Doric archway. Burton's *Calverley Park Crescent*, c. 1830, 17 houses with continuous ground-floor verandah.

Turvey House, *Bedfordshire*. (183.) Large 3-storeyed rectangular house of 7 bays by 4 with plain entrance front marked by Tuscan portico, but rich garden front adorned with emphatic Corinthian order and rinceaux frieze. This elaborate composition, inspired by Nash's style at Buckingham Palace, must be c. 1830 though the core is supposed to date from 1794. Inside, apsed and domed rooms and fine staircase with columnar screen.

Ty Mawr, *Llanfrynach, Powys*. Remodelled in Gothick style, c. 1820, for the Rev. C. Clifton. (Further additions c. 1860–80.)

Tyneholme House, *Pencaitland, Lothian Region*. By W. Burn, 1835, for P. Dudgeon. Modest, asymmetrical, Jacobethan.

Tynemouth, *Tyne and Wear*. Several Regency *terraces*. *Tyne Master Mariners' Asylum*, Tynemouth Road, 1837, Tudor with clock tower.

Tyninghame House, *Lothian Region*. (57, 58.) By W. Burn, 1829–30, for 9th Earl of Haddington. One of the finest and earliest Baronial-style mansions of C19 Scotland. Vast irregular pile in pink sandstone with French tourelles. Excellent and well-preserved interiors. Fine park.

Tyringham Hall, *Buckinghamshire*. (14, 59.) By Soane, 1793–c. 1800, for W. Praed. 7-bay 2-storeyed entrance front with bow ringed with Ionic columns; horizontally channelled rustication (French motif) and bands of incised Greek key decoration. Soane's interiors were unfortunately lost in a remodelling of 1909. Also by Soane the grey stone *Entrance Gateway*, segmental arch flanked by lodges with unfluted Doric columns, a memorable Neo-Classical composition with no curved mouldings, just deeply incised lines. Soane's hump-backed single-arched *bridge* on the drive is similarly austere and marked with incised lines.

Underley Hall, *near Kirkby Lonsdale, Cumbria*. By T. Webster, 1825–8, for A. Mowell. Another early example of Jacobean Revival. (Extended 1872.)

Turvey House, Bedfordshire, c. 1830. A provincial reaction to Nash's metropolitan splendour

Underriver, *Kent. St Julian's*, by J. B. Papworth, 1818–20, for R. Herries. Early example of Jacobean Revival, enlarged by Pennethorne, 1835–7, but spoilt by its recent adaptation as flats.

Upton Hall, *Nottinghamshire*. By W. Donthorn, c. 1830, for T. Wright. Stuccoed Greek Revival villa with Ionic portico.

Ushaw, *Co. Durham. St Cuthbert's College* (RC), extensive Classical ranges by J. Taylor, 1804–8. Chapel begun by Pugin, 1840.

Wakefield, *West Yorkshire*. (92.) *St John*, St John's Square, by C. Watson, 1791–5, Classical. *St James*, Thornes, by S. Sharp, 1829–31, Grecian. *Court House*, by C. Mountain, 1807–10, with Greek Doric portico. (Enlarged 1849–50.) *Mechanics Institution* (now Public Rooms), 1820–1, Grecian. *Grammar School*, Northgate, by R. Lane, 1833–4, Tudor Gothic.

Walberton House, *West Sussex*. By R. Smirke, 1817–18, for R. Prime. Plain Classical house of white stucco with 7-bay front.

Wallasey, *Cheshire. St John*, Liscard Road, Egremont, by H. Edwards, 1832–3, ashlar-faced church with Greek Doric portico.

Walsall, *West Midlands. St Mary* (RC) (73), Vicarage Walk, by J. Ireland, Grecian with shallow coffered vault. *St Matthew*, nave by F. Goodwin, 1820–1, with Gothick fan vault, cast-iron arcade piers and galleries. *Literary and Philosophical Institution* (County Court), Leicester Street, 1830–1, with stuccoed tetrastyle Greek Doric portico.

Wareham, *Dorset. Unitarian church*, South Street, 1830, with tetrastyle Ionic portico.

Wargrave Manor, *Berkshire*. c. 1780–90, for J. Hill, by J. Yenn, a distinguished pupil of Chambers. 3-bay, 3-storeyed stuccoed villa with central 3-bay curved bow and Tuscan colonnade. Regency flavour is perhaps due to later alterations.

Warleigh House, *near Bathford, Avon*. By J. Webb, 1814, for H. Skrine. Asymmetrical Tudor villa.

Warwick. *Warwick Arms Hotel*, High Street, c. 1790, in the Wyatt style, perhaps by W. Eboral; 5-bay ashlar-faced with tripartite windows in blank segmental arches. (Former) *Judge's Lodging*, Northgate Street, by H. Hakewill, 1814–16, plain but austerely refined Classical front of 3 bays with

Ionic porch and horizontally channelled rustication on ground floor. (Former) *Gasworks*, Saltisford, 1822, with elegant 11-bay façade, stuccoed in Parker's Roman cement, flanked by octagonal end pavilions; round-headed windows with Gothick glazing bars. Good early C19 factories in *Saltisford* and *Wallace Street*.

Weedon Barracks, *Northamptonshire*. 1803, extensive yellow brick ranges with Greek Doric details.

Wellington, *Salop. All Saints*, by G. Steuart, 1788–90, good Classical church with tower.

West Bromwich, *West Midlands. Christ Church*, High Street, by F. Goodwin, 1821–8, neo-Perp with tall W tower and galleried interior.

West Cowes, *Isle of Wight. St Mary*, W tower by Nash, 1816, bold design in Greek Revival style unusual for Nash. *St Thomas of Canterbury* (RC), Terminus Road, by T. Gabb, 1796, modest Classical church. *Northwood House*, by G. J. J. Mair, 1838 onwards, for G. H. Ward, in a rather French Neo-Classical style with banded rustication; main range of 9 bays with 3-bay pediment; curious interiors, some of them domed. Greek Revival lodge by Nash.

West Dean Park, *West Sussex*. By J. Wyatt, c. 1804–8, for 1st Lord Selsey. Dull Gothic house of flint, remodelled (especially internally) 1893 by George and Peto.

West Grinstead Park, *West Sussex*. By Nash, c. 1809, for W. Burrell. Castellated with round tower. Enlarged c. 1865 and now ruinous.

West Lodge, *Iwerne Minster, Dorset*. Superbly sited piece of stuccoed Regency panache with portico of attached Tuscan columns.

Westacre High House, *Westacre, Norfolk*. Remodelled by W. Donthorn, 1829, for A. Hammond. Austere Neo-Classical style with 13-bay N front divided by giant pilasters with minimal Classical ornamentation (despite the crenellated parapet). This reductionist style is taken further in the stables, an abstract Soanean composition in white Holkham stock-brick.

Weston, *near Bath, Avon. Partis' College*, by S. F. & P. F. Page, 1825–7, ranges of neo-Greek almshouses with central chapel.

Weymouth, *Dorset*. (43.) The perfect Regency sea-side resort. *St Mary*, St Mary Street, by J. Hamilton, 1815–17, in old fashioned Classical style. *Masonic Hall*, St Thomas Street, by C. B. Fookes, 1834, stuccoed front with 2 Greek Doric columns in antis. *Guildhall*, St Edmund Street, probably by T. Bury, 1836–7, with Ionic portico. Numerous Regency terraces especially along sea-front, often with shallow curved bow windows, e.g. *Royal Terrace, Gloucester Row* (partly by J. Hamilton), *Royal Crescent, Belvidere, Waterloo Place, Brunswick Terrace, Johnstone Row, Devonshire Buildings* and *Pulteney Buildings. St Alban Street*, c. 1800, narrow with bow-window houses on each side. *St Mary's Street* is flanked at N end by large bow-ended stuccoed blocks of shops and houses with tripartite bow windows, c. 1810. In front of this attractive group is the painted Coade stone statue of George III on large stone pedestal inscribed from 'The grateful inhabitants' of Weymouth. Designed by J. Hamilton, erected 1809.

Whaddon Hall, *Buckinghamshire*. Stuccoed mansion, c. 1820, with screen of 2 Erectheion Ionic columns on 5-bay entrance front, and semi-circular bow flanked by tripartite windows on garden front. Impressive stair hall with coffered dome and screens of porphyry scagliola columns beneath segmental arches: a Wyattesque touch.

Wherstead Park, *Suffolk*. 1792, in the Wyatt style. Long low entrance front of grey brick, 7 bays, 2 storeys, with ground-floor windows set in blank arches. Impressive domed staircase with 1st-floor screens of yellow scagliola Ionic columns. Park laid out by Repton by 1795 for Sir R. Harland, Bt.

Whitchurch, *Salop*. St Catherine, Dodington, by E. Haycock, 1836–7, odd entrance façade with portico of 2 Greek Ionic columns in antis; open tower over.

White Hall, *Winestead, Humberside*. Perhaps by C. Mountain, c. 1815, Greek Doric with good interiors.

Whitehill House, *Lasswade, Lothian Region*. By W. Burn, 1839–44, for R. B. Wardlaw Ramsay. Lavish Jacobethan house now somewhat mutilated.

Whitson Court, *Gwent*. By Nash, c. 1794, for W. Phillips. Plain 5-bay Classical box of red brick. (Later alterations.)

Whittinghame House, *Lothian Region*. (50.) By R. Smirke, 1817–18, for J. Balfour. Vast Neo-Classical house in Smirke's most dauntingly cubic Neo-

Classical style with large austere interiors. Elaborated and coarsened by W. Burn, 1827.

Wick, *Highland Region*. St Joachim (RC), by the Rev. J. Lovi, Greek-cross plan.

Widworthy Court, *near Honiton, Devon*. By G. S. Repton, 1830, for Sir E. M. Elton. Plain stone-built Classical box.

Wigan, *Greater Manchester*. St John (RC) (*71*), Standishgate, 1819, attractive 3-bay ashlar front with 8-column Ionic colonnade along the whole ground floor and 3 round-headed windows above; interior, enriched 1849, with impressive apse surrounded by giant Corinthian columns and altar of 1834 by J. J. Scoles. This church forms complete stylistic contrast with *St Mary* (RC) (*70*), Standishgate, 1818, which has solid neo-Perp stone façade, early for its date, and galleried Gothic interior with flat ribbed ceiling.

Wigginton Lodge, *Staffordshire*. By L. W. Wyatt, 1804, for Sir C. Clarke, Bt. Simple stuccoed villa with canopied verandah.

Wigton, *Cumbria*. St Cuthbert (RC), by I. Bonomi, 1837, sandstone Gothic church in lancet style.

Wilcot, *Wiltshire*. Ladies Bridge, by Sir J. Rennie, 1808, single-arched stone bridge prettily ornamented, i.e. not in Rennie's usual style.

Willey Hall, *Salop*. (*48*.) By L. W. Wyatt, 1813–15, for C. Weld-Forester. One of the grandest Neo-Classical houses in the country, beautifully sited in fine parkland. Heavy exterior with giant tetrastyle Corinthian portico. It is the interior planning which is especially memorable: a galleried tunnel-vaulted 2-storeyed Great Hall with oblong glazed lantern leads to the oval stair hall where 2 curved staircases are connected to the galleries by a flying bridge. Interiors in rich and monumental Empire Style, including the noble library with apsed ends and original shelving and furniture.

Wilton Castle, *Cleveland*. By R. Smirke, c. 1807, for Sir J. Lowther, Bt. Symmetrical, castellated, ashlar-faced. (Interiors altered; additions 1887.)

Wilton House, *Wiltshire*. Gothic N front and cloister of this great C17 house are by J. Wyatt, 1801–11, for 11th Earl of Pembroke.

Wimborne Minster, *Dorset*. Allendale House, by Wyatville, 1823, for W. Castleman, simple 3-bay villa with Greek

Doric porch.

Wimpole Hall, *Cambridgeshire*. (59, 61.) Great C18 mansion altered by Soane, 1791–3, for 3rd Earl of Hardwicke, to provide Yellow Drawing Room, remarkable T-shaped domed interior, and Book Room with segmental arches decorated with paterae. Extensive farm buildings also by Soane.

Winchester, *Hampshire*. (101.) *St John's Hospital*, High Street, by W. Garbett, 1817, 1831 and 1833, Gothic. *Library* (formerly Corn Exchange), Jewry Street, by O. B. Carter, 1836–8, with Tuscan portico inspired by Inigo Jones's Covent Garden church. *Winchester College, Headmaster's House*, by G. S. Repton, 1839–41, Gothic, in knapped flint.

Windleston Hall, *Co. Durham*. c. 1834, for Sir R. J. Eden, Bt., perhaps by I. Bonomi. Classical pile with long Tuscan colonnade.

Windsor, *Berkshire*. *Windsor Castle* (10, 15, 49, 77, 79, 80, 80) remodelled externally and internally by Wyatville, 1824–40, for George IV, as perhaps the most complete and extensive architectural expression of the Romantic Revival. Exteriors, including added upper portion of the Round Tower, are Picturesquely medievalising, but interiors are in an eclectic range of styles from the Waterloo Chamber (Gothic), to the Grand Reception Room (French Rococo) and the Green and Crimson Drawing Rooms (late Classical). *Home Park: Frogmore House*, by J. Wyatt, 1792–5, for Queen Charlotte, with later C19 wings and good staircase. Picturesque grounds with lake and temple. *Great Park: Fort Belvedere*, Flitcroft's triangular Shrub Hill Tower, c. 1750, was dramatically enlarged by Wyatville for George IV, 1827–30, with hexagonal towers of varying heights and octagonal dining room. *Royal Lodge* (79), extensive cottage orné by Nash, 1813–16, for the Prince Regent, enlarged by Wyatville, 1823–30, and demolished 1830 save for Wyatville's conservatory and Tudor Gothic dining room which survives as the drawing room of the existing 1840s house on the site. *Ruins* at Virginia Water, composed by Wyatville, 1826–9, as 'Temple of Augustus', from antique fragments from Lepcis Magna, North Africa.

Winslade House, *Clyst St Mary, Devon*. 3-storeyed Italianate block of 5 by 6

bays, c. 1840, pedimented windows and crowning balustrade. Spectacular lodge, c. 1820, 4 pairs of Greek Doric columns.

Wiston Hall, *Wissington, Suffolk*. By Soane, 1791, for S. Beachcroft. Simple 3-bay block of red brick.

Witley Court, *Hereford and Worcester*. Impressive ruins of Italianate palace by S. Daukes, c. 1860, incorporate 2 early C19 unpedimented Ionic porticos; the larger (octostyle) one on W garden front is by Nash, c. 1805, for 3rd Lord Foley.

Woburn Abbey, *Bedfordshire*. (60.) S front, conservatory and Chinese Dairy, by H. Holland, 1787–1802, for 5th Duke of Bedford. Finest room in Holland's S wing is the tripartite library with rich plasterwork and screens of Corinthian columns. In 1801 he added the Greek Ionic Temple of Liberty at E end of his conservatory of 1789 which became a sculpture gallery in 1816 under the direction of Wyatville, who added the domed Temple of the Graces at W end.

Wollaton Hall, *Nottingham*. In grounds of the great Elizabethan house an impressive *Camellia House*, 1823, by Messrs Jones & Clark, metallic hothouse builders of Birmingham. Irregular octagon in plan with corridors barrel-vaulted with curved iron plates.

Wolverhampton, *West Midlands*. *St George*, Bilston Road, by J. Morgan, 1828–30, expensive Classical Commissioners' church. *SS Peter and Paul* (RC) (73), North Street, by J. Ireland, 1827–8, beautiful T-shaped Greek Revival church with domed sanctuary and lunette windows opening into barrel vault. (S transept 1901.)

Wolverley, *Hereford and Worcester*. (96.) *Sebright School*, c. 1830, probably by W. Knight, curious façade with 3 giant Gothic arches.

Wood Hall, *Swine, near Burton Constable, Humberside*. 1814–15, for E. W. Maister, perhaps by Nash and evidently inspired by asymmetrical Italianate villas such as Cronkhill (q.v.)

Woodford House, *Woodford, North-amptonshire*. By C. Bacon, 1813–26, for C. Arbuthnot, MP. Snug Regency villa.

Woolley Park, *Brightwalton, Berkshire*. Remodelled by Wyatville, 1799, for the Rev. P. Wroughton. Rendered Greek Revival house with 5-bay front and good domed staircase. (Wings added c. 1860.)

Wonham Manor, *Betchworth, Surrey*. Remodelled in a simple Gothic style by

L. W. Wyatt, c. 1805-10, for 1st Viscount Templeton.

Worcester. (84.) *St Clement*, Henwick Road, by T. Lee, 1822-3, early example of the Norman Revival. *Shire Hall*, Foregate Street, 1834-8, by Day, Schinkelesque with Greek Ionic portico and good interiors. Regency terraces, e.g. *Britannia Square, St George's Square* and *Lansdowne Crescent*.

Workington, *Cumbria. St John*, Washington Street, by T. Hardwick, 1822-3, with Tuscan portico inspired by Inigo Jones's at St Paul, Covent Garden, which Hardwick had rebuilt after the fire of 1795. (Tower 1847.)

Worksop, *Nottinghamshire. St Mary* (RC), Park Street, by M. E. Hadfield, 1838-9, neo-Perp with 5-bay unaisled nave under hammerbeam roof.

Worlingham Hall, *Suffolk.* By F. Sandys, c. 1800, for R. Sparrow. Main front of 7 bays with semi-circular Tuscan porch below tripartite window. Unusual octagonal stair hall and Soanean library with apsed end screened by columns.

Wormington Grange, *Gloucestershire.* Enlarged by H. Hakewill, 1826-7, for J. Gist. New E entrance front of fine Cotswold stone featuring rectilinear tripartite windows, pilaster strips and delicate 1-storeyed pedimented portico based on the Greek Ionic Temple on the Ilissus, Athens. Chaste neo-Greek interiors with refined plasterwork. Stable block in similarly austere Neo-Classical style.

Worthing, *Sussex.* (43, 107.) *St Paul*, Chapel Road, by J. B. Rebecca, 1812, Greek Revival. *Beach House*, by Rebecca, 1820, stuccoed villa. *Sea Hotel*, by Rebecca, c. 1826. Regency terraces, e.g. *Bedford Row, 1802-5, Ambrose Place*, 1815, *Liverpool Terrace*, c. 1830, by H. Cotton, and, on edge of town, *Park Crescent*, c. 1830, by A. H. Wilds, a bizarre serpentine terrace crowded with heavy Classical detail and approached through triumphal arch flanked by herms. Terrace looks straight into trees and at the end are 2 Swiss Cottages.

Worthy House, *Kings Worthy, Hampshire.* By R. Smirke, 1816, for Sir C. Ogle. Round-headed windows and projecting tower-like bays. Smirke added the Ionic porte-cochère in 1825.

Wrest Park, *Bedfordshire.* 1834-9, designed for himself by Earl de Grey as rare and early example of Louis XV Revival, inspired by Blondel.

Wrotham, *Kent. Court Lodge* (formerly Rectory), by S. Wyatt, 1801-2, for the Rev. G. Moore, elegant stuccoed villa with domed bow.

Wycombe Abbey, *Marlow Hill, High Wycombe, Buckinghamshire.* Remodelled by J. Wyatt, c. 1803-4, for 1st Lord Carrington, as rambling and extensive Gothic romance in stone and flint. Tall Gothic entrance hall; fine landscaped park.

Wyelands, *Gwent.* Regency house, perhaps by R. Lugar, in fine park.

Wynnstay, *Clwyd.* Round *tower* at Nant-y-Belan, by Wyatville, 1810, for Sir Watkin Williams Wynn, Bt., modelled on the Tomb of Cecilia Metella, Appian Way, Rome. *Lodge*, on Chester to Oswestry road, by C. R. Cockerell, 1827-8, small-scale masterpiece, with 3 massive rusticated arches supporting a recessed attic with 3 circular windows.

Wynyard Park, *Co. Durham.* By P. W. Wyatt, 1822-30, for 3rd Marquess of Londonderry, a Durham coal magnate. Impressive Neo-Classical palace with giant octostyle Corinthian portico and central domed octagonal hall directly inspired by B. D. Wyatt's unexecuted plans for a Waterloo Palace for the Duke of Wellington. The magnificently decorated interiors (restored exactly after a fire of 1841) are important early examples of the Louis XIV Revival.

Yaxham Rectory, *Norfolk.* By R. Lugar, 1820-2, for the Rev. Dr. J. Johnson. Front of 3 widely spaced bays with Italianate eaves but Greek Doric porch.

York. (86, 90.) *Retreat* (Friends' Mental Hospital), Heslington Lane, by J. Bevans, 1794-6, Classical with wings and pavilions. *Friends' Meeting House*, Clifford Street, by Watson and Pritchett, 1816-19. (Façade 1885.) *Yorkshire Museum* (91), by Wilkins, 1827-30, with ambitious Greek Doric portico. *Assembly Rooms*, Blake Street, entrance front with Ionic portico added by Watson and Pritchett, 1828 (in place of Lord Burlington's more interesting front of 1731). *St Peter's School* (97), Clifton, begun by J. Harper, 1838, Gothic. *Centenary Methodist Church*, St Saviourgate, by J. Simpson, 1839-40, with large Ionic portico. 3 bridges by P. Atkinson: *Ouse Bridge*, 1810-20; *Foss Bridge*, 1811-12; and *Layerthorpe Bridge*, 1829 (widened 1929).

BIBLIOGRAPHY

Place of publication is London unless
otherwise stated.

Beazley & Howell, P., *The Companion Guide to
North Wales*, 1975.
The Companion Guide to South Wales,
1977.

Bolton, A. T., *The Architecture of Robert and
James Adam*, 2 vols, 1922.

Bracegirdle, B., *The Archaeology of the
Industrial Revolution*, 1973.

Clarke, B. F. L., *Parish Churches of London*,
1966.

Colvin, H. M., *A Biographical Dictionary of
British Architects 1600–1840*, 1978.

Colvin, H. M., ed., *The History of the King's
Works*, 6 vols, 1963–80.

Cornforth, J., *English Interiors 1790–1848, the
Quest for Comfort*, 1978.

Crook, J. M., *The British Museum*, 1972.
The Greek Revival, 1972.

Dunbar, J. G., *The Historic Architecture of
Scotland*, 1968.

Gomme, A., Jenner, M. & Little, B., *Bristol, an
Architectural History*, 1979.

Gomme, A. & Walker, D., *Architecture of
Glasgow*, 1968.

Hay, G., *The Architecture of Scottish Post-
Reformation Churches, 1560–1843*, Oxford,
1957.

Hilling, J. B., *The Historic Architecture of Wales*,
Cardiff, 1976.

Hitchcock, H. R., *Architecture 19th and 20th
centuries*, Harmondsworth, 1958 (revised
edition 1968).

Hobhouse, H., *Thomas Cubitt, Master Builder*,
1971.
A History of Regent Street, 1975.

Hussey, C., *The Picturesque*, 1927.
English Country Houses, Mid Georgian, 1956
(revised edition 1963).
English Country Houses, Late Georgian, 1958.

Jones, B., *Follies and Grottoes*, 1953 (revised
edition 1974).

Linstrum, D., *Sir Jeffry Wyatville*, Oxford,
1972.
West Yorkshire, Architects and Architecture,
1978.

Liscombe, R., *William Wilkins 1778–1839*,
Cambridge, 1980.

Macaulay, J., *The Gothic Revival 1745–1845*,
Glasgow and London, 1975.

Pevsner, N., *The Buildings of England*, 46 vols,
1951–74.

Pilcher, D., *The Regency Style*, 1947.

Port, M. H., *600 New Churches, a Study of the
Church Building Commission, 1818–56*,
1961.

Richards, J. M., *The Functional Tradition in
Early Industrial Buildings*, 1958.

Robinson, J. M., *The Wyatts, an Architectural
Dynasty*, Oxford, 1979.

Royal Commission on Historical Monuments
(England, Scotland and Wales), *Reports
and Inventories*, 1910 onwards.

Saunders, A., *Regent's Park*, Newton Abbot,
1969 (2nd revised edition 1981).

Seaborne, M., *The English School …
1370–1870*, 1971.

Stroud, D., *The Architecture of Sir John Soane*,
1961.
Humphry Repton, 1962.
Henry Holland, 1966.
George Dance, Architect, 1741–1825, 1971.

Summerson, J., *Georgian London*, 1945
(revised edition 1970).
Sir John Soane, 1952.
Architecture in Britain 1530–1830,
Harmondsworth, 1953 (5th edition 1969).
*The Life and Work of John Nash,
Architect*, 1980.

Survey of London (Greater London Council),
1900 onwards, 40 vols to date.

Tait, A. A., *The Landscape Garden in Scotland
1735–1835*, Edinburgh, 1980.

Victoria History of the Counties of England
(University of London, Institute of
Historical Research), 1900 onwards, 166
vols to date.

Watkin, D. J., *Thomas Hope (1769–1831) and
the Neo-Classical Idea*, 1968.
The Life and Work of C. R. Cockerell, RA,
1974.
*The Triumph of the Classical, Cambridge
Architecture 1804–34*, Cambridge, 1977.

Whiffen, M., *Stuart and Georgian Churches
outside London*, 1947–8.

Youngson, A. J., *The Making of Classical
Edinburgh*, Edinburgh, 1966.

INDEX OF ARCHITECTS

ILLUSTRATION ACKNOWLEDGEMENTS

Acknowledgement is made to the following for permission to reproduce copyright photographs on the pages specified:

Brighton Museums and Art Gallery, 6; Christopher Dalton, 23 (b.), 63, 85 (t.); Country Life, 8, 30, 38, 44, 47, 49, 53 (b.), 62 (b.), 64, 83, 136; Department of the Environment, Edinburgh, 94; Elsam, Mann & Cooper, Ltd, 25; Greater London Council, 34, 78–9, 100, 103, 111; A. F. Kersting, 51 (b.), 56, 68, 134, 162; National Monuments Record, 9, 13, 14, 17, 19, 21, 23 (t.), 27, 29, 32, 41, 42, 46, 48, 52, 53 (t.), 54, 55, 60, 61, 66, 67, 69, 70, 71, 72, 74 (b.), 78 (t.), 85 (b.), 86, 87, 90, 91, 93, 95, 98, 101, 102, 105, 106, 113 (t.), 114, 156, 171, 180, 183; Alistair Rowan, 177; Scottish Civic Trust, 74 (t.); Scottish National Monuments Record, 10, 12, 22, 31, 39, 40, 51 (t.), 58, 75, 82, 97, 110 (t.), 113 (b.), 155; Bill Toomey, 35, 92; National Monuments Record, Wales, Crown Copyright, 11, 57, 62 (t.), 88, 109, 110 (b.), 175; Gerald Wilson, 80.

The plans are reproduced, by permission, from the following sources:

Mark Girouard, Life in the English Country House, Yale University Press, New Haven and London, 1978 (Fig. 16), 15, (Fig. 17) 55; John Summerson, John Nash, 1935, 18; A New Description of Sir John Soane's Museum, 1955 (Fig. 2), 20; G. Hemm, St George's Hall, Liverpool, Northern Publishing Co., Liverpool, 1949, 24; R. Dixon & S. Muthesius, Victorian Architecture, Thames & Hudson, London, 1978 (Pl. 67), 26; C. Hussey, English Country Houses, Late Georgian, 1800–1840, Country Life Books, Feltham, 1958 (Pl. 216), 48, (Pl. 148), 53 (Pl. 352) 56; John Summerson, Georgian London, Pleiades Books, London, 1945 (Fig. 29), 68; Malcolm Seaborne, The English School, 1370–1870, Routledge & Kegan Paul, London, and University of Toronto Press, Toronto, 1971 (Fig. 28), 96; Survey of London, Vol. XXXV, Athlone Press/University of London, 1970 (Pl. 26c), 104